Pattern Recognition Algorithms for Data Mining

T0134015

Pattern Recognition Algorithms for Data Mining

Scalability, Knowledge Discovery and Soft
Granular Computing

Sankar K. Pal and Pabitra Mitra

Machine Intelligence Unit
Indian Statistical Institute
Calcutta, India

CRC Press
Taylor & Francis Group
Boca Raton London New York

CRC Press is an imprint of the
Taylor & Francis Group, an **informa** business
A CHAPMAN & HALL BOOK

CRC Press
Taylor & Francis Group
6000 Broken Sound Parkway NW, Suite 300
Boca Raton, FL 33487-2742

First issued in paperback 2019

ISBN-13: 978-1-58488-457-6 (hbk)
ISBN-13: 978-0-367-39424-0 (pbk)
Library of Congress Card Number 2004043539

Library of Congress Cataloging-in-Publication Data

Pal, Sankar K.
    Pattern recognition algorithms for data mining : scalability, knowledge discovery, and soft granular computing / Sankar K. Pal and Pabitra Mitra.
      p. cm.
    Includes bibliographical references and index.
    ISBN 1-58488-457-6 (alk. paper)
    1. Data mining. 2. Pattern recognition systems. 3. Computer algorithms. 4. Granular computing / Sankar K. Pal and Pabita Mitra.

QA76.9.D343P38 2004
006.3'12—dc22   2004043539

Visit the Taylor & Francis Web site at
http://www.taylorandfrancis.com

and the CRC Press Web site at
http://www.crcpress.com

To our parents

Contents

Foreword

Indian Statistical Institute (ISI), the home base of Professors S.K. Pal and P. Mitra, has long been recognized as the world's premier center of fundamental research in probability, statistics and, more recently, pattern recognition and machine intelligence. The halls of ISI are adorned with the names of P.C. Mahalanobis, C.R. Rao, R.C. Bose, D. Basu, J.K. Ghosh, D. Dutta Majumder, K.R. Parthasarathi and other great intellects of the past century–great intellects who have contributed so much and in so many ways to the advancement of science and technology. The work of Professors Pal and Mitra, "Pattern Recognition Algorithms for Data Mining," or PRDM for short, reflects this illustrious legacy. The importance of PRDM is hard to exaggerate. It is a treatise that is an exemplar of authority, deep insights, encyclopedic coverage and high expository skill.

The primary objective of PRDM, as stated by the authors, is to provide a unified framework for addressing pattern recognition tasks which are essential for data mining. In reality, the book accomplishes much more; it develops a unified framework and presents detailed analyses of a wide spectrum of methodologies for dealing with problems in which recognition, in one form or another, plays an important role. Thus, the concepts and techniques described in PRDM are of relevance not only to problems in pattern recognition, but, more generally, to classification, analysis of dependencies, system identification, authentication, and ultimately, to data mining. In this broad perspective, conventional pattern recognition becomes a specialty–a specialty with deep roots and a large store of working concepts and techniques.

Traditional pattern recognition is subsumed by what may be called recognition technology. I take some credit for arguing, some time ago, that development of recognition technology should be accorded a high priority. My arguments may be found in the foreword," Recognition Technology and Fuzzy Logic, "Special Issue on Recognition Technology, IEEE Transactions on Fuzzy Systems, 2001. A visible consequence of my arguments was an addition of the subtitle "Soft Computing in Recognition and Search," to the title of the journal "Approximate Reasoning." What is important to note is that recognition technology is based on soft computing–a coalition of methodologies which collectively provide a platform for the conception, design and utilization of intelligent systems. The principal constitutes of soft computing are fuzzy logic, neurocomputing, evolutionary computing, probabilistic computing, rough set theory and machine learning. These are the methodologies which are described and applied in PRDM with a high level of authority and expository skill. Particularly worthy of note is the exposition of methods in which rough set theory and fuzzy logic are used in combination.

Much of the material in PRDM is new and reflects the authors' extensive experience in dealing with a wide variety of problems in which recognition and analysis of dependencies play essential roles. Such is the case in data mining and, in particular, in the analysis of both causal and non-causal dependencies.

A pivotal issue–which subsumes feature selection and feature extraction– and which receives a great deal of attention in PRDM, is that of feature analysis. Feature analysis has a position of centrality in recognition, and its discussion in PRDM is an order of magnitude more advanced and more insightful than what can be found in the existing literature. And yet, it cannot be claimed that the basic problem of feature selection–especially in the context of data mining–has been solved or is even close to solution. Why? The reason, in my view, is the following. To define what is meant by a feature it is necessary to define what is meant by relevance. Conventionally, relevance is defined as a bivalent concept, that is, if q is a query and p is a proposition or a collection of propositions, then either p is relevant to q or p is not relevant to q, with no shades of gray allowed. But it is quite obvious that relevance is a matter of degree, which is consistent with the fact that in a natural language we allow expressions such as quite relevant, not very relevant, highly relevant, etc. In the existing literature, there is no definition of relevance which makes it possible to answer the question: To what degree is p relevant to q? For example, if q is: How old is Carol? and p is: Carol has a middle-aged mother, then to what degree is the knowledge that Carol has a middle-aged mother, relevant to the query: How old is Carol? As stated earlier, the problem is that relevance is not a bivalent concept, as it is frequently assumed to be; rather, relevance is a fuzzy concept which does not lend itself to definition within the conceptual structure of bivalent logic. However, what can be found in PRDM is a very thorough discussion of a related issue, namely, methods of assessment of relative importance of features in the context of pattern recognition and data mining.

A difficult problem which arises both in assessment of the degree of relevance of a proposition, p, and in assessment of the degree of importance of a feature, f, relates to combination of such degrees. More concretely, if we have two propositions $p-1$ and p_2 with respective degrees of relevance r_1 and r_2, then all that can be said about the relevance of (p_1, p_2) is that it is bounded from below by $\max(r_1, r_2)$. This makes it possible for both p_1 and p_2 to be irrelevant $(r_1 = r_2 = 0)$, and yet the degree of relevance of (p_1, p_2) may be close to 1.

The point I am trying to make is that there are many basic issues in pattern recognition–and especially in relation to its role in data mining–whose resolution lies beyond the reach of methods based on bivalent logic and bivalent–logic-based probability theory. The issue of relevance is a case in point. Another basic issue is that of causality. But what is widely unrecognized is that even such familiar concepts as cluster and edge are undefinable within the conceptual structure of bivalent logic. This assertion is not contradicted by the fact that there is an enormous literature on cluster analysis and edge detection. What cannot be found in this literature are formalized definitions of cluster and edge.

How can relevance, causality, cluster, edge and many other familiar concepts be defined? In my view, what is needed for this purpose is the methodology of computing with words. In this methodology, the objects of computation are words and propositions drawn from a natural language. I cannot be more detailed in a foreword.

Although PRDM does not venture into computing with words directly, it does lay the groundwork for it, especially through extensive exposition of granular computing and related methods of computation. It does so through an exceptionally insightful discussion of advanced methods drawn from fuzzy logic, neurocomputing, probabilistic computing, rough set theory and machine learning.

In summary, "Pattern Recognition Algorithms in Data Mining" is a book that commands admiration. Its authors, Professors S.K. Pal and P. Mitra are foremost authorities in pattern recognition, data mining and related fields. Within its covers, the reader finds an exceptionally well-organized exposition of every concept and every method that is of relevance to the theme of the book. There is much that is original and much that cannot be found in the literature. The authors and the publisher deserve our thanks and congratulations for producing a definitive work that contributes so much and in so many important ways to the advancement of both the theory and practice of recognition technology, data mining and related fields. The magnum opus of Professors Pal and Mitra is a must reading for anyone who is interested in the conception, design and utilization of intelligent systems.

March 2004

Lotfi A. Zadeh
University of California
Berkeley, CA, USA

Foreword

Data mining offers techniques of discovering patterns in voluminous databases. In other words, data mining is a technique of discovering knowledge from large data sets (KDD). Knowledge is usually presented in the form of decision rules easy to understand and used by humans. Therefore, methods for rule generation and evaluation are of utmost importance in this context.

Many approaches to accomplish this have been developed and explored in recent years. The prominent scientist Prof. Sankar K. Pal and his student Dr. Pabitra Mitra present in this valuable volume, in addition to classical methods, recently emerged various new methodologies for data mining, such as rough sets, rough fuzzy hybridization, granular computing, artificial neural networks, genetic algorithms, and others. In addition to theoretical foundations, the book also includes experimental results. Many real life and nontrivial examples given in the book show how the new techniques work and can be used in reality and what advantages they offer compared with classical methods (e.g., statistics).

This book covers a wide spectrum of problems related to data mining, data analysis, and knowledge discovery in large databases. It should be recommended reading for any researcher or practitioner working in these areas. Also graduate students in AI get a very well-organized book presenting modern concepts and tools used in this domain.

In the appendix various basic computing tools and data sets used in experiments are supplied. A complete bibliography on the subject is also included.

The book presents an unbeatable combination of theory and practice and gives a comprehensive view on methods and tools in modern KDD.

The authors deserve the highest appreciation for this excellent monograph.

January 2004

Zdzislaw Pawlak
Polish Academy of Sciences
Warsaw, Poland

Foreword

This is the latest in a series of volumes by Professor Sankar Pal and his collaborators on pattern recognition methodologies and applications. Knowledge discovery and data mining, the recognition of patterns that may be present in very large data sets and across distributed heterogeneous databases, is an application of current prominence. This volume provides a very useful, thorough exposition of the many facets of this application from several perspectives.

The chapters provide overviews of pattern recognition, data mining, outline some of the research issues and carefully take the reader through the many steps that are involved in reaching the desired goal of exposing the patterns that may be embedded in voluminous data sets. These steps include preprocessing operations for reducing the volume of the data and the dimensionality of the feature space, clustering, segmentation, and classification. Search algorithms and statistical and database operations are examined. Attention is devoted to soft computing algorithms derived from the theories of rough sets, fuzzy sets, genetic algorithms, multilayer perceptrons (MLP), and various hybrid combinations of these methodologies.

A valuable expository appendix describes various soft computing methodologies and their role in knowledge discovery and data mining (KDD). A second appendix provides the reader with several data sets for experimentation with the procedures described in this volume.

As has been the case with previous volumes by Professor Pal and his collaborators, this volume will be very useful to both researchers and students interested in the latest advances in pattern recognition and its applications in KDD.

I congratulate the authors of this volume and I am pleased to recommend it as a valuable addition to the books in this field.

February 2004

Laveen N. Kanal
University of Maryland
College Park, MD, USA

Preface

In recent years, government agencies and scientific, business and commercial organizations are routinely using computers not just for computational purposes but also for storage, in massive databases, of the immense volumes of data that they routinely generate or require from other sources. We are in the midst of an information explosion, and there is an urgent need for methodologies that will help us bring some semblance of order into the phenomenal volumes of data. Traditional statistical data summarization and database management techniques are just not adequate for handling data on this scale, and for extracting intelligently information or knowledge that may be useful for exploring the domain in question or the phenomena responsible for the data and providing support to decision-making processes. This quest had thrown up some new phrases, for example, data mining and knowledge discovery in databases (KDD).

Data mining deals with the process of identifying valid, novel, potentially useful, and ultimately understandable patterns in data. It may be viewed as applying pattern recognition (PR) and machine learning principles in the context of voluminous, possibly heterogeneous data sets. Two major challenges in applying PR algorithms to data mining problems are those of "scalability" to large/huge data sets and of "discovering knowledge" which is valid and comprehensible to humans. Research is going on in these lines for developing efficient PR methodologies and algorithms, in different classical and modern computing frameworks, as applicable to various data mining tasks with real life applications.

The present book is aimed at providing a treatise in a unified framework, with both theoretical and experimental results, addressing certain pattern recognition tasks essential for data mining. Tasks considered include data condensation, feature selection, case generation, clustering/classification, rule generation and rule evaluation. Various theories, methodologies and algorithms using both a classical approach and hybrid paradigm (e.g., integrating fuzzy logic, artificial neural networks, rough sets, genetic algorithms) have been presented. The emphasis is given on (a) handling data sets that are large (both in size and dimension) and involve classes that are overlapping, intractable and/or have nonlinear boundaries, and (b) demonstrating the significance of granular computing in soft computing frameworks for generating linguistic rules and dealing with the knowledge discovery aspect, besides reducing the computation time.

It is shown how several novel strategies based on multi-scale data condensation, dimensionality reduction, active support vector learning, granular computing and efficient search heuristics can be employed for dealing with the issue of scaling up in large scale learning problem. The tasks of encoding, extraction and evaluation of knowledge in the form of human comprehensible linguistic rules are addressed in a soft computing framework by different integrations of its constituting tools. Various real life data sets, mainly large in dimension and/or size, taken from varied domains, e.g., geographical information systems, remote sensing imagery, population census, speech recognition and cancer management, are considered to demonstrate the superiority of these methodologies with statistical significance.

Examples are provided, wherever necessary, to make the concepts more clear. A comprehensive bibliography on the subject is appended. Major portions of the text presented in the book are from the published work of the authors. Some references in the related areas might have been inadvertently omitted because of oversight or ignorance.

This volume, which is unique in its character, will be useful to graduate students and researchers in computer science, electrical engineering, system science, and information technology both as a text and a reference book for some parts of the curriculum. The researchers and practitioners in industry and research and development laboratories working in fields such as system design, pattern recognition, data mining, image processing, machine learning and soft computing will also benefit. For convenience, brief descriptions of the data sets used in the experiments are provided in the Appendix.

The text is organized in eight chapters. Chapter 1 describes briefly basic concepts, features and techniques of PR and introduces data mining and knowledge discovery in light of PR, different research issues and challenges, the problems of scaling of PR algorithms to large data sets, and the significance of soft computing in knowledge discovery.

Chapters 2 and 3 deal with the (pre-processing) tasks of multi-scale data condensation and unsupervised feature selection or dimensionality reduction. After providing a review in the respective fields, a methodology based on a statistical approach is described in detail in each chapter along with experimental results. The method of k-NN density estimation and the concept of representation entropy, used therein, are explained in their respective chapters. The data condensation strategy preserves the salient characteristics of the original data at different scales by representing the underlying probability density. The unsupervised feature selection algorithm is based on computing the similarity between features and then removing the redundancy therein without requiring any search. These methods are scalable.

Chapter 4 concerns the problem of learning with support vector machine (SVM). After describing the design procedure of SVM, two active learning strategies for handling the large quadratic problem in a SVM framework are presented. In order to reduce the sample complexity, a statistical query model is employed incorporating a trade-off between the efficiency and robustness in performance.

Chapters 5 to 8 highlight the significance of granular computing for different mining tasks in a soft paradigm. While the rough-fuzzy framework is used for case generation in Chapter 5, the same is integrated with expectation maximization algorithm and minimal spanning trees in Chapter 6 for clustering large data sets. The role of rough sets is to use information granules for extracting the domain knowledge which is encoded in different ways. Since computation is made using the granules (clump of objects), not the individual points, the methods are fast. The cluster quality, envisaged on a multi-spectral image segmentation problem, is also improved owing to the said integration. In Chapter 7, design procedure of a rough self-organizing map (RSOM) is described for clustering and unsupervised linguistic rule generation with a structured network.

The problems of classification, and rule generation and evaluation in a supervised mode are addressed in Chapter 8 with a modular approach through a synergistic integration of four soft computing tools, namely, fuzzy sets, rough sets, neural nets and genetic algorithms. A modular evolutionary rough-fuzzy multi-layered perceptron is described which results in accelerated training, compact network, unambiguous linguistic rules and improved accuracy. Different rule evaluation indices are used to reflect the knowledge discovery aspect.

Finally, we take this opportunity to thank Mr. Robert B. Stern of Chapman & Hall/CRC Press, Florida, for his initiative and encouragement. Financial support to Dr. Pabitra Mitra from the Council of Scientific and Industrial Research (CSIR), New Delhi in the form of Research Associateship (through Grant # 22/346/02-EMR II) is also gratefully acknowledged.

Sankar K. Pal

Pabitra Mitra

September 13, 2003

List of Tables

List of Figures

Chapter 1

Introduction

1.1 Introduction

Pattern recognition (PR) is an activity that we humans normally excel in. We do it almost all the time, and without conscious effort. We receive information via our various sensory organs, which is processed instantaneously by our brain so that, almost immediately, we are able to identify the source of the information, without having made any perceptible effort. What is even more impressive is the accuracy with which we can perform recognition tasks even under non-ideal conditions, for instance, when the information that needs to be processed is vague, imprecise or even incomplete. In fact, most of our day-to-day activities are based on our success in performing various pattern recognition tasks. For example, when we read a book, we recognize the letters, words and, ultimately, concepts and notions, from the visual signals received by our brain, which processes them speedily and probably does a neurobiological implementation of template-matching! [189]

The discipline of pattern recognition (or pattern recognition by machine) essentially deals with the problem of developing algorithms and methodologies/devices that can enable the computer-implementation of many of the recognition tasks that humans normally perform. The motivation is to perform these tasks more accurately, or faster, and perhaps more economically than humans and, in many cases, to release them from drudgery resulting from performing routine recognition tasks repetitively and mechanically. The scope of PR also encompasses tasks humans are not good at, such as reading bar codes. The goal of pattern recognition research is to devise ways and means of automating certain decision-making processes that lead to classification and recognition.

Machine recognition of patterns can be viewed as a two-fold task, consisting of learning the invariant and common properties of a set of samples characterizing a class, and of deciding that a new sample is a possible member of the class by noting that it has properties common to those of the set of samples. The task of pattern recognition by a computer can be described as a transformation from the measurement space $\mathcal{M}$ to the feature space $\mathcal{F}$ and finally to the decision space $\mathcal{D}$; i.e.,

$$\mathcal{M} \to \mathcal{F} \to \mathcal{D}.$$

1

Here the mapping $\delta \; : \; \mathcal{F} \to \mathcal{D}$ is the decision function, and the elements $d \in \mathcal{D}$ are termed as decisions.

PR has been a thriving field of research for the past few decades, as is amply borne out by the numerous books [55, 59, 72, 200, 204, 206] devoted to it. In this regard, mention must be made of the seminal article by Kanal [104], which gives a comprehensive review of the advances made in the field until the early 1970s. More recently, a review article by Jain *et al.* [101] provides an engrossing survey of the advances made in statistical pattern recognition till the end of the twentieth century. Though the subject has attained a very mature level during the past four decades or so, it remains green to the researchers due to continuous cross-fertilization of ideas from disciplines such as computer science, physics, neurobiology, psychology, engineering, statistics, mathematics and cognitive science. Depending on the practical need and demand, various modern methodologies have come into being, which often supplement the classical techniques [189].

In recent years, the rapid advances made in computer technology have ensured that large sections of the world population have been able to gain easy access to computers on account of falling costs worldwide, and their use is now commonplace in all walks of life. Government agencies and scientific, business and commercial organizations are routinely using computers, not just for computational purposes but also for storage, in massive databases, of the immense volumes of data that they routinely generate or require from other sources. Large-scale computer networking has ensured that such data has become accessible to more and more people. In other words, we are in the midst of an information explosion, and there is urgent need for methodologies that will help us bring some semblance of order into the phenomenal volumes of data that can readily be accessed by us with a few clicks of the keys of our computer keyboard. Traditional statistical data summarization and database management techniques are just not adequate for handling data on this scale and for intelligently extracting information, or rather, knowledge that may be useful for exploring the domain in question or the phenomena responsible for the data, and providing support to decision-making processes. This quest has thrown up some new phrases, for example, *data mining* and *knowledge discovery in databases (KDD)* [43, 65, 66, 88, 89, 92].

The massive databases that we are talking about are generally characterized by the presence of not just numeric, but also textual, symbolic, pictorial and aural data. They may contain redundancy, errors, imprecision, and so on. KDD is aimed at discovering natural structures within such massive and often heterogeneous data. Therefore PR plays a significant role in KDD process. However, KDD is visualized as being capable not only of knowledge discovery using generalizations and magnifications of existing and new pattern recognition algorithms, but also of the adaptation of these algorithms to enable them to process such data, the storage and accessing of the data, its preprocessing and cleaning, interpretation, visualization and application of the results, and the modeling and support of the overall human-machine interaction.

Data mining is that part of knowledge discovery which deals with the process of identifying valid, novel, potentially useful, and ultimately understandable patterns in data, and excludes the knowledge interpretation part of KDD. Therefore, as it stands now, data mining can be viewed as applying PR and machine learning principles in the context of voluminous, possibly heterogeneous data sets [189].

The objective of this book is to provide some results of investigations, both theoretical and experimental, addressing certain pattern recognition tasks essential for data mining. Tasks considered include data condensation, feature selection, case generation, clustering, classification and rule generation/evaluation. Various methodologies based on both classical and soft computing approaches (integrating fuzzy logic, artificial neural networks, rough sets, genetic algorithms) have been presented. The emphasis of these methodologies is given on (a) handling data sets which are large (both in size and dimension) and involve classes that are overlapping, intractable and/or having nonlinear boundaries, and (b) demonstrating the significance of granular computing in soft computing paradigm for generating linguistic rules and dealing with the knowledge discovery aspect. Before we describe the scope of the book, we provide a brief review of pattern recognition, knowledge discovery in data bases, data mining, challenges in application of pattern recognition algorithms to data mining problems, and some of the possible solutions.

Section 1.2 presents a description of the basic concept, features and techniques of pattern recognition briefly. Next, we define the KDD process and describe its various components. In Section 1.4 we elaborate upon the data mining aspects of KDD, discussing its components, tasks involved, approaches and application areas. The pattern recognition perspective of data mining is introduced next and related research challenges are mentioned. The problem of scaling pattern recognition algorithms to large data sets is discussed in Section 1.6. Some broad approaches to achieving scalability are listed. The role of soft computing in knowledge discovery is described in Section 1.7. Finally, Section 1.8 discusses the plan of the book.

1.2 Pattern Recognition in Brief

A typical pattern recognition system consists of three phases, namely, *data acquisition, feature selection/extraction* and *classification/clustering*. In the data acquisition phase, depending on the environment within which the objects are to be classified/clustered, data are gathered using a set of sensors. These are then passed on to the feature selection/extraction phase, where the dimensionality of the data is reduced by retaining/measuring only some characteristic features or properties. In a broader perspective, this stage significantly influences the entire recognition process. Finally, in the classification/clustering phase, the selected/extracted features are passed on to the classifying/clustering system that evaluates the incoming information and makes a final decision. This phase basically establishes a transformation between the features and the classes/clusters. Different forms of transformation can be a Bayesian rule of computing *a posterior* class probabilities, nearest neighbor rule, linear discriminant functions, perceptron rule, nearest prototype rule, etc. [55, 59].

1.2.1   Data acquisition

Pattern recognition techniques are applicable in a wide domain, where the data may be qualitative, quantitative, or both; they may be numerical, linguistic, pictorial, or any combination thereof. The collection of data constitutes the data acquisition phase. Generally, the data structures that are used in pattern recognition systems are of two types: *object data vectors* and *relational data*. Object data, a set of numerical vectors, are represented in the sequel as $Y = \{\mathbf{y}_1, \mathbf{y}_2, \ldots, \mathbf{y}_n\}$, a set of n feature vectors in the p-dimensional measurement space Ω_Y. An sth object, $s = 1, 2, \ldots, n$, observed in the process has vector $\mathbf{y}_s$ as its numerical representation; y_{si} is the ith $(i = 1, 2, \ldots, p)$ feature value associated with the sth object. Relational data is a set of n^2 numerical relationships, say $\{r_{sq}\}$, between pairs of objects. In other words, r_{sq} represents the extent to which sth and qth objects are related in the sense of some binary relationship ρ. If the objects that are pairwise related by ρ are called $O = \{o_1, o_2, \ldots, o_n\}$, then $\rho : O \times O \to I\!R$.

1.2.2   Feature selection/extraction

Feature selection/extraction is a process of selecting a map of the form $X = f(Y)$, by which a sample $\mathbf{y}$ $(=[y_1, y_2, \ldots, y_p])$ in a p-dimensional measurement space Ω_Y is transformed into a point $\mathbf{x}$ $(=[x_1, x_2, \ldots, x_{p'}])$ in a p'-dimensional feature space Ω_X, where $p' < p$. The main objective of this task [55] is to retain/generate the optimum salient characteristics necessary for the recognition process and to reduce the dimensionality of the measurement space Ω_Y so that effective and easily computable algorithms can be devised for efficient classification. The problem of feature selection/extraction has two aspects – formulation of a suitable criterion to evaluate the goodness of a feature set and searching the optimal set in terms of the criterion. In general, those features are considered to have optimal saliencies for which interclass/intraclass distances are maximized/minimized. The criterion of a good feature is that it should be unchanging with any other possible variation within a class, while emphasizing differences that are important in discriminating between patterns of different types.

The major mathematical measures so far devised for the estimation of feature quality are mostly statistical in nature, and can be broadly classified into two categories – *feature selection in the measurement space* and *feature selection in a transformed space*. The techniques in the first category generally reduce the dimensionality of the measurement space by discarding redundant or least information carrying features. On the other hand, those in the second category utilize all the information contained in the measurement space to obtain a new transformed space, thereby mapping a higher dimensional pattern to a lower dimensional one. This is referred to as feature extraction.

1.2.3 Classification

The problem of classification is basically one of partitioning the feature space into regions, one region for each category of input. Thus it attempts to assign every data point in the entire feature space to one of the possible classes (say, M) . In real life, the complete description of the classes is not known. We have instead a finite and usually smaller number of samples which often provides partial information for optimal design of feature selector/extractor or classifying/clustering system. Under such circumstances, it is assumed that these samples are representative of the classes. Such a set of typical patterns is called a *training set*. On the basis of the information gathered from the samples in the training set, the pattern recognition systems are designed; i.e., we decide the values of the parameters of various pattern recognition methods. Design of a classification or clustering scheme can be made with labeled or unlabeled data. When the computer is given a set of objects with known classifications (i.e., labels) and is asked to classify an unknown object based on the information acquired by it during training, we call the design scheme *supervised learning*; otherwise we call it *unsupervised learning*. Supervised learning is used for classifying different objects, while clustering is performed through unsupervised learning.

Pattern classification, by its nature, admits many approaches, sometimes complementary, sometimes competing, to provide solution of a given problem. These include *decision theoretic approach* (both *deterministic* and *probabilistic*), *syntactic approach, connectionist approach, fuzzy and rough set theoretic approach* and *hybrid or soft computing approach*.

In the decision theoretic approach, once a pattern is transformed, through feature evaluation, to a vector in the feature space, its characteristics are expressed only by a set of numerical values. Classification can be done by using deterministic or probabilistic techniques [55, 59]. In deterministic classification approach, it is assumed that there exists only one unambiguous pattern class corresponding to each of the unknown pattern vectors. *Nearest neighbor classifier (NN rule)* [59] is an example of this category.

In most of the practical problems, the features are usually noisy and the classes in the feature space are overlapping. In order to model such systems, the features $x_1, x_2, \ldots, x_i, \ldots, x_p$ are considered as random variables in the probabilistic approach. The most commonly used classifier in such probabilistic systems is the *Bayes maximum likelihood classifier* [59].

When a pattern is rich in structural information (e.g., picture recognition, character recognition, scene analysis), i.e., the structural information plays an important role in describing and recognizing the patterns, it is convenient to use syntactic approaches [72] which deal with the representation of structures via sentences, grammars and automata. In the syntactic method [72], the ability of selecting and classifying the simple pattern primitives and their relationships represented by the composition operations is the vital criterion of making a system effective. Since the techniques of composition of primitives into patterns are usually governed by the formal language theory, the approach is often referred to as a linguistic approach. An introduction to a variety of approaches based on this idea can be found in [72].

A good pattern recognition system should possess several characteristics. These are on-line adaptation (to cope with the changes in the environment), handling nonlinear class separability (to tackle real life problems), handling of overlapping classes/clusters (for discriminating almost similar but different objects), real-time processing (for making a decision in a reasonable time), generation of soft and hard decisions (to make the system flexible), verification and validation mechanisms (for evaluating its performance), and minimizing the number of parameters in the system that have to be tuned (for reducing the cost and complexity). Moreover, the system should be made artificially intelligent in order to emulate some aspects of the human processing system. Connectionist approaches (or artificial neural network based approaches) to pattern recognition are attempts to achieve these goals and have drawn the attention of researchers because of their major characteristics such as adaptivity, robustness/ruggedness, speed and optimality.

All these approaches to pattern recognition can again be fuzzy set theoretic [24, 105, 200, 285] in order to handle uncertainties, arising from vague, incomplete, linguistic, overlapping patterns, etc., at various stages of pattern recognition systems. Fuzzy set theoretic classification approach is developed based on the realization that a pattern may belong to more than one class, with varying degrees of class membership. Accordingly, fuzzy decision theoretic, fuzzy syntactic, fuzzy neural approaches are developed [24, 34, 200, 204].

More recently, the theory of rough sets [209, 214, 215, 261] has emerged as another major mathematical approach for managing uncertainty that arises from inexact, noisy, or incomplete information. It is turning out to be methodologically significant to the domains of artificial intelligence and cognitive sciences, especially in the representation of and reasoning with vague and/or imprecise knowledge, data classification, data analysis, machine learning, and knowledge discovery [227, 261].

Investigations have also been made in the area of pattern recognition using genetic algorithms [211]. Like neural networks, genetic algorithms (GAs) [80] are also based on powerful metaphors from the natural world. They mimic some of the processes observed in natural evolution, which include cross-over, selection and mutation, leading to a stepwise optimization of organisms.

There have been several attempts over the last decade to evolve new approaches to pattern recognition and deriving their hybrids by judiciously combining the merits of several techniques [190, 204]. Recently, a consolidated effort is being made in this regard to integrate mainly fuzzy logic, artificial neural networks, genetic algorithms and rough set theory, for developing an efficient new paradigm called *soft computing* [287]. Here integration is done in a cooperative, rather than a competitive, manner. The result is a more intelligent and robust system providing a human-interpretable, low cost, approximate solution, as compared to traditional techniques. Neuro-fuzzy approach is perhaps the most visible hybrid paradigm [197, 204, 287] in soft computing framework. Rough-fuzzy [209, 265] and neuro-rough [264, 207] hybridizations are also proving to be fruitful frameworks for modeling human perceptions and providing means for computing with words. Significance of the recently proposed computational theory of perceptions (CTP) [191, 289] may also be mentioned in this regard.

1.3   Knowledge Discovery in Databases (KDD)

Knowledge discovery in databases (KDD) is defined as [65]:

> *The nontrivial process of identifying valid, novel, potentially useful, and ultimately understandable patterns in data.*

In this definition, the term *pattern* goes beyond its traditional sense to include models or structure in data. *Data* is a set of facts F (e.g., cases in a database), and a *pattern* is an expression E in a language L describing the facts in a subset F_E (or a model applicable to that subset) of F. E is called a pattern if it is simpler than the enumeration of all facts in F_E. A measure of certainty, measuring the *validity* of discovered patterns, is a function C mapping expressions in L to a partially or totally ordered measure space M_C. An expression E in L about a subset $F_E \subset F$ can be assigned a certainty measure $c = C(E, F)$. *Novelty* of patterns can be measured by a function $N(E, F)$ with respect to changes in data or knowledge. Patterns should potentially lead to some *useful* actions, as measured by some utility function $u = U(E, F)$ mapping expressions in L to a partially or totally ordered measure space M_U. The goal of KDD is to make patterns *understandable* to humans. This is measured by a function $s = S(E, F)$ mapping expressions E in L to a partially or totally ordered measure space M_S.

Interestingness of a pattern combines validity, novelty, usefulness, and understandability and can be expressed as $i = I(E, F, C, N, U, S)$ which maps expressions in L to a measure space M_I. A pattern $E \in L$ is called *knowledge* if for some user-specified threshold $i \in M_I$, $I(E, F, C, N, U, S) > i$ [65]. One can select some thresholds $c \in M_C$, $s \in M_S$, and $u \in M_u$ and term a pattern E knowledge

$$\text{iff}\quad C(E,F) > c,\ \text{and}\ S(E,F) > s,\ \text{and}\ U(E,F) > u. \qquad (1.1)$$

The role of interestingness is to threshold the huge number of discovered patterns and report only those that may be of some use. There are two approaches to designing a measure of interestingness of a pattern, *viz.*, objective and subjective. The former uses the structure of the pattern and is generally used for computing *rule interestingness*. However, often it fails to capture all the complexities of the pattern discovery process. The *subjective* approach, on the other hand, depends additionally on the *user* who examines the pattern. Two major reasons why a pattern is interesting from the subjective (user-oriented) point of view are as follow [257]:

- *Unexpectedness*: when it is "surprising" to the user.

- *Actionability*: when the user can act on it to her/his advantage.

Although both these concepts are important, it has often been observed that actionability and unexpectedness are correlated. In literature, unexpectedness is often defined in terms of the dissimilarity of a discovered pattern from a vocabulary provided by the user.

As an example, consider a database of student evaluations of different courses offered at some university. This can be defined as EVALUATE (TERM, YEAR, COURSE, SECTION, INSTRUCTOR, INSTRUCT_RATING, COURSE_RATING). We describe two patterns that are interesting in terms of actionability and unexpectedness respectively. The pattern that "Professor X is consistently getting the overall INSTRUCT_RATING below the overall COURSE_RATING" can be of interest to the chairperson because this shows that Professor X has room for improvement. If, on the other hand, in most of the course evaluations the overall INSTRUCT_RATING is higher than the COURSE_RATING and it turns out that in most of Professor X's ratings overall the INSTRUCT_RATING is lower than the COURSE_RATING, then such a pattern is unexpected and hence interesting. ◇

Data mining is a step in the KDD process that consists of applying data analysis and discovery algorithms which, under acceptable computational limitations, produce a particular enumeration of patterns (or generate a model) over the data. It uses *historical* information to discover regularities and improve future decisions [161].

The overall KDD process is outlined in Figure 1.1. It is interactive and iterative involving, more or less, the following steps [65, 66]:

1. *Data cleaning and preprocessing*: includes basic operations, such as noise removal and handling of missing data. Data from real-world sources are often erroneous, incomplete, and inconsistent, perhaps due to operation error or system implementation flaws. Such low quality data needs to be cleaned prior to data mining.

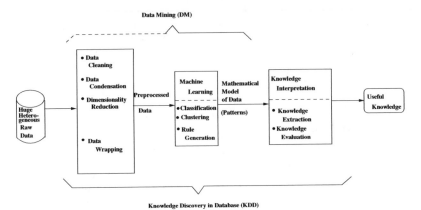

FIGURE 1.1: The KDD process [189].

2. *Data condensation and projection*: includes finding useful features and samples to represent the data (depending on the goal of the task) and using dimensionality reduction or transformation methods.

3. *Data integration and wrapping*: includes integrating multiple, heterogeneous data sources and providing their descriptions (wrappings) for ease of future use.

4. *Choosing the data mining function(s) and algorithm(s)*: includes deciding the purpose (e.g., classification, regression, summarization, clustering, discovering association rules and functional dependencies, or a combination of these) of the model to be derived by the data mining algorithm and selecting methods (e.g., neural networks, decision trees, statistical models, fuzzy models) to be used for searching patterns in data.

5. *Data mining*: includes searching for patterns of interest in a particular representational form or a set of such representations.

6. *Interpretation and visualization*: includes interpreting the discovered patterns, as well as the possible visualization of the extracted patterns. One can analyze the patterns automatically or semiautomatically to identify the truly interesting/useful patterns for the user.

7. *Using discovered knowledge*: includes incorporating this knowledge into the performance system, taking actions based on knowledge.

Thus, KDD refers to the overall process of turning low-level data into high-level knowledge. Perhaps the most important step in the KDD process is data mining. However, the other steps are also important for the successful application of KDD in practice. For example, steps 1, 2 and 3, mentioned above, have been the subject of widespread research in the area of *data warehousing*. We now focus on the data mining component of KDD.

1.4   Data Mining

Data mining involves fitting models to or determining patterns from observed data. The fitted models play the role of inferred knowledge. Deciding whether the model reflects useful knowledge or not is a part of the overall KDD process for which subjective human judgment is usually required. Typically, a data mining algorithm constitutes some combination of the following three components [65].

- **The model**: The function of the model (e.g., classification, clustering) and its representational form (e.g., linear discriminants, neural networks). A model contains parameters that are to be determined from the data.

- **The preference criterion**: A basis for preference of one model or set of parameters over another, depending on the given data. The criterion is usually some form of goodness-of-fit function of the model to the data, perhaps tempered by a smoothing term to avoid overfitting, or generating a model with too many degrees of freedom to be constrained by the given data.

- **The search algorithm**: The specification of an algorithm for finding particular models and parameters, given the data, model(s), and a preference criterion.

A particular data mining algorithm is usually an instantiation of the model/preference/search components.

1.4.1   Data mining tasks

The more common model tasks/functions in current data mining practice include:

1. *Association rule discovery*: describes association relationship among different attributes. The origin of association rules is in market basket analysis. A *market basket* is a collection of items purchased by a customer in an individual *customer transaction*. One common analysis task in a transaction database is to find sets of items, or *itemsets*, that *frequently* appear together. Each pattern extracted through the analysis consists of an itemset and its *support*, i.e., the number of transactions

that contain it. Businesses can use knowledge of these patterns to improve placement of items in a store or for mail-order marketing. The huge size of transaction databases and the exponential increase in the number of potential frequent itemsets with increase in the number of attributes (items) make the above problem a challenging one. The a priori algorithm [3] provided one early solution which was improved by subsequent algorithms using partitioning, hashing, sampling and dynamic itemset counting.

2. *Clustering*: maps a data item into one of several clusters, where clusters are natural groupings of data items based on similarity metrics or probability density models. Clustering is used in several exploratory data analysis tasks, customer retention and management, and web mining. The clustering problem has been studied in many fields, including statistics, machine learning and pattern recognition. However, large data considerations were absent in these approaches. Recently, several new algorithms with greater emphasis on scalability have been developed, including those based on summarized cluster representation called *cluster feature* (Birch [291], ScaleKM [29]), sampling (CURE [84]) and density joins (DBSCAN [61]).

3. *Classification*: classifies a data item into one of several predefined categorical classes. It is used for the purpose of predictive data mining in several fields, e.g., in scientific discovery, fraud detection, atmospheric data mining and financial engineering. Several classification methodologies have already been discussed earlier in Section 1.2.3. Some typical algorithms suitable for large databases are based on Bayesian techniques (AutoClass [40]), and decision trees (Sprint [254], RainForest [75]).

4. *Sequence analysis* [85]: models sequential patterns, like time-series data [130]. The goal is to model the process of generating the sequence or to extract and report deviation and trends over time. The framework is increasingly gaining importance because of its application in bioinformatics and streaming data analysis.

5. *Regression* [65]: maps a data item to a real-valued prediction variable. It is used in different prediction and modeling applications.

6. *Summarization* [65]: provides a compact description for a subset of data. A simple example would be mean and standard deviation for all fields. More sophisticated functions involve summary rules, multivariate visualization techniques and functional relationship between variables. Summarization functions are often used in interactive data analysis, automated report generation and text mining.

7. *Dependency modeling* [28, 86]: describes significant dependencies among variables.

Some other tasks required in some data mining applications are, outlier/ anomaly detection, link analysis, optimization and planning.

1.4.2 Data mining tools

A wide variety and number of data mining algorithms are described in the literature – from the fields of statistics, pattern recognition, machine learning and databases. They represent a long list of seemingly unrelated and often highly specific algorithms. Some representative groups are mentioned below:

1. Statistical models (e.g., linear discriminants [59, 92])

2. Probabilistic graphical dependency models (e.g., Bayesian networks [102])

3. Decision trees and rules (e.g., CART [32])

4. Inductive logic programming based models (e.g., PROGOL [180] and FOIL [233])

5. Example based methods (e.g., nearest neighbor [7], lazy learning [5] and case based reasoning [122, 208] methods)

6. Neural network based models [44, 46, 148, 266]

7. Fuzzy set theoretic models [16, 23, 43, 217]

8. Rough set theory based models [137, 123, 227, 176]

9. Genetic algorithm based models [68, 106]

10. Hybrid and soft computing models [175]

The data mining algorithms determine both the flexibility of the model in representing the data and the interpretability of the model in human terms. Typically, the more complex models may fit the data better but may also be more difficult to understand and to fit reliably. Also, each representation suits some problems better than others. For example, decision tree classifiers can be very useful for finding structure in high dimensional spaces and are also useful in problems with mixed continuous and categorical data. However, they may not be suitable for problems where the true decision boundaries are nonlinear multivariate functions.

1.4.3 Applications of data mining

A wide range of organizations including business companies, scientific laboratories and governmental departments have deployed successful applications of data mining. While early adopters of this technology have tended to be in information-intensive industries such as financial services and direct mail

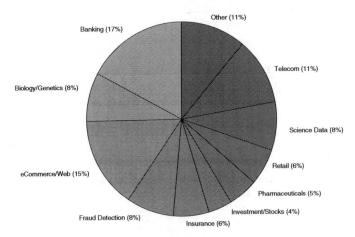

FIGURE 1.2:   Application areas of data mining.

marketing, the technology is applicable to any company looking to leverage a large data warehouse to better manage their operations. Two critical factors for success with data mining are: a large, well-integrated data warehouse and a well-defined understanding of the process within which data mining is to be applied. Several domains where large volumes of data are stored in centralized or distributed databases include the following.

- *Financial Investment*: Stock indices and prices, interest rates, credit card data, fraud detection [151].

- *Health Care*: Several diagnostic information stored by hospital management systems [27].

- *Manufacturing and Production*: Process optimization and trouble shooting [94].

- *Telecommunication network*: Calling patterns and fault management systems [246].

- *Scientific Domain*: Astronomical object detection [64], genomic and biological data mining[15].

- *The World Wide Web*: Information retrieval, resource location [62, 210].

The results of a recent poll conducted at the *www.kdnuggets.com* web site regarding the usage of data mining algorithms in different domains are presented in Figure 1.2.

1.5   Different Perspectives of Data Mining

In the previous section we discussed the generic components of a data mining system, common data mining tasks/tools and related principles and issues that appear in designing a data mining system. At present, the goal of the KDD community is to develop a unified framework of data mining which should be able to model typical data mining tasks, be able to discuss the probabilistic nature of the discovered patterns and models, be able to talk about data and inductive generalizations of the data, and accept the presence of different forms of data (relational data, sequences, text, web). Also, the framework should recognize that data mining is an interactive and iterative process, where comprehensibility of the discovered knowledge is important and where the user has to be in the loop [153, 234].

Pattern recognition and machine learning algorithms seem to be the most suitable candidates for addressing the above tasks. It may be mentioned in this context that historically the subject of knowledge discovery in databases has evolved, and continues to evolve, from the intersection of research from such fields as machine learning, pattern recognition, statistics, databases, artificial intelligence, reasoning with uncertainties, expert systems, data visualization, and high-performance computing. KDD systems incorporate theories, algorithms, and methods from all these fields. Therefore, before elaborating the pattern recognition perspective of data mining, we describe briefly two other prominent frameworks, namely, the database perspective and the statistical perspective of data mining.

1.5.1   Database perspective

Since most business data resides in industrial databases and warehouses, commercial companies view mining as a sophisticated form of database querying [88, 99]. Research based on this perspective seeks to enhance the expressiveness of query languages (rule query languages, meta queries, query optimizations), enhance the underlying model of data and DBMSs (the logical model of data, deductive databases, inductive databases, rules, active databases, semistructured data, etc.) and improve integration with data warehousing systems (online analytical processing (OLAP), historical data, meta-data, interactive exploring). The approach also has close links with search-based perspective of data mining, exemplified by the popular work on association rules [3] at IBM Almaden.

The database perspective has several advantages including scalability to large databases present in secondary and tertiary storage, generic nature of the algorithms (applicability to a wide range of tasks and domains), capability to handle heterogeneous data, and easy user interaction and visualization of mined patterns. However, it is still ill-equipped to address the full range of knowledge discovery tasks because of its inability to mine complex patterns and model non-linear relationships (the database models being of limited richness), unsuitability for exploratory analysis, lack of induction capability, and restricted scope for evaluating the significance of mined patterns [234].

1.5.2 Statistical perspective

The statistical perspective views data mining as computer automated exploratory data analysis of (usually) large complex data sets [79, 92]. The term *data mining* existed in statistical data analysis literature long before its current definition in the computer science community. However, the abundance and massiveness of data has provided impetus to development of algorithms which, though rooted in statistics, lays more emphasis on computational efficiency. Presently, statistical tools are used in all the KDD tasks like preprocessing (sampling, outlier detection, experimental design), data modeling (clustering, expectation maximization, decision trees, regression, canonical correlation etc), model selection, evaluation and averaging (robust statistics, hypothesis testing) and visualization (principal component analysis, Sammon's mapping).

The advantages of the statistical approach are its solid theoretical background, and ease of posing formal questions. Tasks such as classification and clustering fit easily into this approach. What seems to be lacking are ways for taking into account the iterative and interactive nature of the data mining process. Also scalability of the methods to very large, especially tertiary memory data, is still not fully achieved.

1.5.3 Pattern recognition perspective

At present, pattern recognition and machine learning provide the most fruitful framework for data mining [109, 161]. Not only do they provide a wide range of models (linear/non-linear, comprehensible/complex, predictive/descriptive, instance/rule based) for data mining tasks (clustering, classification, rule discovery), methods for modeling uncertainties (probabilistic, fuzzy) in the discovered patterns also form part of PR research. Another aspect that makes pattern recognition algorithms attractive for data mining is their capability of learning or induction. As opposed to many statistical techniques that require the user to have a hypothesis in mind first, PR algorithms automatically analyze data and identify relationships among attributes and entities in the data to build models that allow domain experts to understand the relationship between the attributes and the class. Data preprocessing tasks like instance selection, data cleaning, dimensionality reduction, handling missing data are also extensively studied in pattern recognition framework. Besides these, other data mining issues addressed by PR methodologies include handling of relational, sequential and symbolic data (syntactic PR, PR in arbitrary metric spaces), human interaction (knowledge encoding and extraction), knowledge evaluation (description length principle) and visualization.

Pattern recognition is at the core of data mining systems. However, pattern recognition and data mining are not equivalent considering their original definitions. There exists a gap between the requirements of a data mining system and the goals achieved by present day pattern recognition algorithms. Development of new generation PR algorithms is expected to encompass more massive data sets involving diverse sources and types of data that will support mixed-initiative data mining, where human experts collaborate with the computer to form hypotheses and test them. The main challenges to PR as a unified framework for data mining are mentioned below.

1.5.4　Research issues and challenges

1. *Massive data sets and high dimensionality.* Huge data sets create combinatorially explosive search spaces for model induction which may make the process of extracting patterns infeasible owing to space and time constraints. They also increase the chances that a data mining algorithm will find spurious patterns that are not generally valid.

2. *Overfitting and assessing the statistical significance.* Data sets used for mining are usually huge and available from distributed sources. As a result, often the presence of spurious data points leads to overfitting of the models. Regularization and resampling methodologies need to be emphasized for model design.

3. *Management of changing data and knowledge.* Rapidly changing data, in a database that is modified/deleted/augmented, may make the previously discovered patterns invalid. Possible solutions include incremental methods for updating the patterns.

4. *User interaction and prior knowledge.* Data mining is inherently an interactive and iterative process. Users may interact at various stages, and domain knowledge may be used either in the form of a high level specification of the model, or at a more detailed level. Visualization of the extracted model is also desirable.

5. *Understandability of patterns.* It is necessary to make the discoveries more understandable to humans. Possible solutions include rule structuring, natural language representation, and the visualization of data and knowledge.

6. *Nonstandard and incomplete data.* The data can be missing and/or noisy.

7. *Mixed media data.* Learning from data that is represented by a combination of various media, like (say) numeric, symbolic, images and text.

8. *Integration.* Data mining tools are often only a part of the entire decision making system. It is desirable that they integrate smoothly, both with the database and the final decision-making procedure.

In the next section we discuss the issues related to the large size of the data sets in more detail.

1.6 Scaling Pattern Recognition Algorithms to Large Data Sets

Organizations are amassing very large repositories of customer, operations, scientific and other sorts of data of gigabytes or even terabytes size. KDD practitioners would like to be able to apply pattern recognition and machine learning algorithms to these large data sets in order to discover useful knowledge. The question of *scalability* asks whether the algorithm can process large data sets efficiently, while building from them the best possible models.

From the point of view of complexity analysis, for most scaling problems the limiting factor of the data set has been the number of examples and their dimension. A large number of examples introduces potential problems with both time and space complexity. For time complexity, the appropriate algorithmic question is what is the growth rate of the algorithm's run time as the number of examples and their dimensions increase? As may be expected, time-complexity analysis does not tell the whole story. As the number of instances grows, space constraints become critical, since, almost all existing implementations of a learning algorithm operate with training set entirely in main memory. Finally, the goal of a learning algorithm must be considered. Evaluating the effectiveness of a scaling technique becomes complicated if degradation in the quality of the learning is permitted. Effectiveness of a technique for scaling pattern recognition/learning algorithms is measured in terms of the above three factors, namely, time complexity, space complexity and quality of learning.

Many diverse techniques, both general and task specific, have been proposed and implemented for scaling up learning algorithms. An excellent survey of these methods is provided in [230]. We discuss here some of the broad categories relevant to the book. Besides these, other hardware-driven (parallel processing, distributed computing) and database-driven (relational representation) methodologies are equally effective.

1.6.1 Data reduction

The simplest approach for coping with the infeasibility of learning from a very large data set is to learn from a reduced/condensed representation of the original massive data set [18]. The reduced representation should be as faithful to the original data as possible, for its effective use in different mining tasks. At present the following categories of reduced representations are mainly used:

- *Sampling/instance selection*: Various random, deterministic and density biased sampling strategies exist in statistics literature. Their use in machine learning and data mining tasks has also been widely studied [37, 114, 142]. Note that merely generating a random sample from a large database stored on disk may itself be a non-trivial task from a computational viewpoint. Several aspects of instance selection, e.g., instance representation, selection of interior/boundary points, and instance pruning strategies, have also been investigated in instance-based and nearest neighbor classification frameworks [279]. Challenges in designing an instance selection algorithm include accurate representation of the original data distribution, making fine distinctions at different scales and noticing rare events and anomalies.

- *Data squashing*: It is a form of lossy compression where a large data set is replaced by a small data set and some accompanying quantities, while attempting to preserve its statistical information [60].

- *Indexing data structures*: Systems such as kd-trees [22], R-trees, hash tables, AD-trees, multiresolution kd-trees [54] and cluster feature (CF)-trees [29] partition the data (or feature space) into buckets recursively, and store enough information regarding the data in the bucket so that many mining queries and learning tasks can be achieved in constant or linear time.

- *Frequent itemsets*: They are often applied in supermarket data analysis and require that the attributes are sparsely valued [3].

- *DataCubes*: Use a relational aggregation database operator to represent chunks of data [82].

The last four techniques fall into the general class of representation called *cached sufficient statistics* [177]. These are summary data structures that lie between the statistical algorithms and the database, intercepting the kinds of operations that have the potential to consume large time if they were answered by direct reading of the data set. Case-based reasoning [122] also involves a related approach where salient instances (or descriptions) are either selected or constructed and stored in the case base for later use.

1.6.2   Dimensionality reduction

An important problem related to mining large data sets, both in dimension and size, is of selecting a subset of the original features [141]. Preprocessing the data to obtain a smaller set of representative features, retaining the optimal/salient characteristics of the data, not only decreases the processing time but also leads to more compactness of the models learned and better generalization.

Dimensionality reduction can be done in two ways, namely, *feature selection* and *feature extraction*. As mentioned in Section 1.2.2 feature selection refers to reducing the dimensionality of the measurement space by discarding redundant or least information carrying features. Different methods based on indices like divergence, Mahalanobis distance, Bhattacharya coefficient are available in [30]. On the other hand, feature extraction methods utilize all the information contained in the measurement space to obtain a new transformed space, thereby mapping a higher dimensional pattern to a lower dimensional one. The transformation may be either linear, e.g., principal component analysis (PCA) or nonlinear, e.g., Sammon's mapping, multidimensional scaling. Methods in soft computing using neural networks, fuzzy sets, rough sets and evolutionary algorithms have also been reported for both feature selection and extraction in supervised and unsupervised frameworks. Some other methods including those based on Markov blankets [121], wrapper approach [117], and Relief [113], which are applicable to data sets with large size and dimension, have been explained in Section 3.3.

1.6.3 Active learning

Traditional machine learning algorithms deal with input data consisting of independent and identically distributed (iid) samples. In this framework, the number of samples required (*sample complexity*) by a class of learning algorithms to achieve a specified accuracy can be theoretically determined [19, 275]. In practice, as the amount of data grows, the increase in accuracy slows, forming the learning curve. One can hope to avoid this slow-down in learning by employing selection methods for sifting through the additional examples and filtering out a small non-iid set of relevant examples that contain essential information. Formally, active learning studies the closed-loop phenomenon of a learner selecting actions or making queries that influence what data are added to its training set. When actions/queries are selected properly, the sample complexity for some problems decreases drastically, and some NP-hard learning problems become polynomial in computation time [10, 45].

1.6.4 Data partitioning

Another approach to scaling up is to partition the data, avoiding the need to run algorithms on very large data sets. The models learned from individual partitions are then combined to obtain the final *ensemble* model. Data partitioning techniques can be categorized based on whether they process subsets sequentially or concurrently. Several model combination strategies also exist in literature [77], including boosting, bagging, ARCing classifiers, committee machines, voting classifiers, mixture of experts, stacked generalization,

Bayesian sampling, statistical techniques and soft computing methods. The problems of feature partitioning and modular task decomposition for achieving computational efficiency have also been studied.

1.6.5　Granular computing

Granular computing (GrC) may be regarded as a unified framework for theories, methodologies and techniques that make use of granules (i.e., groups, classes or clusters of objects in a universe) in the process of problem solving. In many situations, when a problem involves incomplete, uncertain and vague information, it may be difficult to differentiate distinct elements and one is forced to consider granules. On the other hand, in some situations though detailed information is available, it may be sufficient to use granules in order to have an efficient and practical solution. Granulation is an important step in the human cognition process. From a more practical point of view, the simplicity derived from granular computing is useful for designing scalable data mining algorithms [138, 209, 219]. There are two aspects of granular computing, one deals with formation, representation and interpretation of granules (algorithmic aspect) while the other deals with utilization of granules for problem solving (semantic aspect). Several approaches for granular computing have been suggested in literature including fuzzy set theory [288], rough set theory [214], power algebras and interval analysis. The rough set theoretic approach is based on the principles of set approximation and provides an attractive framework for data mining and knowledge discovery.

1.6.6　Efficient search algorithms

The most straightforward approach to scaling up machine learning is to produce more efficient algorithms or to increase the efficiency of existing algorithms. As mentioned earlier the data mining problem may be framed as a search through a space of models based on some fitness criteria. This view allows for three possible ways of achieving scalability.

- *Restricted model space*: Simple learning algorithms (e.g., two-level trees, decision stump) and constrained search involve a "smaller" model space and decrease the complexity of the search process.

- *Knowledge encoding*: Domain knowledge encoding, providing an initial solution close to the optimal one, results in fast convergence and avoidance of local minima. Domain knowledge may also be used to guide the search process for faster convergence.

- *Powerful algorithms and heuristics*: Strategies like greedy search, divide and conquer, and modular computation are often found to provide considerable speed-ups. Programming optimization (efficient data structures, dynamic search space restructuring) and the use of genetic algorithms, randomized algorithms and parallel algorithms may also obtain approximate solutions much faster compared to conventional algorithms.

1.7 Significance of Soft Computing in KDD

Soft computing [287] is a consortium of methodologies which works synergistically and provides in one form or another flexible information processing capabilities for handling real life ambiguous situations. Its aim is to exploit the tolerance for imprecision, uncertainty, approximate reasoning and partial truth in order to achieve *tractability, robustness, low cost solutions*, and *close resemblance to human-like decision making*. In other words, it provides the foundation for the conception and design of high MIQ (Machine IQ) systems and therefore forms the basis of future generation computing systems.

In the last section we have discussed various strategies for handling the scalability issue in data mining. Besides scalability other challenges include modeling user interaction and prior knowledge, handling nonstandard, mixed media and incomplete data, and evaluating and visualizing the discovered knowledge. While the scalability property is important for data mining tasks, the significance of the above issues is more with respect to the knowledge discovery aspect of KDD. Soft computing methodolgies, having flexible information processing capability for handling real life ambiguous situations, provide a suitable framework for addressing the latter issues [263, 175].

The main constituents of soft computing, at this juncture, as mentioned in Section 1.2.3, include fuzzy logic, neural networks, genetic algorithms, and rough sets. Each of them contributes a distinct methodology, as stated below, for addressing different problems in its domain.

Fuzzy sets, which constitute the oldest component of soft computing, are suitable for handling the issues related to understandability of patterns, incomplete/noisy data, mixed media information and human interaction and can provide approximate solutions faster. They have been mainly used in clustering, discovering association rules and functional dependencies, summarization, time series analysis, web applications and image retrieval.

Neural networks are suitable in data-rich environments and are typically used for extracting embedded knowledge in the form of rules, quantitative evaluation of these rules, clustering, self-organization, classification and regression. They have an advantage, over other types of machine learning algorithms, for scaling [21].

Neuro-fuzzy hybridization exploits the characteristics of both neural networks and fuzzy sets in generating natural/linguistic rules, handling imprecise and mixed mode data, and modeling highly nonlinear decision boundaries. Domain knowledge, in natural form, can be encoded in the network for improved performance.

Genetic algorithms provide efficient search algorithms to select a model, from mixed media data, based on some preference criterion/objective function. They have been employed in regression and in discovering association rules. Rough sets are suitable for handling different types of uncertainty in data and have been mainly utilized for extracting knowledge in the form of rules.

Other hybridizations typically enjoy the generic and application-specific merits of the individual soft computing tools that they integrate. Data mining functions modeled by such systems include rule extraction, data summarization, clustering, incorporation of domain knowledge, and partitioning. Case-based reasoning (CBR), a novel AI problem-solving paradigm, has recently drawn the attention of both soft computing and data mining communities. A profile of its theory, algorithms, and potential applications is available in [262, 195, 208].

A review on the role of different soft computing tools in data mining problems is provided in Appendix A.

1.8 Scope of the Book

This book has eight chapters describing various theories, methodologies, and algorithms along with extensive experimental results, addressing certain pattern recognition tasks essential for data mining. Tasks considered include data condensation, feature selection, case generation, clustering, classification, and rule generation/evaluation. Various methodologies have been described using both classical and soft computing approaches (integrating fuzzy logic, artificial neural networks, rough sets, genetic algorithms). The emphasis of the methodologies is on handling data sets that are large (both in size and dimension) and involve classes that are overlapping, intractable and/or having nonlinear boundaries. Several strategies based on data reduction, dimensionality reduction, active learning, granular computing and efficient search heuristics are employed for dealing with the issue of 'scaling-up' in learning problem. The problems of handling linguistic input and ambiguous output decision, learning of overlapping/intractable class structures, selection of optimal parameters, and discovering human comprehensible knowledge (in the form of linguistic rules) are addressed in a soft computing framework.

The effectiveness of the algorithms is demonstrated on different real life data sets, mainly large in dimension and/or size, taken from varied domains, e.g., geographical information systems, remote sensing imagery, population census, speech recognition, and cancer management. Superiority of the models over several related ones is found to be statistically significant.

In Chapter 2, the problem of data condensation is addressed. After providing a brief review of diferent data condensation algorithms, such as condensed nearest neighbor rule, learning vector quantization and Astrahan's method, a generic multiscale data reduction methodology is described. It preserves the salient characteristics of the original data set by representing the probability density underlying it. The representative points are selected in a multiresolution fashion, which is novel with respect to the existing density based approaches. A scale parameter (k) is used in non-parametric density estimation so that the data can be viewed at varying degrees of detail depending on the value of k. This type of multiscale representation is desirable in various data mining applications. At each scale the representation gives adequate importance to different regions of the feature space based on the underlying probability density.

It is observed experimentally that the multiresolution approach helps to achieve lower error with similar condensation ratio compared to several related schemes. The reduced set obtained is found to be effective for a number of mining tasks such as classification, clustering and rule generation. The algorithm is also found to be efficient in terms of sample complexity, in the sense that the error level decreases rapidly with the increase in size of the condensed set.

Chapter 3 deals with the task of feature selection. First a brief review on feature selection and extraction methods, including the filter and wrapper approaches, is provided. Then it describes, in detail, an unsupervised feature selection algorithm suitable for data sets, large in both dimension and size. Conventional methods of feature selection involve evaluating different feature subsets using some index and then selecting the best among them. The index usually measures the capability of the respective subsets in classification or clustering depending on whether the selection process is supervised or unsupervised. A problem of these methods, when applied to large data sets, is the high computational complexity involved in searching.

The unsupervised algorithm described in Chapter 3 digresses from the aforesaid conventional view and is based on measuring similarity between features and then removing the redundancy therein. This does not need any search and, therefore, is fast. Since the method achieves dimensionality reduction through removal of redundant features, it is more related to feature selection for compression rather than for classification.

The method involves partitioning of the original feature set into some distinct subsets or clusters so that the features within a cluster are highly similar while those in different clusters are dissimilar. A single feature from each such cluster is then selected to constitute the resulting reduced subset. The algorithm is generic in nature and has the capability of multiscale representation of data sets.

Superiority of the algorithm, over related methods, is demonstrated extensively on different real life data with dimension ranging from 4 to 649. Comparison is made on the basis of both clustering/classification performance and redundancy reduction. Studies on effectiveness of the maximal information compression index and the effect of scale parameter are also presented.

While Chapters 2 and 3 deal with some preprocessing tasks of data mining, Chapter 4 is concerned with its classification/learning aspect. Here we present two active learning strategies for handling the large quadratic programming (QP) problem of support vector machine (SVM) classifier design. The first one is an error-driven incremental method for active support vector learning. The method involves selecting a chunk of q new points, having equal number of correctly classified and misclassified points, at each iteration by resampling the data set, and using it to update the current SV set. The resampling strategy is computationally superior to random chunk selection, while achieving higher classification accuracy. Since it allows for querying multiple instances at each iteration, it is computationally more efficient than those that are querying for a single example at a time.

The second algorithm deals with active support vector learning in a statistical query framework. Like the previous algorithm, it also involves queries for multiple instances at each iteration. The intermediate statistical query oracle, involved in the learning process, returns the value of the probability that a new example belongs to the actual support vector set. A set of q new points is selected according to the above probability and is used along with the current SVs to obtain the new SVs. The probability is estimated using a combination of two factors: the margin of the particular example with respect to the current hyperplane, and the degree of confidence that the current set of SVs provides the actual SVs. The degree of confidence is quantified by a measure which is based on the local properties of each of the current support vectors and is computed using the nearest neighbor estimates.

The methodology in the second part has some more advantages. It not only queries for the error points (or points having low margin) but also a number of other points far from the separating hyperplane (interior points). Thus, even if a current hypothesis is erroneous there is a scope for its being corrected owing to the interior points. If only error points were selected the hypothesis might have actually been worse. The ratio of selected points having low margin and those far from the hyperplane is decided by the confidence factor, which varies adaptively with iteration. If the current SV set is close to the optimal one, the algorithm focuses only on the low margin points and ignores the redundant points that lie far from the hyperplane. On the other hand, if the confidence factor is low (say, in the initial learning phase) it explores a higher number of interior points. Thus, the trade-off between efficiency and robustness of performance is adequately handled in this framework. Also, the efficiency of most of the existing active SV learning algorithms depends on the sparsity ratio (i.e., the ratio of the number of support vectors to the total number of data points) of the data set. Due to the adaptive nature of the query in the proposed algorithm, it is likely to be efficient for a wide range of sparsity ratio.

Experimental results have been presented for five real life classification problems. The number of patterns ranges from 351 to 495141, dimension from

9 to 34, and the sparsity ratio from 0.01 to 0.51. The algorithms, particularly the second one, are found to provide superior performance in terms of classification accuracy, closeness to the optimal SV set, training time and margin distribution, as compared to several related algorithms for incremental and active SV learning. Studies on effectiveness of the confidence factor, used in statistical queries, are also presented.

In the previous three chapters all the methodologies described for data condensation, feature selection and active learning are based on classical approach. The next three chapters (Chapters 5 to 7) emphasize demonstrating the effectiveness of integrating different soft computing tools, e.g., fuzzy logic, artificial neural networks, rough sets and genetic algorithms for performing certain tasks in data mining.

In Chapter 5 methods based on the principle of granular computing in rough fuzzy framework are described for efficient case (representative class prototypes) generation of large data sets. Here, fuzzy set theory is used for linguistic representation of patterns, thereby producing a fuzzy granulation of the feature space. Rough set theory is used to obtain the dependency rules which model different informative regions in the granulated feature space. The fuzzy membership functions corresponding to the informative regions are stored as cases along with the strength values. Case retrieval is made using a similarity measure based on these membership functions. Unlike the existing case selection methods, the cases here are cluster granules, and not the sample points. Also, each case involves a reduced number of relevant (variable) features. Because of this twofold information compression the algorithm has a low time requirement in generation as well as retrieval of cases. Superiority of the algorithm in terms of classification accuracy, and case generation and retrieval time is demonstrated experimentally on data sets having large dimension and size.

In Chapter 6 we first describe, in brief, some clustering algorithms suitable for large data sets. Then an integration of a minimal spanning tree (MST) based graph-theoretic technique and expectation maximization (EM) algorithm with rough set initialization is described for non-convex clustering. Here, rough set initialization is performed using dependency rules generated on a fuzzy granulated feature space. EM provides the statistical model of the data and handles the associated uncertainties. Rough set theory helps in faster convergence and avoidance of the local minima problem, thereby enhancing the performance of EM. MST helps in determining non-convex clusters. Since it is applied on Gaussians rather than the original data points, the time requirement is very low. Comparison with related methods is made in terms of a cluster quality measure and computation time. Its effectiveness is also demonstrated for segmentation of multispectral satellite images into different landcover types.

A rough self-organizing map (RSOM) with fuzzy discretization of feature space is described in Chapter 7. Discernibility reducts obtained using rough set theory are used to extract domain knowledge in an unsupervised framework. Reducts are then used to determine the initial weights of the network, which are further refined using competitive learning. Superiority of this network in terms of quality of clusters, learning time and representation of data is demonstrated quantitatively through experiments over the conventional SOM with both random and linear initializations. A linguistic rule generation algorithm has been described. The extracted rules are also found to be superior in terms of coverage, reachability and fidelity. This methodology is unique in demonstrating how rough sets could be integrated with SOM, and it provides a fast and robust solution to the initialization problem of SOM learning.

While granular computing is performed in rough-fuzzy and neuro-rough frameworks in Chapters 5 and 6 and Chapter 7, respectively, the same is done in Chapter 8 in an evolutionary rough-neuro-fuzzy framework by a synergistic integration of all the four soft computing components. After explaining different ensemble learning techniques, a modular rough-fuzzy multilayer perceptron (MLP) is described in detail. Here fuzzy sets, rough sets, neural networks and genetic algorithms are combined with modular decomposition strategy. The resulting connectionist system achieves gain in terms of performance, learning time and network compactness for classification and linguistic rule generation.

Here, the role of the individual components is as follows. Fuzzy sets handle uncertainties in the input data and output decision of the neural network and provide linguistic representation (fuzzy granulation) of the feature space. Multilayer perceptron is well known for providing a connectionist paradigm for learning and adaptation. Rough set theory is used to extract domain knowledge in the form of linguistic rules, which are then encoded into a number of fuzzy MLP modules or subnetworks. Genetic algorithms (GAs) are used to integrate and evolve the population of subnetworks as well as the fuzzification parameters through efficient searching. A concept of variable mutation operator is introduced for preserving the localized structure of the constituting knowledge-based subnetworks, while they are integrated and evolved. The nature of the mutation operator is determined by the domain knowledge extracted by rough sets.

The modular concept, based on a "divide and conquer" strategy, provides accelerated training, preserves the identity of individual clusters, reduces the catastrophic interference due to overlapping regions, and generates a compact network suitable for extracting a minimum number of rules with high certainty values. A quantitative study of the knowledge discovery aspect is made through different rule evaluation indices, such as interestingness, certainty, confusion, coverage, accuracy and fidelity. Different well-established algorithms for generating classification and association rules are described in this regard for convenience. These include *a priori*, subset, MofN and dynamic itemset counting methods.

The effectiveness of the modular rough-fuzzy MLP and its rule extraction algorithm is extensively demonstrated through experiments along with comparisons. In some cases the rules generated are also validated by domain experts. The network model, besides having significance in soft computing research, has potential for application to large-scale problems involving knowledge discovery tasks, particularly related to mining of linguistic classification rules.

Two appendices are included for the convenience of readers. Appendix A provides a review on the role of different soft computing tools in KDD. Appendix B describes the different data sets used in the experiments.

Chapter 2

Multiscale Data Condensation

2.1 Introduction

The current popularity of data mining and data warehousing, as well as the decline in the cost of disk storage, has led to a proliferation of terabyte data warehouses [66]. Mining a database of even a few gigabytes is an arduous task for machine learning techniques and requires advanced parallel hardware and algorithms. An approach for dealing with the intractable problem of learning from huge databases is to select a small subset of data for learning [230]. Databases often contain redundant data. It would be convenient if large databases could be replaced by a small subset of representative patterns so that the accuracy of estimates (e.g., of probability density, dependencies, class boundaries) obtained from such a reduced set should be comparable to that obtained using the entire data set.

The simplest approach for data reduction is to draw the desired number of random samples from the entire data set. Various statistical sampling methods such as random sampling, stratified sampling, and peepholing [37] have been in existence. However, naive sampling methods are not suitable for real world problems with noisy data, since the performance of the algorithms may change unpredictably and significantly [37]. Better performance is obtained using *uncertainty sampling* [136] and *active learning* [241], where a simple classifier queries for informative examples. The random sampling approach effectively ignores all the information present in the samples not chosen for membership in the reduced subset. An advanced condensation algorithm should include information from all samples in the reduction process.

Some widely studied schemes for data condensation are built upon classification-based approaches, in general, and the k-NN rule, in particular [48]. The effectiveness of the condensed set is measured in terms of the classification accuracy. These methods attempt to derive a minimal consistent set, i.e., a minimal set which correctly classifies all the original samples. The very first development of this kind is the condensed nearest neighbor rule (CNN) of Hart [91]. Other algorithms in this category including the popular IB3, IB4 [4], reduced nearest neighbor and iterative condensation algorithms are summarized in [279]. Recently a local asymmetrically weighted similarity metric (LASM) approach for data compression [239] is shown to have superior

29

performance compared to conventional k-NN classification-based methods. Similar concepts of data reduction and locally varying models based on neural networks and Bayes classifier are discussed in [226] and [144] respectively.

The classification-based condensation methods are, however, specific to (i.e., dependent on) the classification tasks and the models (e.g., k-NN, perceptron) used. Data condensation of more generic nature is performed by classical vector quantization methods [83] using a set of codebook vectors which minimize the quantization error. An effective and popular method of learning the vectors is to use the self-organizing map [118]. However, if the self-organizing map is to be used as a pattern classifier, the codebook vectors may be further refined using the learning vector quantization algorithms [118]. These methods are seen to approximate the density underlying the data [118]. Since learning is inherent in the methodologies, the final solution is dependent on initialization, choice of learning parameters, and the nature of local minima.

Another group of generic data condensation methods are based on the density-based approaches, which consider the density function of the data for the purpose of condensation rather than minimizing the quantization error. These methods do not involve any learning process and therefore are deterministic (i.e., for a given input data set the output condensed set is fixed). Here one estimates the density at a point and selects the points having 'higher' densities, while ensuring a minimum separation between the selected points. These methods bear resemblance to density-based clustering techniques like the DBSCAN algorithm [61], popular for spatial data mining. DBSCAN is based on the principle that a cluster point contains in its neighborhood a minimum number of samples; i.e., the cluster point has density above a certain threshold. The neighborhood radius and the density threshold are user specified. Astrahan [13] proposed a classical data reduction algorithm of this type in 1971, in which he used a hypersphere (disc) of radius d_1 about a point to obtain an estimate of density at that point. The points are sorted based on these estimated densities, and the densest point is selected, while rejecting all points that lie within another disc of radius d_2 about the selected point. The process is repeated until all the samples are covered. However, selecting the values of d_1 and d_2 is a non-trivial problem. A partial solution using a minimal spanning tree-based method is described in [39]. Though the above approaches select the points based on the density criterion, they do not directly attempt to represent the original distribution. The selected points are distributed evenly over the entire feature space irrespective of the distribution. A constant separation is used for instance pruning. Interestingly, Fukunaga [74] suggested a non-parametric algorithm for selecting a condensed set based on the criterion that density estimates obtained with the original set and the reduced set are *close*. The algorithm is, however, search-based and requires large computation time.

Efficiency of condensation algorithms may be improved by adopting a multiresolution representation approach. A multiresolution framework for instance-based learning and regression has been studied in [54] and [178] respectively.

It uses a k-d tree [22] to impose a hierarchy of data partitions that implicitly condense the data into homogeneous blocks having variable resolutions. Each level of the tree represents a partition of the feature space at a particular scale of detail. Prediction for a query point is performed using blocks from different scales; finer scale blocks are used for points close to the query and cruder scale blocks for those far from the query. However, the blocks are constructed by simple median splitting algorithms which do not directly consider the density function underlying the data.

We describe in this chapter a density-based multiresolution data reduction algorithm [165] that uses discs of adaptive radii for both density estimation and sample pruning. The method attempts to accurately represent the entire distribution rather than the data set itself. The accuracy of this representation is measured using nearest neighbor density estimates at each point belonging to the entire data set. It does away with the difficult choice of radii d_1 and d_2 as in Astrahan's method discussed above. Here, k-NN density estimates are obtained for each point and the points having higher density are selected subject to the condition that the point does not lie in a region 'covered' by any other selected point. A selected point 'covers' a disc around it with volume inversely proportional (by a factor σ, say) to the (estimated) density at that point, as illustrated in Figure 2.1. Hence the regions having higher density are represented more accurately in the reduced data sets compared to sparse regions. The proportionality factor (σ) and k used for k-NN density estimation controls the condensation ratio and the accuracy of representation.

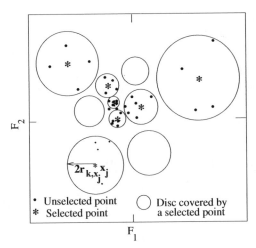

FIGURE 2.1: Multiresolution data reduction.

The condensation algorithm can obtain reduced sets which represent the data at different scales. The parameter k acts as the scale parameter, and the data is viewed at varying degrees of detail depending on the value of k. This type of multiscale representation of data is desirable for various applications like data mining. At each scale the representation gives adequate importance to different regions of the feature space based upon the probability density as mentioned before. The above scheme induces a scale that is both efficient in terms of density estimation error and natural to the data distribution.

It is observed from experiments that the multiresolution approach helps to achieve lower error with similar condensation ratio compared to several related data condensation schemes. The reduced set obtained was found to be effective for a number of data mining applications such as classification, clustering and rule generation. The algorithm is also found to be scalable and efficient in terms of sample complexity, in the sense that the error level decreases quickly with the increase in size of the condensed set.

In Section 2.2 we first describe some of the commonly used data condensation techniques. These include condensed nearest neighbor rule, learning vector quantization method, and Astrahan's algorithm. In Section 2.3 we describe different aspects of multiscale representation. Section 2.4 provides in brief the k-NN density estimation technique. The multiscale data condensation algorithm based on this is explained in Section 2.5. Experimental results and comparisons are presented in Section 2.6, and summary of the chapter is provided in Section 2.7.

2.2   Data Condensation Algorithms

As discussed before, common data condensation algorithms are mainly based on the k-NN rule, competitive learning, or density estimation. We provide below three algorithms, one from each such category, namely, the condensed nearest neighbor rule, learning vector quantization method and Astrahan's algorithm, respectively.

2.2.1   Condensed nearest neighbor rule

The objective of the condensed nearest neighbor technique [91] is to select a minimal subset of points such that the k-NN rule with the selected subset would correctly classify the remaining points in the original data set. Obtaining the 'minimal' subset is computationally infeasible. However, a near minimal subset can be obtained with the following algorithm.

Algorithm:
Set up bins called STORE and GRABBAG. The first k points are placed in STORE; all other samples are placed in GRABBAG. Let n_g denote the

current number of samples in GRABBAG whenever Step 1 of the algorithm is entered.

1. Use the k-NN rule with the current contents of STORE to classify the ith point from GRABBAG. If classified correctly the point is returned to GRABBAG; otherwise, it is placed in STORE. Repeat this operation for $i = 1, 2, \ldots, n_g$.

2. If one complete pass is made through Step 1 with no transfer from GRABBAG to STORE, or the GRABBAG is exhausted then terminate; else go to Step 1.

The final contents of STORE constitute the condensed subset to be used with the k-NN rule. The contents of GRABBAG are discarded.

2.2.2   Learning vector quantization

In vector quantization, the feature space is divided into a number of distinct regions, and for each region a 'reconstruction vector' is defined. Each reconstruction vector can be used to code (represent) the data points belonging to that region. The collection of all these reconstruction vectors constitutes what is called the 'code book' of the vector quantizer. A vector quantizer with the minimum encoding distortion is called a Voronoi or nearest neighbor quantizer. The self-organizing map (SOM) [118] provides an approximate method for computing the Voronoi quantizer in an unsupervised manner using competitive learning. This can be considered as the first step of learning vector quantization. The second stage fine-tunes the SOM [118] by using the class information to move the code book vectors slightly for improving the decision regions of the classifier. The following steps are used in this process.

1. Suppose that the code book vector $\mathbf{w}_c$ is closest to the input vector $\mathbf{x}_i$. Let $C_{\mathbf{w}c}$ denote the class of $\mathbf{w}_c$, and $C_{\mathbf{x}i}$ the class of $\mathbf{x}_i$.

2. The code book vectors are adjusted as follows:

   (a) If $C_{\mathbf{w}c} = C_{\mathbf{x}i}$, then $\mathbf{x}_c(t+1) = \mathbf{w}_c(t) + \alpha_t(\mathbf{x}_i - \mathbf{w}_c(t))$
   (b) If $C_{\mathbf{w}c} \neq C_{\mathbf{x}i}$, then $\mathbf{x}_c(t+1) = \mathbf{w}_c(t) - \alpha_t(\mathbf{x}_i - \mathbf{w}_c(t))$

3. The other (non-closest) code book vectors are not changed.

After convergence of the above learning steps, the final code book vectors constitute the condensed set. The learning parameter α_t usually decreases monotonically with iteration t.

2.2.3   Astrahan's density-based method

This method [13] involves two steps, namely, selecting high density points based on the local density estimates and pruning of other points that lie in the neighborhood of the selected points. The steps are described below.

Select two radii d_1 and d_2, where $d_2 > d_1$. Set up two bins EDIT and SELECT. Initially, EDIT contains all the points in the data set.

1. For every point $\mathbf{x}_i$ of the EDIT set, count the number (n_i) of points in the EDIT set that lie inside a disc of radius d_1 centered at $\mathbf{x}_i$. Move point $\mathbf{x}_j$ having the highest count n_j to the SELECT set. Note that, $\mathbf{x}_j$ is the densest point among $\mathbf{x}_i$s.

2. *Discard* from EDIT all points that lie inside a disc of radius d_2 centered about a selected point $\mathbf{x}_j$. Repeat Step 1, until EDIT is exhausted.

The SELECT set, thus produced, constitutes the condensed set of points.

In the above method, for the purpose of density estimation one may use radius $d_1 = \sqrt{sup_{i=1,..,n}(inf_{j=1,..,n}d(\mathbf{x}_i, \mathbf{x}_j))}$, and radius $d_2 = \gamma d_1$ for pruning, where γ is a tunable parameter controlling the condensation ratio. The above expression for d_1 produces a radius close to that obtained using the minimal spanning tree-based method described in [39].

2.3   Multiscale Representation of Data

Multiscale representation of data refers to visualization of the data at different 'scales,' where the term *scale* may signify either unit, frequency, radius, window size or kernel parameters. The importance of scale has been increasingly acknowledged in the past decade in the areas of image and signal analysis and computer vision with the development of several scale-inspired models such as pyramids, wavelets and multiresolution techniques. Recently scale-based methods have also become popular in clustering [135] and density estimation. In these methodologies, the concept of scale has been implemented using variable width radial basis function Network, annealing-based clustering and variable window density estimates.

The question of scale is natural to data condensation. At a very coarse scale the entire data may be represented by only a few number of points, and at a very fine scale all the sample points may constitute the condensed set, the scales in between representing varying degrees of detail. In many data mining applications (e.g., structure discovery in remotely sensed data, identifying population groups from census data) it is necessary that the data be represented in varying levels of detail. Data condensation is only a preliminary step in the overall data mining process and several higher level learning operations may be performed on the condensed set later. Hence the condensation algorithm should be able to obtain representative subsets at different scales, as demanded, in an *efficient* manner.

The method for data condensation, discussed in Section 2.1, obtains condensed sets of different degrees of detail by varying a scale parameter k. It may be noted that such variable detail representation may be achieved by other approaches also, including random sampling. However, unlike random sampling the scales induced by the density-based multiscale method are not prespecified by the sizes of the condensed sets but follow the natural characteristics of the data. As far as efficiency of the scaling procedure is concerned, it may be noted that in most of the multiscale schemes for representing data or signal, including wavelets, efficiency is achieved by a lenient representation of the 'unimportant' regions and a detailed representation of the 'important' regions, where the notion of importance may vary from problem to problem. The condensation algorithm follows a similar principle where at each scale the different regions of the feature space are represented in the condensed set based on the densities of those regions estimated at that particular scale. Figure 2.2 illustrates the concept of variable scale representation. The data consists of 2000 points selected randomly from two nonoverlapping circles of radius 1 unit and centers at $(2,0)$ and $(5,0)$ respectively (Figure 2.2(a)). Figures 2.2(b)−(e) shows representation of the data by condensed sets at different levels of detail. It can be seen that in Figure 2.2(b) only two points cover the entire data set. In Figure 2.2(c) four points are used to represent the entire data set. Figure 2.2(d) and (e) are more detailed representations of the data.

For a particular scale the basic principle of the density-based multiscale data condensation algorithm involves sorting the points based on *estimated densities*, selecting the denser points and removing other points that lie within certain distances of the selected points in a multiresolution manner. A nonparametric method of estimating a probability density function is the k-nearest neighbor method. In k-NN-based estimation technique the density of a point is computed based upon the volume of disc about that point which includes a fixed number, say k, other points [145]. Hence, the radius of the disc is smaller in a densely populated region than in a sparse region. The volume of the disc is inversely proportional to the probability density function at the center point of the disc. This behavior is advantageous for the present problem from the point of view of multiresolution representation over different regions of feature space. This is the reason that the k-NN density estimate is considered in the condensation algorithm.

Before we present the multiscale data condensation algorithm, we describe in brief the k-NN-based density estimation technique in the next section.

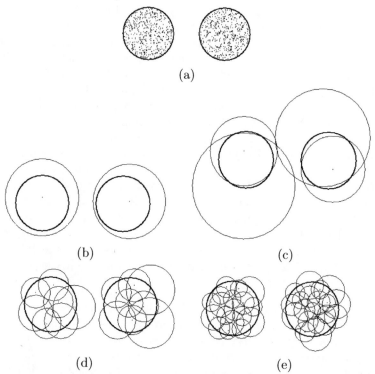

FIGURE 2.2: Representation of data set at different levels of detail by the condensed sets. '.' is a point belonging to the condensed set; the circles about the points denote the discs covered that point. The two bold circles denote the boundaries of the data set.

2.4 Nearest Neighbor Density Estimate

Let $x_1, x_2, \ldots, x_N$ be independent observations on a p-dimensional random variable X, with a continuous probability density function f. The problem is to estimate f at a point z.

Let $d(x, z)$ represent the Euclidean distance between x and z. A p-dimensional hypersphere of radius r about z is designated by $S_{r,z}$, i.e., $S_{r,z} = \{x | d(x, z) \leq r\}$. The volume or Lebesgue measure of the hypersphere $S_{r,z}$ will be called A_r. Let us describe a non-parametric method for estimating f suggested by Loftsgaarden [145].

Let $k(N)$ be a sequence of positive integers such that $\lim_{N \to \infty} k(N) = \infty$, and $\lim_{N \to \infty} k(N)/N = 0$. Once $k(N)$ is chosen and a sample set $\{x_1, x_2, \ldots x_N\}$ is available, $r_{k(N),z}$ is determined as the distance from z to the $(k(N) + 1)$th nearest neighbor of z among $x_1, x_2, \ldots x_N$. Hence, an estimate of f is given by

$$\hat{f}_N(z) = \frac{k(N)}{N} \times \frac{1}{A_{r_{k(N),z}}} \qquad (2.1)$$

It can be proved [145] that the density estimate given by Equation 2.1 is asymptotically unbiased and consistent. It may however be noted that k-NN estimates suffer from the 'curse of dimensionality' problem in high dimensional spaces.

A condensation algorithm should obtain a subset that is representative of the original data distribution. We discuss below some measures of accuracy of such representations in terms of the error in k-NN density estimate discussed above.

Measures of error in density estimate:

Let $x_1, \ldots, x_N$ be N independent samples drawn from a distribution f. The closeness between two estimates g_1 and g_2 of f is measured by a criterion of the form

$$\hat{J} = \frac{1}{N} \sum_{i=1}^{N} D(g_1(x_i), g_2(x_i)) \,,$$

where x_i is the ith sample, and $D(., .)$ is a measure of the distance between $g_1(x_i)$ and $g_2(x_i)$. It may be noted that $\hat{J}$ is a random variable, and an estimate of the quantity J, where

$$J = E(\hat{J}) = \int D(g_1(z), g_2(z)) f(z) dz$$

Here one obtains a density estimate $\hat{f}_N$ for f, from $\{x_1, \ldots x_N\}$ using the k-NN density estimation method already described. The next step is to choose n points, $n \ll N$, from $x_1, \ldots, x_N$ such that the density estimate $\hat{\alpha}_n$ obtained from this n points is close to $\hat{f}_N$ where n is not predetermined. In the next section, we present a method that automatically provides the value for n and the set of n points for a given $\{\mathbf{x}_1, \ldots, \mathbf{x}_N\}$. It may be noted that $\hat{J}$ measures the difference between estimates $\hat{f}_N$ and $\hat{\alpha}_n$ and not the error of each of these estimates with respect to the actual distribution. However, if N is large it is known that $\hat{f}_N$ is a consistent estimate of f [145] (for suitable values of k as mentioned in Equation 2.1). Hence, a small value of $\hat{J}$ indicate closeness of $\hat{\alpha}_n$ to the actual distribution f.

For computing D an expression, similar to log-likelihood ratio used in classification [74],

$$D(\hat{f}_N(\mathbf{x}_i), \hat{\alpha}_n(\mathbf{x}_i)) = \left| \ln \frac{\hat{f}_N(\mathbf{x}_i)}{\hat{\alpha}_n(\mathbf{x}_i)} \right| ,$$
(2.2)

is considered. A second possibility for computing D is to use a modified version of the kernel of the Kullback-Liebler information number [74], which attaches more weight to the high density region of the distribution

$$D(\hat{f}_N(\mathbf{x}_i), \hat{\alpha}_n(\mathbf{x}_i)) = \left| \hat{\alpha}_N(\mathbf{x}_i).\ln \frac{\hat{f}_N(\mathbf{x}_i)}{\hat{\alpha}_n(\mathbf{x}_i)} \right| .$$
(2.3)

These quantities can be used to measure the efficacy of the reduction algorithms. If the density estimates are close enough, each of the quantities will be almost zero.

2.5   Multiscale Data Condensation Algorithm

The multiscale data condensation algorithm [165] involves estimating the density at a point using the methods described in the previous section, sorting the points based on the density criterion, selecting a point according to the sorted list, and pruning all points lying within a disc about a selected point with radius inversely proportional to the density at that point.

Algorithm:

Let $B_N = \{\mathbf{x}_1, \mathbf{x}_2, \ldots, \mathbf{x}_N\}$ be the original data set. Choose a positive integer k.

1. For each point $\mathbf{x}_i \in B_N$ calculate the distance of the kth nearest neighbor of $\mathbf{x}_i$ in B_N. Denote it by $r_{k,\mathbf{x}_i}$.

2. Select the point $\mathbf{x}_j \in B_N$, having the lowest value of $r_{k,\mathbf{x}_j}$ and place it in the reduced set E. Ties in lowest value of $r_{k,\mathbf{x}_j}$ may be resolved by

a convention, say according to the index of the samples. From Equation 2.1 it is evident that $\mathbf{x_j}$ corresponds to the point having the highest density $\hat{f}_N(\mathbf{x}_j)$.

3. Remove all points from B_N that lie within a disc of radius $2r_{k,\mathbf{x}_j}$ centered at $\mathbf{x}_j$, and the set consisting of the remaining points be renamed as B_N. Note that since $r_{k,\mathbf{x}_j}^p$ (where p is the dimension of the feature space) is inversely proportional to the estimate of the probability density at $\mathbf{x}_j$, regions of higher probability density are covered by smaller discs and sparser regions are covered by larger discs. Consequently, more points are selected from the regions having higher density.

4. Repeat Step 2 on B_N till B_N becomes a null set.

The $\mathbf{x}_j$'s thus selected and the corresponding $r_{k,\mathbf{x}_j}$ constitute the condensed (reduced) set. $\Box$

The procedure is illustrated in Figure 2.1 in $F_1 - F_2$ space. As shown in the figure, each selected point (marked '*') is at the center of a disc that covers some region in the feature space. All other points (marked as '.') lying within the disc except the center are discarded. It can be seen that the selected points lying in high density regions have discs of smaller radii, while points in sparser regions correspond to larger discs; i.e., the data are represented in a multiscale manner over the feature space.

Remarks:

1. The algorithm not only selects the denser data points but does so in a manner such that the separation between two points is inversely proportional to the probability density of the points. Hence, regions in the feature space having higher density are represented by more points than sparser regions. This provides a better representation of the data distribution than random sampling because different regions of the feature space are given variable importance on the basis of the probability density of that region; i.e., the representation is of multiresolution nature. A technique for performance enhancement and computational time reduction using such multiresolution representation is discussed in [54].

2. The condensed set obtained may be used to obtain an estimate of the probability density function of the data. This may be done using the k-NN density estimation method discussed in Section 2.4.

3. The parameter k acts as a scale-parameter for the condensation algorithm. The size of the neighborhood, used for density estimate, as well as the pruning radii are dependent on k, and therefore vary with scale. Smaller the value of k more refined is the scale and vice versa. However, independent of the chosen scale, the representation gives adequate importance to the different regions of the feature space depending on

their estimated densities at that scale. This type of multiresolution representation helps preserve salient features that are natural to the data over a wide range of scales. In many situations the scale to be used for condensation is dictated by the application. However, if no such application-specific requirements exist, the condensed set may be selected from the region where the error versus scale curve (which is exponentially decaying in nature) begins to flatten.

4. It may be noted that the choice of k is a classical problem for k-NN-based methods for finite sample sets. Theoretically, the value of k should increase with the size of the data set (N), but at a slower rate than N itself. For data condensation using the density based multiscale method it has also been observed that the value of k should be increased as the data set size N increases to achieve a constant condensation ratio (CR), though the exact nature of the k versus CR curve is distribution dependent. In the experimental results presented in Section 2.6.6 it is observed that at high values of k (i.e., low values of CR) the k versus CR curve is sufficiently robust over different data sets.

5. The accuracy of k-NN density depends on the value of k used. Admissible values of k may be obtained from considerations discussed above. However, for very small data sets the choice of lower admissible limit of k is dictated by the size of the data set.

2.6   Experimental Results and Comparisons

In this section we present the results of experiments [165] conducted on some well-known data sets of varying dimension and size. Among them the Forest cover type data represents forest cover of 30m × 30m cells obtained from US Forest Service (USFS) Region 2 Resource Information System (RIS). It contains 581012 instances having 54 attributes representing cartographic variables. Each observation is labeled as belonging to one of the 7 different classes (forest cover types). Among the other data sets, the Satellite Image data consists of four 512 × 512 gray scale images of different spectral bands obtained by the Indian Remote Sensing satellite of the city of Calcutta in India. Each pixel represents a 36.25m × 36.25m region. The third large data set used is the PUMS census data for the Los Angeles and Long Beach area. The data contains 133 attributes, mostly categorical, and 320000 samples were used. The other data sets, e.g., Wisconsin breast cancer (medical domain data), Pima Indian (also medical domain data), Vowel (speech data), Iris (flower classification data), Ringnorm and Twonorm (artificial data), are benchmark data sets widely used in literature. The *Norm* data was artificially generated by drawing 500 i.i.d samples from a normal distribution with mean $= \begin{bmatrix} 0 \\ 0 \end{bmatrix}$ and covariance matrix $= \begin{bmatrix} 1 & 0 \\ 0 & 1 \end{bmatrix}$. The data sets are described in detail in Appendix B.

The organization of the results is as follows. First we present and compare the results concerning error in density estimate and condensation ratio for all ten data sets. Next, the efficacy of the multiscale condensation method for three diverse tasks namely classification, clustering and rule generation is demonstrated on the three large data sets. The Forest cover type data is considered to evaluate the *classification* performance, the Satellite image data is considered for *clustering*, and the PUMS Los Angeles census data is considered for *rule generation*. The choice of tasks for the three large data sets described above has been guided by studies performed on them in existing literature as well as the nature of the data sets. Finally an empirical study is provided regarding the scalability property of the algorithm in terms of sample complexity, i.e., the number of samples in the condensed set required to achieve a particular accuracy level.

2.6.1 Density estimation

The error between density estimates obtained using the original data set and the reduced set is studied here. The density-based multiscale condensation algorithm is compared with three representative data reduction schemes (random sampling, vector quantization based and clustering based) described below. Classification-based data reduction methods such as Condensed Nearest Neighbor are not compared, as error in density estimates is not the optimality criterion for such methods. The methods compared are random sampling with replacement, the self-organizing map (SOM) [118] and Astrahan's clustering based uniform scale method [13] (Section 2.2.3). The following quantities are compared for each algorithm:

1. The condensation ratio (CR), measured as the ratio of the cardinality of the condensed set and the original set, expressed as percentage.

2. The log-likelihood (LLR) ratio for measuring the error in density estimate with the original set and the reduced set as described in Equation 2.2.

3. The Kullback-Liebler information number (KLI), also for measuring the error in density estimate (Equation 2.3).

2.6.2 Test of statistical significance

Results presented here correspond to the case when for each data 90% of the samples are selected as training set and the remaining samples are used as test set. Ten such independent random training-test set splits are obtained, and the mean and standard deviation (SD) of the errors are computed over ten runs. Tests of significance were performed for the inequality of means (of the errors) obtained using the multiscale algorithm and the other condensation schemes compared. Since both mean pairs and the variance pairs are unknown and different, a generalized version of t-test is appropriate in this context. The above problem is the classical Behrens-Fisher problem in hypothesis testing; a suitable test statistic is described and tabled in [12]. The test statistic is of the form

$$v = \frac{\bar{x}_1 - \bar{x}_2}{\sqrt{\lambda_1 s_1^2 + \lambda_2 s_2^2}}, \qquad (2.4)$$

where $\bar{x}_1, \bar{x}_2$ are the means, s_1, s_2 the standard deviations and $\lambda_1 = 1/n_1, \lambda_2 = 1/n_2$, n_1, n_2 are the number of observations. $\square$

Tables 2.1−2.4 report the individual means and SD's, and the value of test statistic computed and the corresponding tabled values at an error probability level of 0.05. If the computed value is greater than the tabled value the means are significantly different.

Results are presented for different values of condensation ratios for each algorithm. However, in Tables 2.1 and 2.2, comparison is presented on the basis of error in density estimate for similar values of CR. Alternatively one could have also compared CR for similar values of error in density estimate. In Tables 2.1 and 2.2, results are presented for two different sets of values of CR, e.g., 0.1-3% and 5-20% (of the original data set and not the training set) respectively. The error values were computed using Equations 2.2 and 2.3 with the same value of k as used for condensation. It may be noted that the optimal choice of k is a function of the data size.

It is seen from the results (Tables 2.1 and 2.2) that the density-based multiscale method achieves consistently better performance than Astrahan's method, random sampling and SOM for both sets of condensation ratios. For each condensation ratio (two condensation ratios are considered), for each index of comparison (two indices are considered) of density estimation error and for each data set (eleven data sets including three large data sets), the multiscale method is found to provide better performance than each of the other three data condensation methodologies compared. Regarding statistical significance tests it can be seen from Tables 2.1 and 2.2 that, out of 132 comparisons, the multiscale method is found to provide *significantly* better results in 127 comparisons. Only while comparing with SOM for the *Norm*, Vowel and Ringnorm data sets, the performance of the multiscale method is found to be better, but not significantly. (The corresponding entries are marked bold in Tables 2.1 and 2.2.) Similar performance has also been observed for other values of the condensation ratio (e.g., 40% and 60%).

For the purpose of comparison, the condensed sets obtained using different algorithms are also used for kernel density estimates. The kernel estimate is

TABLE 2.1: Comparison of κ-NN density estimation error of condensation algorithms (lower CR)

Data set	Multiscale Algorithm			Uniform Scale method [13]			SOM			Random sampling		
	CR (Mean SD)	LLR (Mean SD)	KLI (Mean SD)	CR (Mean SD)	LLR (Mean SD)	KLI (Mean SD)	CR	LLR (Mean SD)	KLI (Mean SD)	CR	LLR (Mean SD)	KLI (Mean SD)
Norm	3.0 0.001	1.16 0.09	0.16 0.04	3.0 0.001	1.33 0.12 (3.76, 1.72)	0.20 0.04 (2.34, 1.71)	3.0	**1.21 0.08 (1.69, 1.73)**	**0.17 0.004 (0.02, 1.81)**	3.0	1.38 0.27 (2.56, 1.78)	0.25 0.10 (2.77, 1.77)
Iris	2.5 0.000	1.83 0.08	0.40 0.04	2.5 0.000	2.02 0.17 (3.35, 1.76)	0.68 0.08 (10.38, 1.76)	2.5	2.00 0.01 (7.0, 1.81)	0.44 0.005 (3.29, 1.81)	2.5	2.85 0.98 (3.44, 1.81)	1.01 0.23 (8.66, 1.81)
Vowel	3.4 0.00	1.40 0.16	0.10 0.01	3.4 0.001	1.67 0.28 (2.77, 1.74)	0.165 0.01 (15.24, 1.71)	3.4	**1.43 0.005 (0.88, 1.81)**	0.11 0.00 (3.32, 1.81)	3.4	1.95 0.55 (3.18, 1.78)	0.41 0.11 (9.30, 1.81)
Pima	3.2 0.002	1.15 0.11	18.1 1.03	3.2	1.31 0.17 (2.62, 1.73)	21.1 4.0 (2.55, 1.78)	3.2	1.24 0.04 (2.55, 1.78)	20.4 1.01 (5.22, 1.71)	3.2	1.99 0.91 (3.04, 1.81)	25.1 9.1 (2.53, 1.81)
Cancer	4.3 0.002	1.37 0.17	17.1 1.4	4.3	1.61 0.28 (2.43, 1.76)	19.0 1.04 (3.80, 1.72)	4.3	1.54 0.11 (2.23, 1.81)	19.4 0.50 (5.35, 1.78)	4.3	1.805 0.57 (2.43, 1.81)	24.0 9.01 (2.54, 1.81)
Monk	4.1 0.00	0.64 0.01	0.65 0.04	4.1	0.70 0.04 (3.62, 1.72)	0.72 0.05 (2.23, 1.81)	4.1	0.67 0.01 (7.03, 1.71)	0.68 0.01 (2.43, 1.81)	4.1	0.83 0.16 (1.86, 1.81)	0.88 0.16 (2.61, 1.81)
Tnorm	1.0 0.00	0.43 0.01	1.70 0.10	1.0	0.57 0.07 (6.56, 1.81)	1.97 0.17 (4.54, 1.73)	1.0	0.46 0.00 (9.95, 1.81)	1.81 0.01 (1.86, 1.81)	1.0	0.59 0.19 (5.86, 1.81)	2.01 0.56 (1.81, 1.78)
Rnorm	2.0 0.00	0.40 0.05	2.11 0.22	2.0	0.54 0.07 (5.40, 1.81)	2.95 0.22 (8.95, 1.71)	2.0	**0.41 0.001 (0.63, 1.81)**	2.24 0.001 (3.30, 1.81)	2.0	0.70 0.15 (6.23, 1.78)	3.01 0.91 (3.19, 1.81)
Forest	0.1 0.001	0.82 0.01	2.71 0.02	0.1	2.0 0.02 (175, 1.76)	4.7 0.55 (11.99, 1.81)	0.1	1.40 0.00 (192.36, 1.81)	3.20 0.01 (1.96, 1.81)	0.1	3.8 1.7 (5.81, 1.81)	7.0 2.50 (5.69, 1.81)
Sat.Img.	0.2 0.001	0.78 0.01	1.18 0.09	0.2	0.92 0.02 (20.76, 1.76)	1.40 0.25 (8.21, 1.81)	0.2	0.88 0.01 (23.45, 1.71)	1.28 0.00 (72.68, 1.76)	0.2	1.09 0.15 (6.84, 1.81)	1.79 0.27 (7.10, 1.78)
Census	0.1 0.002	0.27 0.00	1.55 0.10	0.1 0.004	0.31 0.02 (6.63, 1.81)	1.70 0.15 (2.76, 1.72)	0.1	0.30 0.01 (14.07, 1.81)	1.61 0.01 (1.98, 1.81)	0.1	0.40 0.17 (2.53, 1.81)	1.90 0.45 (2.52, 1.81)

'CR' denotes condensation ratio in %, 'LLR' denotes the log-likelihood error, and 'KLI' denotes the Kullback-Liebler information number. The numbers in the parentheses indicate the computed and tabled values of the test statistic, respectively. A higher computed value compared to tabled value indicates statistical significance. The values marked bold denote lack of statistical significance.

TABLE 2.2: Comparison of k-NN density estimation error of condensation algorithms (higher CR)

Data set	Multiscale Algorithm			Uniform Scale method [13]			SOM			Random sampling		
	CR Mean SD	LLR Mean SD	KLI Mean SD	CR Mean SD	LLR Mean SD	KLI Mean SD	CR	LLR Mean SD	KLI Mean SD	CR	LLR Mean SD	KLI Mean SD
Norm	20 0.001	0.38 0.001	0.08 0.00	20 0.002	0.43 0.002 (74.16, 1.76)	0.10 0.001 (61.59, 1.78)	20	0.40 0.001 (46.9, 1.72)	0.09 0.00 (74.16, 1.76)	20	0.49 0.09 (4.05, 1.81)	0.11 0.01 (9.94, 1.81)
Iris	20 0.001	0.82 0.001	0.19 0.001	20 0.001	0.91 0.001 (211, 1.72)	0.25 0.001 (140, 1.72)	20	0.87 0.001 (117, 1.72)	0.22 0.001 (9.90, 1.81)	20	1.04 0.40 (1.82, 1.81)	0.40 0.16 (4.35, 1.81)
Vowel	20 0.002	0.88 0.07	0.05 0.001	20 0.002	0.97 0.10 (2.61, 1.74)	0.09 0.001 (93.8, 1.72)	20	**0.90 0.001** (0.93, 1.81)	0.07 0.001 (46.90, 1.72)	20	1.25 0.25 (4.73, 1.81)	0.21 0.04 (13.2, 1.81)
Pima	20 0.001	0.50 0.05	8.8 0.32	20 0.002	0.62 0.09 (3.86, 1.78)	10.0 0.81 (4.56, 1.76)	20	0.59 0.002 (5.96, 1.81)	9.1 0.10 (2.96, 1.81)	20	0.81 0.25 (4.16, 1.81)	14.03 4.1 (14.21, 1.81)
Cancer	20 0.001	0.68 0.05	9.1 0.4	20 0.002	0.81 0.07 (5.01, 1.76)	10.4 0.70 (5.34, 1.74)	20	0.77 0.01 (5.85, 1.81)	9.8 0.01 (5.63, 1.81)	20	0.92 0.22 (3.52, 1.81)	11.9 2.09 (4.36, 1.81)
Monk	20 0.002	0.31 0.001	0.32 0.005	20 0.002	0.34 0.002 (44.5, 1.78)	0.35 0.002 (18.47, 1.78)	20	0.32 0.001 (33.01, 1.81)	0.33 0.001 (6.40, 1.81)	20	0.42 0.04 (9.11, 1.81)	0.44 0.04 (9.87, 1.81)
Tnorm	20 0.000	0.22 0.001	0.80 0.005	10 0.001	0.29 0.005 (45.53, 1.81)	1.04 0.02 (38.61, 1.81)	10	0.25 0.00 (70.35, 1.71)	0.88 0.01 (26.40, 1.81)	10	0.35 0.08 (5.40, 1.81)	1.21 0.17 (7.99, 1.81)
Rnorm	20 0.000	0.25 0.005	0.91 0.002	10 0.001	0.29 0.01 (11.86, 1.78)	1.07 0.07 (7.57, 1.81)	10	0.26 0.00 (6.63, 1.81)	1.01 0.00 (32.52, 1.81)	10	0.32 0.09 (2.57, 1.81)	1.21 0.35 (2.84, 1.81)
Forest	5 0.001	0.54 0.005	0.91 0.002	5 0.002	0.62 0.005 (37.5, 1.72)	1.71 0.007 (364, 1.81)	5	0.57 0.002 (18.4, 1.78)	1.04 0.005 (80.0, 1.76)	5	1.72 0.25 (15.6, 1.81)	4.91 1.17 (11.4, 1.81)
Sat.Img.	5 0.001	0.41 0.005	0.71 0.01	5 0.001	0.50 0.007 (34.70, 1.76)	0.81 0.02 (14.83, 1.76)	5	0.47 0.002 (36.95, 1.78)	0.80 0.01 (21.10, 1.71)	5	0.62 0.10 (6.95, 1.81)	0.92 0.14 (4.96, 1.81)
Census	5 0.002	0.17 0.001	0.80 0.01	5 0.002	0.22 0.002 (74.16, 1.76)	0.91 0.007 (27.98, 1.78)	5	0.19 0.00 (46.90, 1.81)	0.88 0.005 (21.95, 1.78)	5	0.28 0.01 (36.3, 1.81)	1.00 0.17 (3.89, 1.81)

given by

$$\hat{\beta}_n(\mathbf{x}) = \frac{1}{n} \sum_{j=1}^{n} K(\mathbf{x}, \mathbf{u}_j),$$

where $\mathbf{u}_j$'s are points belonging to the reduced set and $K(\cdot, \cdot)$ is the kernel function. We used a Gaussian kernel of the form

$$K(\mathbf{x}, \mathbf{u}_j) = \left[(h^2 2\pi)^{-p/2} \right] \exp\left\{ -\frac{1}{2h^2} \delta(\mathbf{x}, \mathbf{u}_j) \right\},$$

where p is the dimension, h bandwidth and $\delta(\mathbf{x}, \mathbf{u}_j)$ the Euclidean distance between $\mathbf{x}$ and $\mathbf{u}_j$. The bandwidth h is chosen as

$$h = \sqrt{ \sup_{i=1,..,n} \left(\inf_{j=1,..,n} d(\mathbf{u}_i, \mathbf{u}_j) \right) },$$

where $\mathbf{u}_i$ and $\mathbf{u}_j$ are points in the condensed set. The reason for selecting the above bandwidth can be explained in terms of minimal spanning trees [39]. The bandwidth satisfies both the conditions for consistent kernel density estimation. The error measures are presented in Tables 2.3 and 2.4 for the same two groups of condensed sets as considered in Tables 2.1 and 2.2, respectively. It is seen from Tables 2.3 and 2.4 that when using kernel estimates, the multiscale algorithm produces less error than all the related schemes for all data sets. Statistical significance tests are also presented for all the comparisons, and in 129, of 132 comparisons, the multiscale method performs significantly better than the other three algorithms. The cases for which statistical significance could not be established are denoted by bold entries in Tables 2.3 and 2.4.

The multiscale algorithm was also compared with Fukunaga's non-parametric data condensation algorithm [74] only for the *Norm* data set. For a log-likelihood error of 0.5 the condensation ratio achieved by this method is 50%, while the corresponding figure is 23.4% for the multiscale method. On the *Norm* data set while the CPU time required by the multiscale algorithm is 8.10 secs, the above mentioned algorithm is found to require 2123.05 secs.

Figure 2.3 shows plots of the points in the condensed set along with the discs covered by them at different condensation ratios for the multiscale algorithm and for Astrahan's method. The objective is to demonstrate the multiresolution characteristics of the algorithm in contrast to a fixed resolution method. It is observed that the multiscale algorithm represents the original data in a multiresolution manner; the denser regions are more accurately represented compared to the sparser regions. The regions covered by the representative points are uniform for Astrahan's method [13]. It may be observed from the figure that multiscale representation is most effective in terms of error when the condensed set is sparse; i.e., the condensation ratio is low (Figure 2.3(a)).

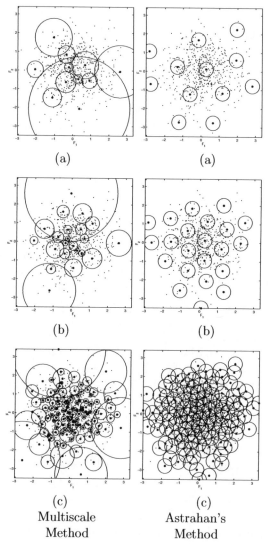

FIGURE 2.3: Plot of the condensed points (of the **Norm** data) for the multiscale algorithm and Astrahan's method, for different sizes of the condensed set. Bold dots represent a selected point and the discs represent the area of $F_1 - F_2$ plane covered by a selected point at their center.

2.6.3   Classification: Forest cover data

As mentioned in Appendix B, the said data represents forest cover types of
30m × 30m cells obtained from US Forest Service (USFS) Region 2 Resource
Information System (RIS). There are 581,012 instances, with 54 attributes
representing cartographic variables (hillshade, distance to hydrology, elevation, soil type, etc.), of which 10 are quantitative and 44 binary. The quantitative variables were scaled to the range $[0, 1]$. The task is to classify the
observations into seven categories representing the forest cover types, namely
Spruce/Fir, Lodgepole Pine, Ponderosa Pine, Cottonwood/Willow, Aspen,
Douglas-fir, Krummholz. About 80% of the observations belong to classes
Spruce/Fir and Lodgepole Pine.

The training set is condensed using different condensation algorithms including the multiscale one. The different condensed sets obtained are then
used to design a k-NN classifier (1-NN for LASM) and a multilayer perceptron
(MLP) for classifying the test set. The goal is to provide evidence that the
performance of the multiresolution condensation algorithm does not depend
on the final use of the condensed set. The following data reduction methods
are compared:

1. Random sampling: Sampling with replacement is used to obtain a specific condensation ratio. The condensed set is a representative of the
   underlying distribution.

2. Stratified sampling: Instead of sampling uniformly over the entire population, subclasses of interest (*strata*) are identified and treated differ-
   ently. For the given data we considered *class stratification*; i.e., the
   number of samples selected from each class is proportional to the size
   of the class in the original set.

3. Condensed nearest neighbor (CNN) [91]: The condensation ratio is varied by changing the parameter k used for k-NN classification. The condensed set obtains a high concentration of points near the class boundaries. It may be mentioned that arbitrarily low condensation ratios
   cannot be achieved using CNN.

4. Local asymmetrically weighted similarity metric (LASM) [239]: The
   condensed set is obtained by random sampling, but the metric used
   for nearest neighbor classification varies locally and is learned from the
   training set. The value of reinforcement rate used is $\alpha = 0.2$ and the
   punishment rate used is $\beta = 1.0$.

5. Method of Astrahan [13]: As explained in Section 2.2.3 this is a uniform
   scale density based method.

6. Learning vector quantization [118]: The method is described in Section 2.2.2. Initial codebook vectors obtained using a self-organizing
   map are refined here using the LVQ algorithm.

As in the case of density estimate experiments (Section 2.6.1), 90% of the data is randomly selected as a training set and the remaining data is used as a test set. Such data splits are performed 10 times independently and the mean and standard deviation (SD) of the classification accuracy on the test set, and condensation ratios (CR) obtained for each such split are presented. Statistical significance tests are also performed to test the inequality of means of the classification accuracy. As before, the computed value of the test statistic and the tabled value are presented. If the computed value is greater than the tabled value the means are significantly different. The CPU time required by the condensation algorithms on a Digital Alpha 800MHz workstation is also presented. The figures shown here are the average values taken over 10 runs.

In Table 2.5, the effect of each method on classification accuracy is studied for condensation ratios of 0.1% and 5%. Note that the lowest condensation ratio that could be achieved for the Forest data using CNN is 3.1%; hence, comparison with CNN is presented only for the 5% case.

It can be seen from Table 2.5 that the multiscale algorithm achieves higher classification accuracy than the other methods and that this difference is statistically significant. For classification, the same value of k as that used for condensation is considered, except for LASM where 1-NN is used. For classification using MLP, the multiscale method and LVQ perform similarly. Results for LASM are not presented for MLP, since if no specialized metric is used LASM represents just a random subset. The performances of both random sampling and stratified sampling are found to be catastrophically poor. The uniform scale method of Astrahan performs more poorly than the multiscale method, LVQ and LASM.

2.6.4 Clustering: Satellite image data

The satellite image data (Appendix B) contains observations of the Indian Remote Sensing (IRS) satellite for the city of Calcutta, India. The data contains images of four spectral bands. We present in Figure 2.4(a), for convenience, the image for band 4. Here the task is to segment the image into different land cover regions, using four features (spectral bands). The image mainly consists of six classes, e.g., clear water (ponds, fisheries), turbid water (the river Ganges flowing through the city), concrete (buildings, roads, airport tarmacs), habitation (concrete structures but less in density), vegetation (crop, forest areas) and open spaces (barren land, playgrounds). Fuzzy segmentation of the image is reported in detail in [198].

Using the multiscale condensation algorithm six prototype points are extracted from the entire data set. The remaining points are placed in the cluster of the prototype point to whose sphere (disc) of influence the particular point belongs. Thus the condensation process implicitly generates a clustering (partition/segmentation) of the image data.

The performance of the multiscale algorithm is compared with two other related clustering methods, namely, k-means algorithm [59] and Astrahans density based uniform scale method [13]. For the k-means algorithm $k = 6$ is considered, since there are six classes, and the best result (as evaluated by a cluster quality index) obtained out of ten random initializations is presented. In Astrahan's method six prototype points are obtained; the remaining pixels are then classified by minimum distance classification with these six points.

The results are presented in Figures 2.4(b)–(d). Figure 2.4(d) is seen to have more structural details compared to Figures 2.4(b) and 2.4(c). From the segmented image obtained using the multiscale method more landmarks known from ground truths can be detected by visual inspection. The segmentation results of the remote sensing images obtained above are also evaluated quantitatively using an index β .

Let n_i be the number of pixels in the ith $(i = 1, \ldots, c)$ region obtained by the segmentation method. Let X_{ij} be the vector (of size 4×1) of the gray values of the jth pixel $(j = 1, \ldots, n_i)$ for all the images in region i, and $\bar{X}_i$ the mean of n_i gray values of the ith region. Then β is defined as [198]:

$$\beta = \frac{\sum_{i=1}^{c} \sum_{j=1}^{n_i} (X_{ij} - \bar{X})^T (X_{ij} - \bar{X})}{\sum_{i=1}^{c} \sum_{j=1}^{n_i} (X_{ij} - \bar{X}_i)^T (X_{ij} - \bar{X}_i)} \tag{2.5}$$

where, n is the size of the image and $\bar{X}$ is the mean gray value of the image. It may be noted that X_{ij}, $\bar{X}$ and $\bar{X}_i$ are all 4×1 vectors.

Note that the above measure is nothing but the ratio of the total variation and within-class variation and is widely used for feature selection and cluster analysis [198]. For a given image and c (number of clusters) value, the higher the homogeneity within the segmented regions, the higher would be the β value. The multiscale method has the highest β value as can be seen in Table 2.6.

2.6.5   Rule generation: Census data

The original source for this data set is the IPUMS project. The data (Appendix B) contains 320000 samples and 133 attributes, mostly categorical (integer valued). A study commonly performed on census data is to identify contrasting groups of populations and study their relations. For this data two groups of population, namely, those who have undergone/not undergone 'higher education,' measured in terms of number of years in college are investigated. It is interesting and useful to generate logical rules depending on the other available attributes that classify these groups. We have considered the attribute educational record, '*edrec,*' and investigated two sets of population, one having more than $4\frac{1}{2}$ years of college education, and the other below that. The task is to extract logical inference rules for the sets.

As a similarity measure between two samples a *Value Difference Metric* (VDM) [279] is used. Using the VDM, the distance between two values x and v of a single attribute a is defined as

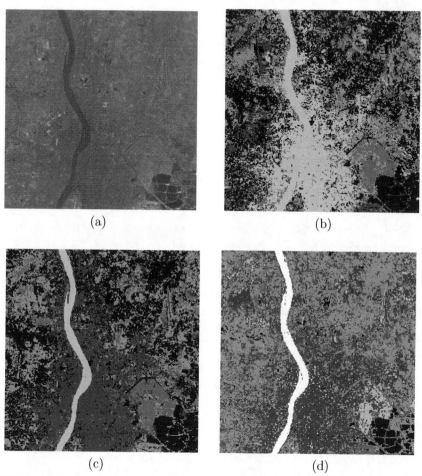

FIGURE 2.4: IRS images of Calcutta: (a) original Band 4 image, and segmented images using (b) k-means algorithm, (c) Astrahan's method, (d) multiscale algorithm.

$$vdm_a(x, v) = \sum_{a=1}^{M} \left(\frac{N_{a,x,c}}{N_{a,x}} - \frac{N_{a,v,c}}{N_{a,v}} \right)^2 \qquad (2.6)$$

where $N_{a,x}$ is the number of times attribute a had value x; $N_{a,x,c}$ is the number of times attribute a had value x and the output class was c; and M is the number of output classes (2 in this case). Using this distance measure, two values of an attribute are considered to be closer if they have more similar classifications, regardless of the magnitude of the values. Using the value difference metric, the distance between two points having p independent attributes is defined as

$$\text{VDM}(\mathbf{x}, \mathbf{v}) = \sqrt{\sum_{a=1}^{p} vdm_a^2(\mathbf{x}_a, \mathbf{v}_a)}. \qquad (2.7)$$

The popular C4.5 [232] program is used to generate logical rules from the condensed data sets. The size of the rules is restricted to conjunction of 3 variables only. As before, 90% of the data is selected as training set and the rules are evaluated on the remaining data. Eleven such splits are obtained and the means and standard deviations (SD) are presented.

For the purpose of comparison with the multiscale method, the C4.5 program is also run on condensed sets obtained using random sampling, stratified sampling, density based uniform scale method of Astrahan [13] and condensed nearest neighbor [91]. Following quantities are computed in Table 2.7:

1. Condensation ratio (CR)

2. Number of rules generated

3. Accuracy of classification on test set (we also present statistical tests of significance for comparing the other methods with the multiscale method)

4. Percentage of uncovered samples

5. CPU time

The comparison is performed for a constant condensation ratio of 0.1%. However, for CNN a CR of only 2.2% could be achieved by varying k. The classification accuracy of the multiscale method is higher than random sampling, stratified sampling and CNN; it is also significantly higher than Astrahan's method. It is also observed that the uncovered region is minimum for the rules generated from the subset obtained by the multiscale algorithm. The rule base size is far smaller than random, statistical sampling and Astrahan's method. Therefore the rules generated from the condensed set are compact yet have high accuracy and cover as compared to other sets.

2.6.6   Study on scalability

For studying the scaling property of the condensation algorithm its *sample complexity*, i.e., the size of condensed set required to achieve an accuracy level (measured as error in density estimate), is examined. In Figure 2.5 the log-likelihood error is plotted against the cardinality of the condensed set (as a fraction of the original set), for three typical data sets, namely, *Norm* (of known distribution), Vowel (highly overlapping), Wisconsin (large dimension). The solid curve is for the multiscale methodology while the dotted one is for random sampling. It can be seen that the multiscale methodology is superior to random sampling.

2.6.7   Choice of scale parameter

In Section 2.5 we have described the role of k in the multiscale algorithm. As k increases, the size of condensed set reduces and vice versa. Here we provide some experimental results in support of the discussion. The effect of varying parameter k on the condensation ratio (CR) is shown in Figure 2.6, for the three aforesaid data sets (Section 2.6.7). It can be observed that for values of k in the range $\approx$ 7–20 the curves attain low CR values and are close to each other for all the three data sets. For the Vowel data, a CR value of 3.4% was obtained at $k = 31$. It may be noted that the curve for the *Norm* (smallest) data set is shifted to the left compared to the other two curves.

2.7   Summary

In this chapter, after describing briefly some of the commonly used data condensation techniques like condensed nearest neighbor rule, learning vector quantization method and Astrahan's algorithm, we have presented a methodology for non-parametric data condensation in detail. The algorithm follows the basic principles of non-parametric data reduction present in literature, but the sample pruning step is done in a multiresolution manner rather than with uniform resolution. It is based on the density underlying the data. The approach is found to have superior performance as compared to some existing data reduction schemes in terms of error in density estimate both for small and large data sets having dimension ranging from 2 to 133. The performance of classification, clustering and rule generation using the condensation algorithm is studied for three large data sets. The algorithm does not require the difficult choice of radii d_1 and d_2, which are critical for Astrahan's method, only the choice of parameter k is necessary. Choice of k is guided by the size of the original data set and the accuracy/condensation ratio desired. The parameter k also provides a parametrization of the concept of scale in data

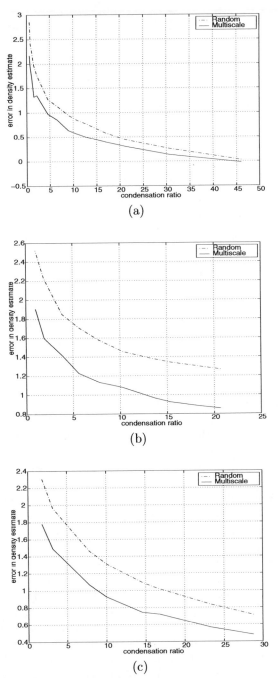

FIGURE 2.5:   Variation in error in density estimate (log-likelihood measure) with the size of the Condensed Set (expressed as percentage of the original set) with the corresponding, for (a) the Norm data, (b) Vowel data, (c) Wisconsin Cancer data.

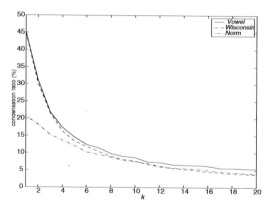

FIGURE 2.6: Variation of condensation ratio CR (%) with k.

condensation, and the scales induced follow the natural characteristics of the data and, hence, are efficient.

As far as the computational complexity is concerned, the algorithm can be considered to have three computational steps. In the first step, for each point in the original set the distance of the kth nearest neighbor is computed. In the second step, the point having the minimum value of the distance is selected, and in the third step, all points lying within a radius of $2r_{k,\mathbf{x_j}}$ of a selected point are removed. It is observed that the computation time required for second and third steps decreases with iteration, since the size of the original set decreases progressively (the rate is dependent on k and the data distribution). The first step is the most time consuming one and it requires $(\mathcal{O}(kN^2))$, where N is the number of data points. A way of reducing the time complexity of nearest neighbor calculation is to use approximate nearest neighbor (ANN) computations using specialized data structures like k-d trees [11]. Probabilistic nearest neighbor search methods have also been suggested [63], having expected $\mathcal{O}(1)$ time complexity and $\mathcal{O}(N)$ storage complexity.

The guiding principle of the multiscale algorithm is to minimize the error in terms of density estimate rather than the classification score. The justification is to obtain a generic representative condensed set independent of the task performed with it later. In many data mining applications the final task is not always known beforehand or there may be multiple tasks to be performed. In the above circumstances such a condensed representation is more useful.

The condensation methodology, described in Section 2.5, involves non-parametric density estimation and data reduction. The asymptotic convergence of the condensation procedure and its finite sample error rate need to be analyzed. It may be noted that k-nearest neighbor density estimation together with its convergence for finite and non-i.i.d. samples is an open research area which has drawn recently the attention of researchers from different fields.

A way of reducing the time complexity of the aforesaid algorithm is to use approximate nearest neighbor (ANN) computations using specialized data structures like k-d trees [11]. Probabilistic nearest neighbor search methods [63], having expected $\mathcal{O}(1)$ time complexity and $\mathcal{O}(N)$ storage complexity, may also be used for this purpose.

TABLE 2.3: Comparison of kernel (Gaussian) density estimation error of condensation algorithms (lower CR, same condensed set as Table 2.1)

Data set	Multiscale Algorithm		Uniform Scale method [13]		SOM		Random sampling	
	LLR Mean SD	KLI Mean SD	LLR Mean SD	KLI Mean SD	LLR Mean SD	KLI Mean SD	LLR Mean SD	KLI Mean SD
Norm	1.04 0.07	0.14 0.03	1.15 0.09 (3.05, 1.74)	0.17 0.03 (2.24, 1.74)	1.10 0.07 (1.92, 1.72)	**0.15 0.004** (**1.04, 1.81**)	1.29 0.25 (3.05, 1.81)	0.23 0.09 (3.67, 1.78)
Iris	1.72 0.05	0.37 0.02	1.91 0.14 (4.04, 1.78)	0.59 0.04 (15.56, 1.76)	1.88 0.01 (9.92, 1.81)	0.41 0.002 (6.29, 1.81)	2.78 0.95 (3.52, 1.81)	0.98 0.17 (11.27, 1.81)
Vowel	1.35 0.09	0.09 0.005	1.61 0.17 (4.27, 1.76)	0.16 0.01 (19.8, 1.76)	**1.38 0.002** (**1.05, 1.81**)	0.10 0.00 (6.32, 1.81)	1.88 0.47 (3.50, 1.81)	0.37 0.08 (11.05, 1.81)
Pima	1.07 0.08	17.2 0.81	1.27 0.11 (4.65, 1.74)	19.9 2.2 (3.64, 1.78)	1.18 0.01 (4.31, 1.81)	19.1 0.88 (5.02, 1.72)	1.91 0.90 (2.94, 1.81)	23.2 8.9 (2.12, 1.81)
Cancer	1.34 0.16	16.8 1.4	1.57 0.20 (2.84, 1.74)	18.8 0.91 (3.78, 1.78)	1.51 0.09 (2.92, 1.78)	19.1 0.47 (4.93, 1.79)	1.78 0.55 (2.43, 1.81)	23.3 8.80 (2.31, 1.81)
Monk	0.62 0.01	0.63 0.04	0.68 0.03 (6.00, 1.78)	0.71 0.04 (4.47, 1.74)	0.66 0.01 (8.94, 1.74)	0.67 0.01 (3.08, 1.81)	0.82 0.11 (6.00, 1.81)	0.87 0.14 (5.21, 1.81)
Tnorm	0.42 0.01	1.64 0.05	0.56 0.05 (8.68, 1.81)	1.92 0.11 (6.51, 1.74)	0.45 0.00 (9.49, 1.81)	1.78 0.001 (5.53, 1.81)	0.57 0.10 (4.72, 1.81)	1.97 0.44 (2.33, 1.81)
Rnorm	0.38 0.03	2.02 0.17	0.53 0.05 (8.13, 1.76)	2.80 0.19 (6.51, 1.74)	0.40 0.001 (9.49, 1.81)	2.19 0.01 (5.53, 1.81)	0.69 0.09 (4.72, 1.81)	2.89 0.82 (2.33, 1.81)
Forest	0.80 0.007	2.69 0.01	1.95 0.01 (325, 1.74)	4.4 0.53 (10.2, 1.81)	1.38 0.00 (366, 1.81)	3.10 0.01 (91, 1.72)	3.70 1.43 (6.55, 1.81)	7.0 2.50 (5.45, 1.81)
Sat.Img	0.75 0.005	1.09 0.02	0.88 0.01 (36.77, 1.76)	1.28 0.09 (6.52, 1.81)	0.82 0.005 (31.3, 1.72)	1.22 0.00 (20.55, 1.81)	0.98 0.10 (7.26, 1.81)	1.72 0.22 (9.02, 1.81)
Census	0.25 0.00	1.46 0.04	0.29 0.01 (12.6, 1.81)	1.59 0.09 (4.17, 1.78)	0.27 0.005 (12.6, 1.81)	1.52 0.005 (4.71, 1.81)	0.37 0.10 (3.79, 1.81)	1.82 0.40 (2.83, 1.81)

TABLE 2.4: Comparison of kernel (Gaussian) density estimation error of condensation algorithms (higher CR, same condensed set as Table 2.2)

Data set	Multiscale Algorithm LLR Mean SD	Multiscale Algorithm KLI Mean SD	Uniform Scale method [13] LLR Mean SD	Uniform Scale method [13] KLI Mean SD	SOM LLR Mean SD	SOM KLI Mean SD	Random sampling LLR Mean SD	Random sampling KLI Mean SD
Norm	0.35 0.001	0.07 0.00	1.40 0.001 (117, 1.72)	0.09 0.001 (66, 1.81)	0.37 0.001 (47, 1.72)	0.08 0.001 (33.1, 1.81)	0.47 0.05 (7.95, 1.81)	0.10 0.01 (9.94, 1.81)
Iris	0.79 0.001	0.17 0.001	0.88 0.001 (211, 1.72)	0.23 0.001 (140, 1.72)	0.86 0.001 (33.1, 1.81)	0.21 0.001 (93.8, 1.72)	1.00 0.28 (2.48, 1.81)	0.37 0.10 (6.63, 1.81)
Vowel	0.86 0.05	0.04 0.001	0.95 0.09 (2.90, 1.74)	0.08 0.001 (93.8, 1.72)	**0.88 0.001** (**1.32, 1.81**)	0.05 0.001 (23.45, 1.72)	1.17 0.22 (4.55, 1.81)	0.20 0.04 (13.26, 1.81)
Pima	0.47 0.04	8.20 0.28	0.60 0.07 (5.34, 1.74)	0.56 0.54 (4.90, 1.74)	0.56 0.001 (7.46, 1.81)	8.8 0.04 (23.45, 1.72)	0.80 0.17 (6.27, 1.81)	14.00 4.10 (4.68, 1.81)
Cancer	0.67 0.04	8.70 0.35	0.79 0.05 (6.21, 1.76)	9.80 0.76 (4.66, 1.74)	0.74 0.005 (5.75, 1.81)	9.50 0.01 (7.57, 1.81)	0.90 0.19 (3.92, 1.78)	11.5 2.01 (4.55, 1.81)
Monk	0.30 0.001	0.31 0.004	0.34 0.001 (93.8, 1.72)	0.34 0.001 (24.1, 1.81)	0.31 0.001 (23.4, 1.72)	0.32 0.001 (8.04, 1.78)	0.41 0.03 (12.15, 1.81)	0.44 0.02 (21.14, 1.81)
Thorm	0.21 0.001	0.78 0.004	0.28 0.004 (56.3, 1.81)	0.99 0.01 (64.6, 1.78)	0.23 0.00 (66.3, 1.81)	0.86 0.005 (41.4, 1.76)	0.34 0.05 (8.62, 1.81)	1.19 0.10 (13.5, 1.81)
Rnorm	0.23 0.002	0.88 0.001	0.28 0.005 (30.8, 1.78)	1.02 0.05 (9.28, 1.81)	0.24 0.001 (14.8, 1.78)	0.97 0.001 (211, 1.72)	0.31 0.05 (4.64, 1.81)	1.17 0.28 (3.43, 1.81)
Forest	0.53 0.004	0.90 0.002	0.61 0.004 (46.9, 1.72)	1.70 0.005 (492, 1.78)	0.55 0.001 (16.08, 1.79)	0.98 0.004 (59.3, 1.74)	1.70 0.17 (22.8, 1.81)	4.90 1.00 (13.2, 1.81)
Sat.Img	0.40 0.004	0.70 0.005	0.47 0.007 (28.8, 1.74)	0.80 0.01 (16.08, 1.79)	0.45 0.001 (40, 1.78)	0.77 0.005 (32, 1.72)	0.59 0.05 (12.5, 1.81)	0.90 0.10 (6.62, 1.81)
Census	0.16 0.001	0.78 0.01	0.22 0.001 (140, 1.72)	0.91 0.005 (35, 1.76)	0.17 0.00 (33.1, 1.81)	0.87 0.004 (27.7, 1.78)	0.27 0.01 (36.3, 1.81)	0.98 0.11 (6.00, 1.81)

TABLE 2.5:   Classification performance for Forest cover type data

Condensation Algorithm	Condensation Ratio (%)		Classification Accuracy (%) using k-NN			Classification Accuracy (%) using MLP			CPU time (hrs)
	Mean	SD	Mean	SD	(test stat.)	Mean	SD	(test stat.)	
Multiscale method	0.1	0.004	83.10	1.90		70.01	0.90		4.29
LVQ	0.1	-	75.01	1.01	(12.50, 1.76)	68.08	0.80	(3.33, 1.72)	2.02
LASM	0.1	-	74.50	2.52	(9.08, 1.72) (1-NN)	-	-		5.90
Astrahan	0.1	0.004	66.90	2.10	(18.97, 1.72)	59.80	0.53	(32.81, 1.73)	4.10
Stratified sampling	0.1	-	44.20	5.9	(20.81, 1.81)	36.10	5.95	(18.75, 1.81)	-
Random sampling	0.1	-	37.70	10.04	(14.73, 1.81)	29.80	8.2	(16.16, 1.81)	-
Multiscale method	5.0	0.01	97.00	1.81		80.02	1.40		4.52
LVQ	5.0	-	88.01	1.04	(14.34, 1.76)	74.00	0.92	(11.99, 1.73)	4.05
LASM	5.0	-	87.55	2.50	(10.17, 1.73) (1-NN)	-	-		7.11
Astrahan	5.0	0.01	82.09	2.53	(16.05, 1.73)	66.00	1.4	(23.48, 1.71)	4.40
CNN	5.05	1.01	81.17	3.80	(2.64, 1.73)	75.02	4.1	(1.52, 1.78)	5.51
Stratified sampling	5.0	-	55.20	7.1	(18.92, 1.81)	40.10	7.01	(18.52, 1.81)	-
Random sampling	5.0	-	44.70	8.02	(21.09, 1.81)	35.80	8.8	(16.40, 1.81)	-

TABLE 2.6: β value and CPU time of different clustering methods

Method	k-means	Astrahan's	Multiscale
β	5.30	7.02	9.88
CPU time (hrs)	0.11	0.71	0.75

TABLE 2.7:   Rule generation performance for the Census data

Condensation method	CR(%)		# of Rules (rounded to integer)		Classification accuracy (%)			Uncovered samples (%)		CPU time (hrs)
	Mean	SD	Mean	SD	Mean	SD	(Test Stat.)	Mean	SD	
Random sampling	0.1	-	448	88	32.1	8.8	(8.43, 1.81)	40.01	5.5	-
Stratified sampling	0.1	-	305	45	38.8	5.5	(9.71, 1.78)	37.0	5.5	-
CNN	2.2	0.050	270	53	32.0	4.1	(17.55, 1.78)	55.0	4.1	2.80
Astrahan [13]	0.1	0.004	245	50	48.8	4.0	(4.89, 1.78)	25.0	3.1	4.22
Multiscale	0.1	0.004	178	30	55.1	1.5		20.2	1.80	4.10

Figures in parentheses indicate the computed value of test statistic and tabled value, respectively.

Chapter 3

Unsupervised Feature Selection

3.1 Introduction

An important problem related to mining large data sets, both in dimension and size, is of selecting a subset of the original features [66]. Preprocessing the data to obtain a smaller set of representative features and retaining the optimal salient characteristics of the data not only decrease the processing time but also leads to more compactness of the models learned and better generalization. Dimensionality reduction can be done in two ways, namely, *feature selection* and *feature extraction*. As mentioned in Section 1.2.2, feature selection refers to reducing the dimensionality of the measurement space by discarding redundant or least information carrying features. One uses supervised feature selection when class labels of the data are available; otherwise unsupervised feature selection is appropriate. In many data mining applications class labels are unknown, thereby indicating the significance of unsupervised feature selection there. On the other hand, feature extraction methods utilize all the information contained in the measurement space to obtain a new transformed space, thereby mapping a higher dimensional pattern to a lower dimensional one.

In this chapter we describe an unsupervised feature selection algorithm based on measuring similarity between features and then removing the redundancy therein [166], for data mining applications. This does not need any search and, therefore, is fast. The method involves partitioning of the original feature set into some distinct subsets or clusters so that the features within a cluster are highly similar while those in different clusters are dissimilar. A single feature from each such cluster is then selected to constitute the resulting reduced subset. Before we describe the methodology and experimental results (Sections 3.4.2 and 3.6), we provide in Sections 3.2 and 3.3, in brief, different methods of feature extraction and feature selection for pattern recognition.

3.2   Feature Extraction

Feature extraction is a process of selecting a map of the form $X = f(Y)$, by which a sample $\mathbf{y}$ ($=[y_1, y_2, \ldots, y_p]$) in a p-dimensional measurement space Ω_Y is transformed into a point $\mathbf{x}$ ($=[x_1, x_2, \ldots, x_{p'}]$) in a p'-dimensional feature space Ω_X, where $p' < p$. Strategies involved in feature extraction include basic linear transformation of the input variables, e.g., principal component analysis (PCA), singular value decomposition (SVD), linear discriminant analysis (LDA), independent component analysis (ICA); more sophisticated linear transforms like spectral transforms (Fourier, Hadamard), wavelet transforms or convolution of kernels; and applying non-linear functions to subsets of variables, e.g., non-linear principal component analysis, Sammon's mapping and neural networks. Two distinct goals may be pursued for feature extraction: achieving the best reconstruction of the data or extracted features being the most efficient for making predictions. The first one is usually an unsupervised learning problem, while the second one is supervised.

The pioneering research on feature selection mostly deals with statistical tools. Later, the thrust of the research shifted to the development of various other approaches to feature selection, including fuzzy and neural approaches [200, 203, 243]. Principal component analysis [55] is the most well-known statistical method for feature extraction. It involves a linear orthogonal transform from a p-dimensional feature space to a p'-dimensional space, $p' \leq p$, such that the features in the new p'-dimensional space are uncorrelated and maximal amount of variance of the original data is preserved by only a small number of features.

Some of the recent attempts made for feature extraction are based on connectionist approaches using neural models like multilayer feedforward networks [20, 49, 50, 147, 154, 194, 229, 243, 247, 251] and self-organizing networks [125, 128, 154]. The methods based on multilayer feedforward networks include, among others, determination of saliency (usefulness) of input features [229, 243], development of Sammon's nonlinear discriminant analysis (NDA) network, and linear discriminant analysis (LDA) network [154]. On the other hand, those based on self-organizing networks include development of nonlinear projection (NP-SOM) based Kohonen's self-organizing feature map [154], distortion tolerant Gabor transformations followed by minimum distortion clustering by multilayer self-organizing maps [128], and a nonlinear projection method based on Kohonen's topology preserving maps [125].

Pal et al. [194] have proposed a neuro-fuzzy system for feature evaluation, both in supervised [49] and unsupervised [50] frameworks, along with its theoretical analysis. A fuzzy set theoretic feature evaluation index is defined in terms of individual class membership. Then a connectionist model, which incorporates weighted distance for computing class membership values, is used to perform the task of minimizing the fuzzy evaluation index. This optimization process results in a set of weighting coefficients representing the importance of the individual features. These weighting coefficients lead to a transformation of the feature space for better modeling the class structures. The upper and lower bounds of the evaluation index, and its relation with interclass distance (e.g., Mahalanobis distance) and weighting coefficient were theoretically established.

The aforesaid neuro-fuzzy system has been extended to perform feature extraction in an unsupervised framework [50]. For this purpose, a set of different linear transformation functions is applied on the original feature space and the computation of the aforesaid evaluation index has been made on the transformed spaces. The similarity between two patterns in the transformed space is computed using a set of weighting coefficients. A layered network is designed where the transformation functions are embedded. An optimum transformed space along with the degrees of individual importance of the transformed (extracted) features are obtained through connectionist minimization. All these operations are performed in a single network where the number of nodes in its second hidden layer determines the desired number of extracted features.

Demartines et al. [52] have described a new strategy called "curvilinear component analysis (CCA)" for dimensionality reduction and representation of multidimensional data sets. The principle of CCA is implemented in a self-organized neural network performing two tasks: *vector quantization* of the submanifold in the data set (input space) and *nonlinear projection* of these quantized vectors toward an output space, providing a revealing unfolding of the submanifold. After learning, the network has the ability to continuously map any new point from one space into another.

The decision boundary feature extraction method, proposed by Lee et al. [131, 132], is based on the fact that all the necessary features for classification can be extracted from the decision boundary between a pair of pattern classes. The algorithm can take advantage of characteristics of neural networks which can solve complex problems with arbitrary decision boundaries without assuming the underlying probability distribution functions of the data.

Chatterjee et al. [38] have described various self-organized learning algorithms and associated neural networks to extract features that are effective for preserving *class separability*. An adaptive algorithm for the computation of $Q^{-1/2}$ (where Q is the correlation or covariance matrix of a random vector sequence) is described. Convergence of this algorithm with probability one is established by using stochastic approximation theory. A single layer linear network, called $Q^{-1/2}$ network, for this algorithm is described. Networks with different architectures are designed for extracting features for different cases.

Principal component analysis network of Rubner and Tavan [242] performs the task of feature extraction through the well-known principal component analysis. The network consists of two layers, viz., input and output. The weights of the network are adjusted through local learning rules.

Hornik et al. [97] have demonstrated the asymptotic behavior of a general class of on-line principal component analysis (PCA) learning networks which are based strictly on local learning rules [242]. It is established that the behavior of the algorithms is intimately related to an ordinary differential equation which is obtained by suitable averaging over the training patterns. They have studied the equilibria of these equations and their local stability properties. It has been shown that local PCA algorithms should always incorporate hierarchical rather than more competitive, symmetric decorrelation, for providing their superior performance.

Recently, support vector machine (SVM) is also becoming popular for feature extraction in high dimensional spaces. In pattern recognition, SVM constructs nonlinear decision functions by training a classifier to perform a linear separation in some high dimensional space which is nonlinearly related to the input space. A Mercer kernel is used for mapping the input space to the high dimensional space [253]. The same type of kernel has been used to develop a nonlinear principal component analysis technique, namely, the Kernel PCA [160], which can efficiently extract polynomial features of arbitrary order by computing the projections onto principal components in the high dimensional space obtained by the kernels.

Many of the aforesaid feature extraction algorithms are, however, not suitable for data mining applications. Statistical methods like PCA fail for high dimensional data as they need to determine the eigenvalues of a large dimensional sparse matrix. Some of the connectionist approaches involve time-consuming learning iterations and require very high computational time for large data sets. Still so far, the literature on feature extraction algorithms, specifically suitable for data mining, is quite scarce.

3.3   Feature Selection

Conventional methods of feature selection involve evaluating different feature subsets using some index and selecting the best among them. The index usually measures the capability of the respective subsets in classification or clustering depending on whether the selection process is supervised or unsupervised. A problem of these methods, when applied to large data sets, is the high computational complexity involved in searching. The complexity is exponential in terms of the data dimension for an exhaustive search. Several heuristic techniques have been developed to circumvent this problem. Among them the branch and bound algorithm, suggested by Fukunaga and Narendra [55], obtains the optimal subset in expectedly less than exponential computations when the feature evaluation criterion used is monotonic in nature. Greedy algorithms like sequential forward and backward search [55] are also popular. These algorithms have quadratic complexity, but they perform poorly for non-monotonic indices. In such cases, sequential floating searches

[231] provide better results, though at the cost of a higher computational complexity. Beam search variants of the sequential algorithms [6] are also used to reduce computational complexity. Recently robust methods for finding the optimal subset for arbitrary evaluation indices are being developed using genetic algorithms (GAs) [211]. GA-based feature selection methods [126] are usually found to perform better than other heuristic search methods for large and medium sized data sets; however they also require considerable computation time for large data sets. Other attempts to decrease the computational time of feature selection include probabilistic search methods like random hill climbing [258] and Las Vegas Filter (LVF) approach [141]. Comparison and discussion of some of the above methods for many real life data sets may be found in [126].

Feature selection algorithms are sometimes denoted as either *filter* or *wrapper* based depending on the way of computing the feature evaluation indices. The algorithms which do not perform classification/clustering of the data in the process of feature evaluation constitute what is called the *filter* approach. In contrast to this, *wrapper* approach [117] directly uses the classification accuracy of some classifier as the evaluation criterion. The latter one often performs better than the filter approach, though much more time consuming. In the next two sections we briefly discuss some algorithms of filter and wrapper approaches.

3.3.1 Filter approach

We discuss here some of the filter methods for unsupervised feature selection. They can be broadly classified into two categories. Methods in one such category involve maximization of clustering performance, as quantified by some index. These include the sequential unsupervised feature selection algorithm [141], maximum entropy based method and the recently developed neuro-fuzzy approach [194]. The other category considers selection of features based on feature dependency and relevance. The principle is that any feature carrying little or no additional information beyond that subsumed by the remaining features is redundant and should be eliminated. Various dependence measures like correlation coefficients [87], measures of statistical redundancy [96], or linear dependence [47] have been used. Recently the Relief algorithm [113] and its extensions [124] which identify statistically relevant features have been reported. A fast feature selection algorithm based on an information fuzzy network is described in [129]. Another algorithm based on conditional independence uses the concept of Markov blanket [121]. All these methods involve search and require significantly high computation time for large data sets. In [112] an algorithm which does not involve search and selects features by hierarchically merging similar feature pairs is described. However, the algorithm is crude in nature and performs poorly on real life data sets. It may be noted that principal component analysis (PCA) [55] also performs unsupervised dimensionality reduction based on information content of features. However, PCA involves feature transformation and obtains a set of transformed features rather than a subset of the original features.

3.3.2 Wrapper approach

In its most general formulation, the wrapper methodology consists of using the prediction performance of a given learning machine to assess the relative usefulness of different subsets of variables. In practice, one needs to define: (i) how to search the space of all possible variable subsets; (ii) how to assess the prediction performance of a learning machine to guide the search and halt it; and (iii) which predictor to use. A wide range of search strategies can be used, including breadth-first, branch-and-bound, simulated annealing and genetic algorithms [117]. Performance assessments are usually done using a validation set or by cross-validation methods such as leave-one-out and hold out. Popular predictors include decision trees, naive Bayes, least square linear predictors and support vector machines.

Wrappers are often criticized because they seem to be a "brute force" method requiring massive amounts of computation. Efficient search strategies may be devised to circumvent this. Using such strategies does not necessarily mean sacrificing prediction performance. In fact, it appears to be the converse in some cases; e.g., coarse search strategies may alleviate the problem of over-fitting and increase the accuracy. Since wrappers use the learning machine as a black box, they are remarkably universal and simple. An efficient but less universal version of the wrapper methods is the *embedded* technique, which performs variable selection in the process of training, but it is dependent on the learning machines used.

3.4 Feature Selection Using Feature Similarity (FSFS)

Here we describe an unsupervised algorithm, FSFS [166], belonging to the filter approach. The method uses feature dependency/similarity for redundancy reduction but requires no search. It involves partitioning of the original feature set into some distinct subsets or clusters so that the features within a cluster are highly similar while those in different clusters are dissimilar. A single feature from each such cluster is then selected to constitute the resulting reduced subset. A novel similarity measure, called maximal information compression index, is used in clustering. Its comparison with two other measures namely, correlation coefficient and least square regression error, is made. It is also explained how 'representation entropy' can be used for quantifying redundancy in a set.

The nature of both the feature clustering algorithm and the feature similarity measure is geared towards two goals – minimizing the information loss (in terms of second order statistics) incurred in the process of feature reduction and minimizing the redundancy present in the reduced feature subset. The feature selection algorithm owes its low computational complexity to two factors – (a) unlike most conventional algorithms, search for the best subset (requiring multiple evaluation of indices) is not involved, (b) the feature similarity measure can be computed in much less time compared to many indices used in other supervised and unsupervised feature selection methods. Since the method achieves dimensionality reduction through removal of redundant features, it is more related to feature selection for compression rather than for classification.

Superiority of the algorithm, over four related methods, viz., branch and bound algorithm, sequential floating forward search, sequential forward search and stepwise clustering, is demonstrated extensively on nine real life data of both large and small sample sizes and dimension ranging from 4 to 649. Comparison is made on the basis of both clustering/classification performance and redundancy reduction. Effectiveness of the maximal information compression index and the effect of scale parameter are also studied.

In Section 3.4.1 we describe measures of similarity between a pair of features. Section 3.4.2 describes the feature selection algorithm using the similarity measure. Some feature evaluation indices are presented in Section 3.5. In Section 3.6 we provide experimental results along with comparisons.

3.4.1 Feature similarity measures

In this section we discuss some criteria for measuring similarity between two random variables, based on linear dependency between them. In this context we present a novel measure called *maximal information compression index* to be used for feature selection.

There are broadly two possible approaches to measure similarity between two random variables. One is to non-parametrically test the closeness of probability distributions of the variables. Walds-Wolfowitz test and the other run tests [236] may be used for this purpose. However, these tests are sensitive to both location and dispersion of the distributions, hence not suited for the purpose of feature selection. Another approach is to measure the amount of functional (linear or higher) dependency between the variables. There are several benefits of choosing linear dependency as a feature similarity measure. It is known that if some of the features are linearly dependent on the others, and if the data is linearly separable in the original representation, the data is still linearly separable if all but one of the linearly dependent features are removed [47]. As far as the information content of the variables is concerned, second order statistics of the data is often the most important criterion after mean values [236]. All the linear dependency measures that we will discuss are related to the amount of error in terms of second order statistics, in predicting one of the variables using the other. We discuss below two existing [236] linear dependency measures before explaining the *maximal information compression index*.

3.4.1.1   Correlation coefficient (ρ)

The most well-known measure of similarity between two random variables is the correlation coefficient. Correlation coefficient ρ between two random variables x_1 and x_2 is defined as $\rho(x_1, x_2) = \frac{\text{cov}(x_1, x_2)}{\sqrt{\text{var}(x_1)\text{var}(x_2)}}$, where var( ) denotes the variance of a variable and cov( ) the covariance between two variables. If x_1 and x_2 are completely correlated, i.e., exact linear dependency exists, $\rho(x_1, x_2)$ is 1 or -1. If x_1 and x_2 are totally uncorrelated, $\rho(x_1, x_2)$ is 0. Hence, $1 - |\rho(x_1, x_2)|$ can be used as a measure of similarity between two variables x_1 and x_2. The following can be stated about the measure:

1. $0 \leq 1 - |\rho(x_1, x_2)| \leq 1$.

2. $1 - |\rho(x_1, x_2)| = 0$ if and only if x_1 and x_2 are linearly related.

3. $1 - |\rho(x_1, x_2)| = 1 - |\rho(x_2, x_1)|$ (symmetric).

4. If $u = \frac{x_1 - a}{c}$ and $v = \frac{x_2 - b}{d}$ for some constants a, b, c, d, then $1 - |\rho(x_1, x_2)| = 1 - |\rho(u, v)|$ i.e., the measure is *invariant to scaling and translation* of the variables.

5. The measure is *sensitive to rotation* of the scatter diagram in (x_1, x_2) plane.

Although the correlation coefficient contains many desirable properties as a feature similarity measure, properties 4 and 5, mentioned above, make it somewhat unsuitable for feature selection. Since the measure is invariant to scaling, two pairs of variables having different variances may have the same value of the similarity measure, which is not desirable as variance has high information content. Sensitivity to rotation is also not desirable in many applications.

3.4.1.2   Least square regression error (e)

Another measure of the degree of linear dependency between two variables x_1 and x_2 is the error in predicting x_2 from the linear model $x_2 = a + bx_1$. a and b are the regression coefficients obtained by minimizing the mean square error $e(x_1, x_2)^2 = \frac{1}{n} \sum (e_i(x_1, x_2))^2$, $e_i(x_1, x_2) = x_{2i} - a - bx_{1i}$. The coefficients are given by $a = \bar{x}_2$ and $b = \frac{\text{cov}(x_1, x_2)}{\text{var}(x_1)}$ and the mean square error $e(x_1, x_2)$ is given by $e(x_1, x_2) = \text{var}(x_2)(1 - \rho(x_1, x_2)^2)$. If x_2 and x_1 are linearly related $e(x_1, x_2) = 0$, and if x_1 and x_2 are completely uncorrelated $e(x_1, x_2) = \text{var}(x_2)$. The measure e^2 is also known as the *residual variance*. It is the amount of variance of x_2 unexplained by the linear model. Some properties of e are:

1. $0 \leq e(x_1, x_2) \leq \text{var}(x_2)$.

2. $e(x_1, x_2) = 0$ if and only if x_1 and x_2 are linearly related.

3. $e(x_1, x_2) \neq e(x_2, x_1)$ (unsymmetric).

4. If $u = x_1/c$ and $v = x_2/d$ for some constant a, b, c, d, then $e(x_1, x_2) = d^2 e(u, v)$, i.e., the measure e is *sensitive to scaling* of the variables. It is also clear that e is *invariant to translation* of the variables.

5. The measure e is *sensitive to rotation* of the scatter diagram in $x_1 - x_2$ plane.

Note that the measure e is not symmetric (property 3). Moreover, it is sensitive to rotation (property 5).

Now we present a measure of linear dependency which has many desirable properties for feature selection not present in the above two measures.

3.4.1.3 Maximal information compression index (λ_2)

Let Σ be the covariance matrix of random variables x_1 and x_2. Define, *maximal information compression index* as $\lambda_2(x_1, x_2) =$ smallest eigenvalue of Σ, i.e.,

$$2\lambda_2(x_1, x_2) = (\text{var}(x_1) + \text{var}(x_2) - \sqrt{(\text{var}(x_1) + \text{var}(x_2))^2 - 4\text{var}(x_1)\text{var}(x_2)(1 - \rho(x_1, x_2)^2)}.$$

The value of λ_2 is zero when the features are linearly dependent and increases as the amount of dependency decreases. It may be noted that the measure λ_2 is nothing but the eigenvalue for the direction normal to the principle component direction of feature pair (x_1, x_2). It is shown in [55] that maximum information compression is achieved if multivariate (in this case bivariate) data are projected along its principal component direction. The corresponding loss of information in reconstruction of the pattern (in terms of second order statistics) is equal to the eigenvalue along the direction normal to the principal component. Hence, λ_2 is the amount of reconstruction error committed if the data is projected to a reduced (in this case reduced from two to one) dimension in the best possible way. Therefore, it is a measure of the *minimum amount of information loss* or the *maximum amount of information compression* possible.

The significance of λ_2 can also be explained geometrically in terms of linear regression. It can be easily shown [236] that the value of λ_2 is equal to the sum of the squares of the perpendicular distances of the points (x_1, x_2) to the best fit line $x_2 = \hat{a} + \hat{b}x_1$, obtained by minimizing the sum of the squared perpendicular distances. The coefficients of such a best fit line are given by $\hat{a} = \bar{x}_1 \cot\theta + \bar{x}_2$ and $\hat{b} = -\cot\theta$, where $\theta = 2 \tan^{-1}\left(\frac{2\text{cov}(x_1, x_2)}{\text{var}(x_1)^2 - \text{var}(x_2)^2}\right)$. The nature of errors and the best fit lines for least square regression and

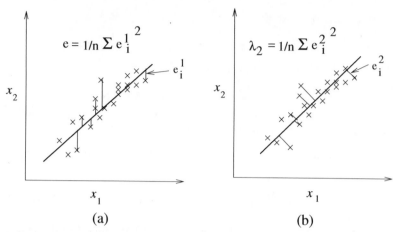

FIGURE 3.1: Nature of errors in linear regression, (a) Least square fit (e), (b) Least square projection fit (λ_2).

principal component analysis are illustrated in Figure 3.1. λ_2 has the following properties:

1. $0 \leq \lambda_2(x_1, x_2) \leq 0.5(\text{var}(x_1) + \text{var}(x_2))$.

2. $\lambda_2(x_1, x_2) = 0$ if and only if x_1 and x_2 are linearly related.

3. $\lambda_2(x_1, x_2) = \lambda_2(x_2, x_1)$ (symmetric).

4. If $u = \frac{x_1}{c}$ and $v = \frac{x_2}{d}$ for some constant a, b, c, d, then $\lambda_2(x_1, x_2) \neq \lambda_2(u, v)$; i.e., the measure is *sensitive to scaling* of the variables. Since the expression of λ_2 does not contain mean, but only the variance and covariance terms, it is *invariant to translation* of the data set.

5. λ_2 is *invariant to rotation* of the variables about the origin (this can be easily verified from the geometric interpretation of λ_2 considering the property that the perpendicular distance of a point to a line does not change with rotation of the axes).

The measure λ_2 possesses several desirable properties such as symmetry (property 3), sensitivity to scaling (property 4), and invariance to rotation (property 5). It is a property of the variable pair (x_1, x_2) reflecting the amount of error committed if maximal information compression is performed by reducing the variable pair to a single variable. Hence, it may be suitably used in redundancy reduction.

3.4.2   Feature selection through clustering

The task of feature selection involves two steps, namely, partitioning the original feature set into a number of homogeneous subsets (clusters) and selecting a representative feature from each such cluster. Partitioning of the features is done based on the k-NN principle using one of the feature similarity measures described in Section 3.4.1. In doing so, the k nearest features of each feature are computed first. Among them the feature having the most compact subset (as determined by its distance to the farthest neighbor) is selected, and its k neighboring features are discarded. The process is repeated for the remaining features until all of them are either selected or discarded.

While determining the k nearest neighbors of features a constant error threshold (ϵ) is assigned; ϵ is set equal to the distance of the kth nearest neighbor of the feature selected in the first iteration. In subsequent iterations, it is checked whether the λ_2 value, corresponding to the subset of a feature, is greater than ϵ or not. If yes, the value of k is decreased. Therefore k may be varying over iterations. The concept of clustering features into homogeneous groups of varying sizes is illustrated in Figure 3.2. The algorithm may be stated as follows:

Algorithm:

Let the original number of features be P, and the original feature set be $A = \{F_i, i = 1, \ldots, P\}$. Represent the dissimilarity between features F_i and F_j by $S(F_i, F_j)$. The higher the value of S is, the more dissimilar are the features. The measures of linear dependency (e.g., ρ, e, λ_2) described in Section 3.4.1 may be used in computing S. Let r_i^k represent the dissimilarity between feature F_i and its kth nearest neighbor feature in R. Then

Step 1: Choose an initial value of $k \leq P - 1$. Initialize the reduced feature subset R to the original feature set A; i.e., $R \leftarrow A$.

Step 2: For each feature $F_i \in R$, compute r_i^k.

Step 3: Find feature $F_{i'}$ for which $r_{i'}^k$ is minimum. *Retain* this feature in R and *discard* k nearest features of $F_{i'}$. (Note: $F_{i'}$ denotes the feature for which removing k nearest neighbors will cause minimum error among all the features in R.) Let $\epsilon = r_{i'}^k$.

Step 4: If $k >$ cardinality$(R) - 1$: $k =$ cardinality$(R) - 1$.

Step 5: If $k = 1$: **Go to Step 8.**

Step 6: **While** $r_{i'}^k > \epsilon$ **do**:

    (a) $k = k - 1$.

    $r_{i'}^k = \inf_{F_i \in R} r_i^k$.

    ('k' is decremented by 1, until the 'kth nearest neighbor' of at least one of the features in R is less than ϵ-dissimilar with the feature)

    (b) If $k = 1$: **Go to Step 8.**

    (if no feature in R has less than ϵ-dissimilar 'nearest neighbor' select all the remaining features in R)

        End While

Step 7: **Go to Step 2.**

Step 8: Return feature set R as the reduced feature set. □

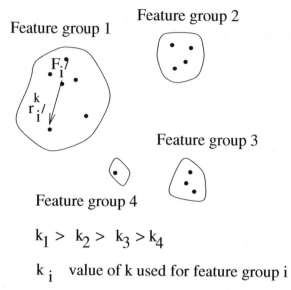

Feature group 1

Feature group 2

Feature group 3

Feature group 4

$$k_1 > k_2 > k_3 > k_4$$

k_i value of k used for feature group i

FIGURE 3.2:   Feature clusters.

Remarks:

Computational complexity. The algorithm has low computational complexity with respect to both number of features and number of samples of the original data. With respect to the dimension (P) the method has complexity $\mathcal{O}(P^2)$. Among the existing search-based schemes only sequential forward and backward search have complexity $\mathcal{O}(P^2)$, though each evaluation is more time consuming. Other algorithms such as plus-l-take-r, sequential floating search and branch and bound algorithm [55] have complexity higher than quadratic. Most probabilistic search algorithms also require more than quadratic number of evaluations.

The second factor that contributes to the speed-up achieved by the similarity based algorithm is the low computational complexity of evaluating the linear dependency measures of feature similarity. If the data set contains n samples, evaluation of the similarity measure for a feature pair is of complexity $\mathcal{O}(n)$. Thus the feature selection scheme has overall complexity $\mathcal{O}(P^2 n)$. Almost all other supervised and unsupervised feature evaluation indices (e.g., entropy, class separability, K-NN classification accuracy) have at least $\mathcal{O}(n^2)$ complexity of computation. Moreover, evaluation of the linear dependency measures involves computation using one-dimensional variables only, while the other measures often involve distance computations at higher dimensions. All these factors contribute to the large speed-up achieved by the similarity-based algorithm compared to other feature selection schemes.

Notion of scale in feature selection and choice of k: In similarity-based feature selection algorithm k controls the size of the reduced set. Since k determines the error threshold (ϵ), the representation of the data at different degrees of details is controlled by its choice. This characteristic is useful in data mining where *multiscale* representation of the data is often necessary. Note that the said property may not always be possessed by other algorithms where the input is usually the desired size of the reduced feature set. The reason is that changing the size of the reduced set may not necessarily result in any change in the levels of details. In contrast, for the similarity-based algorithm, k acts as a scale parameter that controls the degree of details in a more direct manner.

Non-metric nature of similarity measure: The similarity measures used in the feature selection algorithm need not be a metric. Unlike conventional agglomerative clustering algorithms it does not utilize the metric property of the similarity measures. Also unlike the stepwise clustering method [112] used previously for feature selection, the clustering algorithm described in this section is partitional and non-hierarchical in nature.

3.5 Feature Evaluation Indices

Let us now describe some indices that may be considered for evaluating the effectiveness of the selected feature subsets. The first three indices, namely, class separability, K-NN classification accuracy and naive Bayes classification accuracy, do need class information of the samples while the remaining three, namely, entropy, fuzzy feature evaluation index and representation entropy, do not. Before we discuss them, we mention, for convenience, the following notations: Let n be the number of sample points in the data set, M be the number of classes present in the data set, P be the number of features in the original feature set A, p be the number of features in the reduced feature set R, Ω_A be the original feature space with dimension P, and Ω_R be the transformed feature space with dimension p.

3.5.1 Supervised indices

1. *Class separability* [55]: Class separability S of a data set is defined as $S = trace(S_b^{-1}S_w)$. S_w is the within-class scatter matrix and S_b is the between-class scatter matrix, defined as:

$$S_w = \sum_{j=1}^{M} \pi_j E\{(\mathbf{x} - \mu_j)(\mathbf{x} - \mu_j)^T | \omega_j\} = \sum_{j=1}^{M} \pi_j \Sigma_j$$

$$S_b = \sum_{j=1}^{M} (\mu_j - \bar{\mathbf{x}})(\mu_j - \bar{\mathbf{x}})^T$$

$$\bar{\mathbf{x}} = E\{\mathbf{x}\} = \sum_{j=1}^{M} \pi_j \mu_j \qquad (3.1)$$

where π_j is the a priori probability that a pattern belongs to class ω_j, $\mathbf{x}$ is the feature vector, μ_j is the sample mean vector of class ω_j, $\bar{\mathbf{x}}$ is the sample mean vector for the entire data points, Σ_j is the sample covariance matrix of class ω_j, and $E\{.\}$ is the expectation operator. A lower value of the separability criteria S ensures that the classes are well separated by their scatter means.

2. *K-NN classification accuracy*: Here the K-NN rule is used for evaluating the effectiveness of the reduced set for classification. Cross-validation is performed in the following manner – randomly select 90% of the data as training set and classify the remaining 10% points. Ten such independent runs are performed, and the average classification accuracy on test set is used. The value of K, chosen for the K-NN rule, is the square root of the number of data points in the training set.

3. *Naive Bayes classification accuracy*: A Bayes maximum likelihood classifier [55], assuming normal distribution of classes, is also used for evaluating the classification performance. Mean and covariance of the classes are estimated from a randomly selected 10% training sample, and the remaining 90% of the points are used as a test set. Ten such independent runs are performed and the average classification accuracy on the test set is provided.

3.5.2   Unsupervised indices

1. *Entropy*: Let the distance between two data points i, j be

$$\mathcal{D}_{ij} = \left[\sum_{l=1}^{p} \left(\frac{x_{i,l} - x_{j,l}}{max_l - min_l} \right)^2 \right]^{1/2},$$

where $x_{i,l}$ denotes feature value for i along lth direction, and max_l, min_l are the maximum and minimum values computed over all the samples along lth axis, and p is the number of features. Similarity between i, j is given by $\text{sim}(i, j) = e^{-\alpha \mathcal{D}_{ij}}$, where α is a positive constant. A possible value of α is $\frac{-\ln 0.5}{\bar{\mathcal{D}}}$. $\bar{\mathcal{D}}$ is the average distance between data points computed over the entire data set. Entropy is defined as [141]:

$$E = -\sum_{i=1}^{n} \sum_{j=1}^{n} (\text{sim}(i,j) \times \log \text{sim}(i,j) + (1 - \text{sim}(i,j)) \times \log (1 - \text{sim}(i,j)))$$

$$(3.2)$$

where n is the number of sample points. If the data are uniformly distributed in the feature space entropy is maximum. When the data has well-formed clusters uncertainty is low and so is entropy.

2. *Fuzzy feature evaluation index.* Fuzzy feature evaluation index (FFEI) is defined as [194]:

$$FFEI = \frac{2}{n(n-1)} \sum_{i} \sum_{i \neq j} \frac{1}{2} \left[\mu_{ij}^R (1 - \mu_{ij}^A) + \mu_{ij}^A (1 - \mu_{ij}^R) \right] \qquad (3.3)$$

where μ_{ij}^A and μ_{ij}^R are the degrees that both patterns i and j belong to the same cluster in the feature spaces Ω_A and Ω_R, respectively. Membership function μ_{ij} may be defined as

$$\begin{aligned} \mu_{ij} &= 1 - \frac{d_{ij}}{\mathcal{D}_{max}} && \text{if } d_{ij} \leq \mathcal{D}_{max} \\ &= 0, && \text{otherwise.} \end{aligned}$$

d_{ij} is the distance between patterns i and j, and $\mathcal{D}_{max}$ is the maximum separation between patterns in the respective feature spaces.

The value of FFEI decreases as the intercluster/intracluster distances increase/ decrease. Hence, the lower the value of FFEI, the more crisp is the cluster structure.

Note that the first two indices, class separability and K-NN accuracy, measure the effectiveness of the feature subsets for classification, while the indices entropy and fuzzy feature evaluation index evaluate the clustering performance of the feature subsets. Let us now describe a quantitative index which measures the amount of redundancy present in the reduced subset.

3.5.3 Representation entropy

Let the eigenvalues of the $p \times p$ covariance matrix of a feature set of size p be $\lambda_l, l = 1, \ldots, p$. Let $\tilde{\lambda}_l = \frac{\lambda_l}{\sum_{l=1}^{p} \lambda_l}$. $\tilde{\lambda}_l$ has similar properties like probability, namely, $0 \leq \tilde{\lambda}_l \leq 1$ and $\sum_{l=1}^{p} \tilde{\lambda}_l = 1$. Hence, an entropy function can be defined as

$$H_R = -\sum_{l=1}^{p} \tilde{\lambda}_l \log \tilde{\lambda}_l. \qquad (3.4)$$

The function H_R attains a minimum value (zero) when all the eigenvalues except one are zero, or in other words when all the information is present along a single co-ordinate direction. If all the eigenvalues are equal, i.e., information is equally distributed among all the features, H_R is maximum and so is the uncertainty involved in feature reduction.

The above measure is known as *representation entropy*. It is a property of the *data set as represented by a particular set of features* and is a measure of the amount of information compression possible by dimensionality reduction. This is equivalent to the amount of redundancy present in that particular representation of the data set. Since the feature similarity based algorithm involves partitioning of the original feature set into a number of homogeneous (highly compressible) clusters, it is expected that representation entropy of the individual clusters are as low as possible, while that of the final reduced set of features has low redundancy, i.e., a high value of representation entropy.

It may be noted that among all the p dimensional subspaces of an original P dimensional data set, the one corresponding to the Karhunen-Loeve coordinates [55] (for the first p eigenvalues) has the highest representation entropy, i.e., is least redundant. However, for large dimensional data sets K-L transform directions are difficult to compute. Also, K-L transform results in general transformed variables and not exact subsets of the original features.

3.6 Experimental Results and Comparisons

Organization of the experimental results is as follows [166]: First the performance of the similarity-based feature selection algorithm (FSFS) in terms of the feature evaluation indices, presented in Section 3.5, is compared with five other feature selection schemes. Then the redundancy reduction aspect of the algorithm is quantitatively discussed along with comparisons. Effect of varying the parameter k, used in feature clustering, is also shown.

Three categories of real life public domain data sets are considered: low dimensional ($P \leq 10$) (e.g., Iris, Wisconsin cancer, and Forest cover type (considering numerical features only) data), medium dimensional ($10 < P \leq 100$) (e.g., Ionosphere, Waveform and Spambase data), and high dimensional ($P > 100$) (e.g., Arrhythmia, Multiple features and Isolet data), containing both large and relatively smaller number of points. Their characteristics are described in Appendix B.

3.6.1 Comparison: Classification and clustering performance

Four indices, viz., entropy (Equation 3.2), fuzzy feature evaluation index (Equation 3.3), class separability (Equation 3.1), K-NN and naive Bayes classification accuracy are considered to demonstrate the efficacy of the FSFS algorithm and for comparing it with other methods. Four unsupervised feature selection schemes considered for comparison are:

1. Branch and Bound Algorithm (BB) [55]: A search method in which all possible subsets are implicitly inspected without exhaustive search.

If the feature selection criterion is monotonic BB returns the optimal subset.

2. Sequential Forward Search (SFS) [55]: A suboptimal search procedure where one feature at a time is added to the current feature set. At each stage, the feature to be included in the feature set is selected from among the remaining available features so that the new enlarged feature set yields a maximum value of the criterion function used.

3. Sequential Floating Forward Search (SFFS) [231]: A near-optimal search procedure with lower computational cost than BB. It performs sequential forward search with provision for backtracking.

4. Stepwise Clustering (using correlation coefficient) (SWC) [112]: A non-search-based scheme which obtains a reduced subset by discarding correlated features.

In the experiments, entropy (Equation 3.2) is mainly used as the feature selection criterion with the first three search algorithms.

Comparisons in terms of five indices are reported for different sizes of the reduced feature subsets. Tables 3.1, 3.2 and 3.3 provide such a comparative result corresponding to high, medium and low dimensional data sets when the size of the reduced feature subset is taken to be about half of the original size as an example. Comparison for other sizes of the reduced feature set is provided in Figure 3.3 considering one data set from each of the three categories, namely, multiple features (high), ionosphere (medium) and cancer (low). The CPU time required by each of the algorithms on a Sun UltraSparc 350 MHz workstation are also reported in Tables 3.1–3.3. Since the branch and bound (BB) and the sequential floating forward search (SFFS) algorithms require infeasibly high computation time for the large data sets, the figures for them could not be provided in Table 3.1. For the classification accuracies (using K-NN and Bayes), both mean and standard deviations (SD) computed for ten independent runs are presented.

Compared to the search-based algorithms (BB, SFFS and SFS), the performance of the feature similarity-based (FSFS) scheme is comparable or slightly superior, while the computational time requirement is much less for the FSFS scheme. On the other hand, compared to the similarity-based SWC method the performance of the FSFS algorithm is much superior, keeping the time requirement comparable. It is further to be noted that the superiority in terms of computational time increases as the dimensionality and sample size increase. For example, in the case of low dimensional data sets, the speed-up factor of the FSFS scheme compared to BB and SFFS algorithms is about 30−50, for Forest data which is low dimensional but has large sample size the factor is about 100, for medium dimensional data sets, BB and SFFS are about 100 times slower and SFS about 10 times slower, while for the high dimensional data sets SFS is about 100 times slower, and BB and SFFS could not be compared as they require infeasibly high run time.

TABLE 3.1:   Comparison of feature selection algorithms for large dimensional data sets

Data set	Method	Evaluation Criteria					CPU
		E	FFEI	S	KNNA (%) Mean SD	BayesA (%) Mean SD	Time (sec)
Isolet p=310 P=617 $k = 305$	SFS	0.52	0.41	1.09	95.02 0.89	92.03 0.52	14.01 $\times 10^4$
	SWC	0.71	0.55	2.70	72.01 0.71	68.01 0.44	431
	Relief-F	0.70	0.52	2.24	95.81 0.81	95.52 0.47	5.03 $\times 10^3$
	FSFS	0.50	0.40	1.07	96.00 0.78	95.01 0.52	440
Mult. Feat. p=325 P=649 $k = 322$	SFS	0.67	0.47	0.45	77.01 0.24	75.02 0.14	5.00 $\times 10^4$
	SWC	0.79	0.55	0.59	52.00 0.19	50.05 0.10	401
	Relief-F	0.71	0.50	0.52	78.37 0.22	75.25 0.11	1.10 $\times 10^3$
	FSFS	0.68	0.48	0.45	78.34 0.22	75.28 0.10	451
Arrhythmia p=100 P=195 $k = 95$	SFS	0.74	0.44	0.25	52.02 0.55	50.21 0.43	1511
	SWC	0.82	0.59	0.41	40.01 0.52	38.45 0.38	70
	Relief-F	0.78	0.55	0.27	56.04 0.54	54.55 0.40	404
	FSFS	0.72	0.40	0.17	58.93 0.54	56.00 0.41	74

E: Entropy, FFEI: Fuzzy Feature Evaluation Index, S: Class Separability, KNNA: k-NN classification accuracy, BayesA: naive Bayes classification accuracy, SD: standard deviation. SFS: Sequential Forward Search, SWC: Stepwise Clustering, FSFS: Feature selection using feature similarity. p: number of selected features, P: number of original features, k: parameter used by the similarity-based method.

TABLE 3.2:   Comparison of feature selection algorithms for medium dimensional data sets

Data set	Method	Evaluation Criteria					CPU
		E	FFEI	S	KNNA (%) Mean SD	BayesA (%) Mean SD	Time (sec)
Spambase p=29 P=57 $k = 27$	BB	0.50	0.30	0.28	90.01 0.71	88.17 0.55	1579
	SFFS	0.50	0.30	0.28	90.01 0.72	88.17 0.55	1109
	SFS	0.52	0.34	0.29	87.03 0.68	86.20 0.54	121.36
	SWC	0.59	0.37	0.41	82.04 0.68	79.10 0.55	11.02
	Relief-F	0.59	0.36	0.34	87.04 0.70	86.01 0.52	70.80
	FSFS	0.50	0.30	0.28	90.01 0.71	88.19 0.52	13.36
Waveform p=20 P=40 $k = 17$	BB	0.67	0.47	0.29	78.02 0.47	62.27 0.41	1019
	SFFS	0.68	0.48	0.31	77.55 0.45	62.22 0.41	627
	SFS	0.69	0.49	0.37	74.37 0.44	59.01 0.42	71.53
	SWC	0.72	0.55	0.41	62.03 0.40	47.50 0.40	8.01
	Relief-F	0.73	0.54	0.38	74.88 0.41	62.88 0.40	50.22
	FSFS	0.68	0.48	0.30	75.20 0.43	63.01 0.40	8.28
Ionosphere p=16 P=32 $k = 11$	BB	0.65	0.44	0.07	75.96 0.35	65.10 0.28	150.11
	SFFS	0.65	0.44	0.08	74.73 0.37	65.08 0.31	50.36
	SFS	0.65	0.44	0.10	69.94 0.32	62.00 0.27	10.70
	SWC	0.66	0.47	0.22	62.03 0.32	59.02 0.25	1.04
	Relief-F	0.62	0.47	0.15	72.90 0.34	64.55 0.27	8.20
	FSFS	0.64	0.43	0.10	78.77 0.35	65.92 0.28	1.07

BB: Branch and Bound, SFFS: Sequential Floating Forward Search

TABLE 3.3: Comparison of feature selection algorithms for low dimensional data sets

Data set	Method	Evaluation Criteria					CPU
		E	FFEI	S	KNNA (%)	BayesA (%)	Time (sec)
					Mean SD	Mean SD	
	BB	0.65	0.40	0.90	64.03 0.41	63.55 0.40	4.01×10^4
Forest	SFFS	0.64	0.39	0.81	67.75 0.43	66.22 0.41	3.02×10^4
	SFS	0.64	0.41	0.98	62.03 0.41	61.09 0.40	7.00×10^3
p=5	SWC	0.68	0.45	1.00	54.70 0.37	53.25 0.35	50.03
P=10	Relief-F	0.65	0.40	0.90	64.03 0.41	63.55 0.40	2.80×10^4
k = 5	FSFS	0.65	0.40	0.90	64.03 0.41	63.55 0.40	55.50
	BB	0.59	0.36	1.84	94.90 0.17	94.45 0.14	3.39
Cancer	SFFS	0.59	0.36	1.84	94.90 0.17	94.45 0.14	6.82
	SFS	0.61	0.37	2.68	92.20 0.17	91.05 0.15	1.16
p=4	SWC	0.60	0.37	2.69	90.01 0.19	89.11 0.17	0.10
P=9	Relief-F	0.59	0.36	1.84	94.90 0.17	94.25 0.17	0.91
k = 5	FSFS	0.56	0.34	1.70	95.56 0.17	94.88 0.17	0.10
	BB	0.55	0.34	22.0	96.80 0.14	97.33 0.10	0.56
Iris	SFFS	0.55	0.34	22.0	96.80 0.14	97.33 0.10	0.71
	SFS	0.57	0.35	27.0	92.55 0.17	93.10 0.14	0.25
p=2	SWC	0.60	0.37	29.2	92.19 0.19	93.02 0.17	0.01
P=4	Relief-F	0.55	0.34	22.0	96.80 0.14	97.33 0.10	0.14
k = 2	FSFS	0.55	0.34	22.0	96.80 0.14	97.33 0.10	0.01

It may be noted that the aforesaid unsupervised feature selection algorithms (viz., BB, SFFS, SFS) usually consider 'entropy' as the selection criterion. Keeping this in mind detailed results are provided in Tables 3.1–3.3. However, some results using another unsupervised measure, namely, fuzzy feature evaluation index (FFEI) (Equation 3.3) are also depicted in Table 3.4. These are shown, as an illustration, only for the four large data sets (Isolet, Multiple features, Arrhythmia and Forest cover type). These results corroborate the findings obtained using entropy.

For comparing the performance with that of a supervised method, Relief-F, which is widely used, 50% of the samples were used as design set. Results are presented in Tables 3.1–3.3. The Relief-F algorithm provides classification performance comparable to the similarity-based scheme in spite of using class label information. Moreover, it has a much higher time requirement, especially for data sets with large number of samples, e.g., the Forest data. Its performance in terms of the unsupervised indices is also poorer.

Statistical significance of the classification performance of the similarity-based method compared to those of the other algorithms is tested. Means and SD values of the accuracies, computed over 10 independent runs, are used for this purpose. The test statistics described in Section 2.6.2 is used. It is observed that the FSFS method has significantly better performance compared to the SWC algorithm for all the data sets, and the SFS algorithm for most of the data sets. For the other algorithms, namely, Relief-F, BB and SFFS, the performance is comparable; i.e., the difference of the mean values of the classification scores is statistically insignificant.

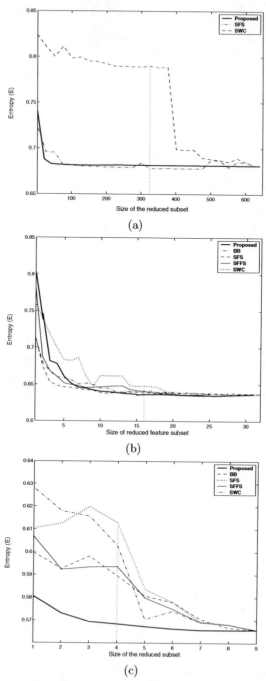

FIGURE 3.3: Variation in classification accuracy with size of the reduced subset for (a) Multiple features, (b) Ionosphere, and (c) Cancer data sets. The vertical dotted line marks the point for which results are reported in Tables 3.1−3.3.

TABLE 3.4: Comparison of feature selection algorithms for large data sets when search algorithms use FFEI as the selection criterion

Data set	Method	Evaluation Criteria					CPU
		FFEI	E	S	KNNA (%) Mean SD	BayesA (%) Mean SD	Time (sec)
Isolet	SFS	0.40	0.54	0.98	95.81 0.82	92.19 0.72	28.01×10^4
p=310, P=617	FSFS	0.40	0.50	1.07	96.00 0.78	95.01 0.52	440
Mult. Feat.	SFS	0.44	0.67	0.44	77.71 0.44	75.81 0.17	9.20×10^4
p=325, P=649	FSFS	0.48	0.68	0.45	78.34 0.22	75.28 0.10	451
Arrhythmia	SFS	0.40	0.77	0.21	53.22 0.59	52.25 0.44	2008
p=100, P=195	FSFS	0.40	0.72	0.17	58.93 0.54	56.00 0.41	74
	BB	0.40	0.65	0.90	64.03 0.41	63.55 0.40	9.21×10^4
Forest	SFFS	0.40	0.66	0.83	67.01 0.45	66.00 0.44	7.52×10^4
	SFS	0.43	0.66	1.01	61.41 0.44	60.01 0.41	17.19×10^3
p=5, P=10	FSFS	0.40	0.65	0.90	64.03 0.41	63.55 0.40	55.50

TABLE 3.5: Representation entropy H_R^s of subsets selected using some algorithms

Data set	BB	SFFS	SFS	SWC	Relief-F	FSFS
Isolet	-	-	2.91	2.87	2.89	3.50
Mult. Ftrs.	-	-	2.02	1.90	1.92	3.41
Arrhythmia	-	-	2.11	2.05	2.02	3.77
Spambase	2.02	1.90	1.70	1.44	1.72	2.71
Waveform	1.04	1.02	0.98	0.81	0.92	1.21
Ionosphere	1.71	1.71	1.70	0.91	1.52	1.81
Forest	0.91	0.82	0.82	0.77	0.91	0.91
Cancer	0.71	0.71	0.55	0.55	0.59	0.82
Iris	0.47	0.47	0.41	0.31	0.47	0.47

3.6.2 Redundancy reduction: Quantitative study

As mentioned before, the FSFS algorithm involves partitioning the original feature set into a certain number of homogeneous groups and then replacing each group by a single feature, thereby resulting in the reduced feature set. Representation entropy (H_R), defined in Section 3.5, is used to measure the redundancy in both the homogeneous clusters and the final selected feature subset. H_R when computed over the individual clusters should be as low as possible (indicating high redundancy among the features belonging to a single cluster), while giving as high value as possible for the selected subset (indicating minimum redundancy). Let us denote the average value of H_R computed over the homogeneous groups by H_R^g and the value of H_R for the final selected subset by H_R^s.

Table 3.5 shows the comparative results of the FSFS method with other feature selection algorithms in terms of H_R^s. It is seen that the subset obtained by the FSFS scheme is least redundant having the highest H_R^s values.

To demonstrate the superiority of the *maximal information compression index* λ_2, compared to the other two feature similarity measures (ρ and e) used

TABLE 3.6:   Redundancy reduction using different feature similarity measures

Data set	Similarity Measure: λ_2		Similarity Measure: e		Similarity Measure: ρ	
	H_R^g	H_R^s	H_R^g	H_R^s	H_R^g	H_R^s
Isolet	0.001	3.50	0.007	3.01	0.003	3.41
Mult. Ftrs.	0.002	3.41	0.008	2.95	0.007	3.01
Arrhythmia	0.007	3.77	0.017	2.80	0.010	3.41
Spambase	0.04	2.71	0.07	2.01	0.05	2.53
Waveform	0.10	1.21	0.14	1.04	0.11	1.08
Ionosphere	0.05	1.81	0.07	1.54	0.07	1.54
Forest	0.10	0.91	0.17	0.82	0.11	0.91
Cancer	0.19	0.82	0.22	0.71	0.19	0.82
Iris	0.17	0.47	0.22	0.31	0.17	0.47

H_R^g: average representation entropy of feature groups, H_R^s: representation entropy of selected subset, λ_2: maximal information compression index, e: least square regression error, ρ: correlation coefficients.

previously, Table 3.6 is provided, where both H_R^s and H_R^g values obtained using each of the similarity measures are compared, in the feature clustering algorithm. It is seen from Table 3.6 that λ_2 has superior information compression capability compared to the other two measures as indicated by the lowest and highest values of H_R^g and H_R^s, respectively.

3.6.3   Effect of cluster size

In the FSFS algorithm the size of the reduced feature subset and hence the scale of details of data representation is controlled by the parameter k. Figure 3.4 illustrates such an effect for three data sets – multiple features, ionosphere and cancer, considering one data from each of the high, medium and low categories. As expected, the size of the reduced subset decreases overall with increase in k. However, for medium and particularly large dimensional data (Figure 3.4a) it is observed that for certain ranges of k at the lower side, there is no change in the size of the reduced subset; i.e., no reduction in dimension occurs. Another interesting fact observed in all the data sets considered is that, for all values of k in the case of small dimensional data sets, and for high values of k in the case of medium and large dimensional data sets, the size of the selected subset varies linearly with k. Further, it is seen in those cases, $p + k \approx P$, where p is the size of the reduced subset and P is the size of the original feature set.

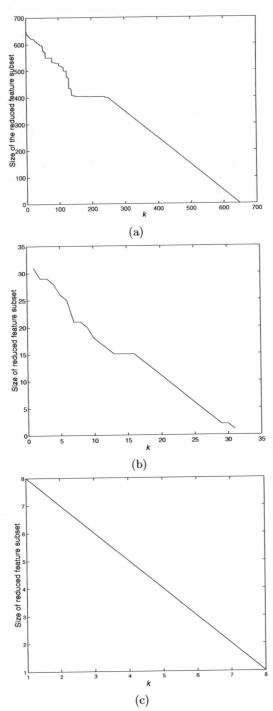

FIGURE 3.4: Variation in size of the reduced subset with parameter k for (a) multiple features, (b) ionosphere, and (c) cancer data.

3.7   Summary

After providing a brief review on various feature selection and feature extraction methodologies, an algorithm for unsupervised feature selection using feature similarity measures is described, in detail, for data mining applications. The novelty of the scheme, as compared to other conventional feature selection algorithms, is the absence of search process which contributes to the high computational time requirement of those feature selection algorithms. The algorithm is based on pairwise feature similarity measures, which are fast to compute. It is found to require several orders less CPU time compared to other schemes. Unlike other approaches that are based on optimizing either classification or clustering performance explicitly, here one determines a set of maximally independent features by discarding the redundant ones. In other words, the method is more related to feature selection for information compression rather than for classification/clustering. This enhances the applicability of the resulting features to compression and other tasks such as forecasting, summarization, association mining in addition to classification/clustering. Another characteristic of the aforesaid algorithm is its capability of multiscale representation of data sets. The scale parameter k used for feature clustering efficiently parametrizes the trade-off between representation accuracy and feature subset size. All these make it suitable for a wide variety of data mining tasks involving large (in terms of both dimension and size) data sets.

The feature clustering algorithm uses a novel feature similarity measure called *maximal information compression index*. One may note that the definition of the said parameter is not new; it is its use in feature subset selection framework which is novel. The superiority of this measure for feature selection is established experimentally. It is also demonstrated through extensive experiments that *representation entropy* can be used as an index for quantifying both redundancy reduction and information loss in a feature selection method.

The information loss in this filter approach is measured in terms of second order statistics. The similarity measure used for feature selection is selected/defined accordingly. One may modify these measures suitably in case even higher order statistics are used. In this regard modifications of correlation indices [236] which measure higher order polynomial dependency between variables may be considered. Also the similarity measure is valid only for numeric features; its extension to accommodate other kinds of variables (e.g., symbolic, categorical, hybrid) as input may also be investigated for data mining applications.

Chapter 4

Active Learning Using Support Vector Machine

4.1 Introduction

In the previous two chapters we have dealt with some preprocessing tasks of data mining. The present chapter is concerned with its classification/learning aspect. Here we present two active learning strategies [164, 167] for handling the large quadratic programming problem of designing support vector machine classifier.

The support vector machine (SVM) [35, 275] has been successful as a high performance classifier in several domains including pattern recognition, data mining and bioinformatics. It has strong theoretical foundations and good generalization capability. Another advantage of SVM is that, as a byproduct of learning, it obtains a set of support vectors (SVs) that characterizes a given classification task or compresses a labeled data set. Often the number of the SVs is only a small fraction of that of the original data set.

A limitation of the SVM design algorithm, particularly for large data sets, is the need to solve a quadratic programming (QP) problem involving a dense $n \times n$ matrix, where n is the number of points in the data set. Since most QP routines have quadratic complexity, SVM design requires huge memory and computational time for large data applications. Several approaches exist for circumventing the above shortcomings. These include simpler optimization criterion for SVM design, e.g., the linear SVM [30] and the kernel adatron [70], specialized QP algorithms sush as the conjugate gradient method [107], decomposition techniques which break down the large QP problem into a series of smaller QP sub-problems [188], and sequential minimal optimization (SMO) algorithm [225] and its various extensions.

A simple method to solve the SVM QP problem has been described by Vapnik [275], which is known as 'chunking.' The chunking algorithm uses the fact that the solution of the SVM problem remains the same if one removes the points that correspond to zero Lagrange multipliers of the QP problem (the non-SV points). The large QP problem can thus be broken down into a series of smaller QP problems, whose ultimate goal is to identify all of the non-zero Lagrange multipliers (SVs) while discarding the zero Lagrange multipliers (non-SVs). At every step, chunking solves a QP problem that consists of the non-zero Lagrange multiplier points from the previous step, and a chunk of q other points. At the final step, the entire set of non-zero Lagrange multipliers has been identified, thereby solving the large QP problem. Several variations of chunking algorithm exist depending upon the method of forming the chunks [35, 249]. Chunking greatly reduces the training time compared to batch learning of SVMs. However, it may not handle large-scale training problems due to slow convergence of the chunking steps when q new points are chosen randomly.

Recently, active learning has become a popular paradigm for reducing the sample complexity of large-scale learning tasks [10, 45]. Here, instead of learning from samples selected randomly, the learner has the ability to select its own training data. This is done iteratively, and the output of a step is used to select the examples for the next step. Several active learning strategies exist in practice, e.g., error driven techniques, uncertainty sampling, version space reduction and adaptive resampling.

In the context of support vector machine, active learning can be used to speed up chunking algorithms. In [36], a query learning strategy for large margin classifiers is presented which iteratively requests the label of the data point closest to the current separating hyperplane. This accelerates the learning drastically compared to random sampling. An active learning strategy based on version space splitting is presented in [272]. The points that split the current version space into two halves having equal volumes are selected at each step, as they are likely to be the actual support vectors. Three heuristics for approximating the above criterion are described; the simplest among them selects the point closest to the current hyperplane as in [36]. A greedy optimal strategy for active SV learning is described in [252]. Here, logistic regression is used to compute the class probabilities, which is further used to estimate the expected error after adding an example. The example that minimizes this error is selected as a candidate SV. Here also two heuristics are suggested for practical implementation by focusing only on the informative dimensions and selecting examples based on their proximity to the separating hyperplane. Although these active learning strategies query only for a single point at each step, several studies have noted that the gain in computational time can be obtained by querying multiple instances at a time. This motivates the formulation of active learning strategies which query for multiple points.

Another major limitation of all the above strategies is that they are essentially greedy methods where the selection of a new point is influenced only by the current hypothesis (separating hyperplane) available. In the above setup, learning may be severely hampered in two situations: a 'bad' example is queried which drastically worsens the current hypothesis, and the current hypothesis itself is far from the optimal hypothesis (e.g., in the initial phase of learning). As a result, the examples queried are less likely to be the actual support vectors.

The model of *learning from statistical queries* captures the natural notion of learning algorithms that construct a hypothesis based on statistical properties of large samples rather than the idiosyncrasies of a particular sample [108]. Such a model of active learning seems intuitively more robust than those that are willing to make radical alterations to their hypothesis on the basis of individual examples. Here, instead of the original oracle which provides random examples of the target hypothesis, the learner interacts with an intermediate oracle whose goal is to enforce restriction on the learner's use of the examples. The intermediate oracle provides an estimate of the probability (with an allowed approximation error) that an example belongs to the target hypothesis i.e., provides answers to statistical queries rather than exact membership queries. The probability of a point's being selected for learning may be set equal to that answer. The statistical query model has been theoretically demonstrated to provide efficient and robust learning in noisy environments [108].

The chapter has two parts. First we present an error-driven incremental method [164] for active support vector learning. The method involves selecting a chunk of q new points, having equal number of correctly classified and misclassified points, at each iteration by resampling the data set, and using it to update the current SV set. The resampling strategy is computationally superior to random chunk selection, while achieving higher classification accuracy. Since it allows for querying multiple instances at each iteration, it is computationally more efficient than those that are querying for a single example at a time.

The second part of this chapter provides a method for active support vector learning in statistical query framework [167]. Like the previous algorithm, it also involves queries for multiple instances at each iteration. The intermediate statistical query oracle, involved in the learning process, returns the value of the probability that a new example belongs to the actual support vector set. A set of q new points is selected according to the above probability, and is used along with the current SVs to obtain the new SVs. The probability is estimated using a combination of two factors: the margin of the particular example with respect to the current hyperplane, and the degree of confidence that the current set of SVs provides the actual SVs. The degree of confidence is quantified by a measure which is based on the local properties of each of the current support vectors and is computed using the nearest neighbor estimates.

The methodology in the second part has some more advantages. It not only queries for the error points (or points having low margin) but also a number of other points far from the separating hyperplane (interior points). Thus, even if a current hypothesis is erroneous there is a scope for its being corrected owing to the interior points. If only error points were selected the hypothesis might have actually been worse. The ratio of selected points having low margin and those far from the hyperplane is decided by the confidence factor, which varies adaptively with iteration. If the current SV set is close to the optimal one, the algorithm focuses only on the low margin points and ignores the redundant points that lie far from the hyperplane. On the other hand, if the confidence factor is low (say, in the initial learning phase) it explores a higher number of interior points. Thus, the trade-off between efficiency and robustness of performance is adequately handled in this framework. Also, the efficiency of most of the existing active SV learning algorithms depends on the sparsity ratio (i.e., the ratio of the number of support vectors to the total number of data points) of the data set. Due to the adaptive nature of the query in the StatQSVM algorithm, it is likely to be efficient for a wide range of sparsity ratio.

Experiment results are presented for five real life classification problems. The sample size ranges from 351 to 495141, dimension from 9 to 34, and the sparsity ratio from 0.01 to 0.51. The algorithms described are found to provide superior performance and faster convergence compared to several related algorithms for incremental and active SV learning.

The organization of the chapter is as follows. In the next section we describe briefly the basic support vector machine algorithm for classification. Then we describe the algorithm of incremental support vector learning in Section 4.3. In Section 4.4 we provide a formal description of the learning with statistical query framework along with a methodology for estimating the associated confidence factor. The algorithm for active learning with statistical queries is described in Section 4.5. Some experimental results are presented in Section 4.6, and finally the summary is provided in Section 4.7.

4.2 Support Vector Machine

Support vector machines are a general class of learning architectures inspired from statistical learning theory that perform *structural risk minimization* on a nested set structure of separating hyperplanes [275]. Given training data, the SVM training algorithm obtains the optimal separating hyperplane in terms of generalization error. Though SVMs may also be used for regression and multiclass classification, in this study we concentrate only on two-class classification problems.

Algorithm: Suppose we are given a set of labelled examples $(\mathbf{x}_1, y_1), (\mathbf{x}_2, y_2), \ldots, (\mathbf{x}_i, y_i) \ldots, (\mathbf{x}_n, y_n), \mathbf{x}_i \in R^P, y_i \in \{-1, +1\}$. We consider functions of the form $sgn((\mathbf{w} \cdot \mathbf{x}) + b)$, in addition we impose the condition

$$\inf_{i=1,\ldots,n} |(\mathbf{w} \cdot \mathbf{x}_i) + b| = 1. \tag{4.1}$$

We would like to find a decision function $f_{\mathbf{w},b}$ with the properties $f_{\mathbf{w},b}(\mathbf{x}_i) = y_i; \ i = 1, \ldots, n$. If such a function exists, condition (4.1) implies

$$y_i((\mathbf{w} \cdot \mathbf{x}_i) + b) \geq 1, \quad \forall \, i = 1, \ldots, n. \tag{4.2}$$

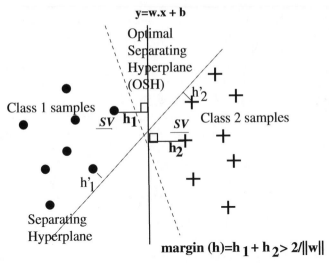

FIGURE 4.1: SVM as maximum margin classifier (linearly separable case).

In many practical situations, a separating hyperplane does not exist. To allow for possibilities of violating Equation 4.2, slack variables are introduced like

$$\xi_i \geq 0, \quad i = 1, \ldots, n \tag{4.3}$$

to get

$$y_i((\mathbf{w} \cdot \mathbf{x}_i) + b) \geq 1 - \xi_i, \quad i = 1, \ldots, n. \tag{4.4}$$

The support vector approach for minimizing the generalization error consists of the following:

Minimize : $\quad \Phi(\mathbf{w}, \xi) = (\mathbf{w} \cdot \mathbf{w}) + C \sum_{i=1}^{n} \xi_i \tag{4.5}$

subject to the constraints (4.3) and (4.4).

It can be shown that minimizing the first term in Equation 4.5 amounts to minimizing the VC-dimension or maximizing the margin (Figure 4.1), while minimizing the second term corresponds to minimizing the misclassification error [35]. SVMs provide the maximum margin classifiers for a given misclassification on the training set. This is illustrated in Figure 4.1.

The above minimization problem can be posed as a constrained quadratic programming (QP) problem. The solution gives rise to a decision function of the form:

$$f(\mathbf{x}) = sgn \left[\sum_{i=1}^{n} y_i \alpha_i (\mathbf{x} \cdot \mathbf{x_i}) + b \right],$$

where α_i's are positive numbers. Only a small fraction of the α_i coefficients are non-zero. The corresponding pairs of $< \mathbf{x_i}, y_i >$ entries are known as *support vectors* and they fully define the decision function. The support vectors are geometrically the points lying near the class boundaries as illustrated in [35]. We use linear kernels for SVM. However, nonlinear kernels such as polynomial, sigmoidal and radial basis functions may also be used.

We briefly mention below an alternate explanation of SVM learning, applicable to hard margin cases, which provides a better insight of the incremental SV learning procedure. The approach is due to Tong and Koller [272]. Consider a feature space $\mathcal{F}$ and the parameter space $\mathcal{W}$. If the training data is linearly separable in the feature space, the set of hyperplanes that separate the data is called the *version space* $\mathcal{V}$, defined as

$$\mathcal{V} = \{\mathbf{w} \in \mathcal{W} |\ \|\mathbf{w}\| = 1, y_i(\mathbf{w} \cdot \mathbf{x}_i) > 0,\ i = 1, \ldots, n\}. \tag{4.6}$$

There exists a duality between the feature space $\mathcal{F}$ and the parameter space $\mathcal{W}$: points in $\mathcal{F}$ correspond to hyperplanes in $\mathcal{W}$ and *vice versa*. Also, the version space is a connected region on the surface of a hypersphere in parameter space. Using the above facts and considering the SVM optimality criterion, it can be shown that SVMs find the center of the largest hypersphere whose center can be placed in version space and whose surface does not intersect with the hyperplanes corresponding to the training instances. The hyperplanes that are touched by the maximal radius hypersphere correspond to support vectors, and the radius of the hypersphere is the margin of the SVM. Thus if one queries for the training instances which maximally reduce the size of the current version space, the SVM obtained would eventually lie close to the actual SVM. It can be shown that maximal reduction in size of the version space takes place if $\mathcal{V}_i^- = \mathcal{V}_i^+$, where $\mathcal{V}_i^-$ and $\mathcal{V}_i^+$ denote the resulting version spaces if instance i is added and has labels -1 and $+1$, respectively.

4.3 Incremental Support Vector Learning with Multiple Points

The objective of the algorithm [164] is to select a minimal subset of support vectors such that the corresponding SVM would provide minimum misclassification on the remaining points in the sample set. The methodology is motivated from the condensation technique proposed by Hart [91] (Section 2.2.1) for reducing the computational complexity and storage requirements of k-NN classifiers.

Algorithm 1:

Set up data bins called STORE and GRABBAG. Initially, k randomly selected samples are placed in STORE; all other samples are placed in GRAB-

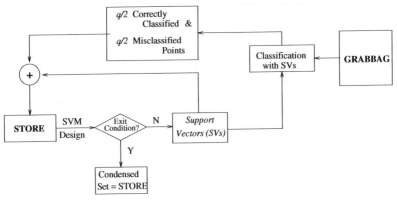

FIGURE 4.2: Incremental support vector learning with multiple points (Algorithm 1).

BAG. k is chosen arbitrarily, such that STORE contains at least one point from each class.

Step 1: Design a SVM using the samples in STORE. Retain the *support vectors* in STORE, and discard other points in STORE.

Step 2: Resample GRABBAG. From GRABBAG select $q/2$ points that are correctly classified and $q/2$ points that are misclassified by the SVM obtained in Step 1. Append the (q) resampled points to STORE obtained after Step 1. Repeat Step 1, until the required accuracy is achieved on a test set, or GRABBAG is exhausted. □

The algorithm is illustrated in Figure 4.2. ◇

In the next section we describe briefly the model of learning using statistical queries. This is useful in understanding the second algorithm (Algorithm 2) for active support vector learning, described in Section 4.5.

4.4 Statistical Query Model of Learning

Let $\mathcal{C}$ be a (concept) class of $\{0, 1\}$ valued functions over an input space X. In trying to design a learning algorithm for the class $\mathcal{C}$, we assume that there is a fixed but arbitrary and unknown target probability distribution $\mathcal{P}$ over X that governs the generation of random examples. The standard supervised learning model (PAC model [275]), when executed on the target concept $f \in \mathcal{C}$, a learning algorithm will be given access to an oracle $EX(f, \mathcal{P})$ that on each call draws an input $\mathbf{x}$ randomly and independently according to $\mathcal{P}$, and returns the labeled example $< \mathbf{x}, f(\mathbf{x}) >$.

In the statistical query model [108] the standard examples oracle $EX(f, \mathcal{P})$

is replaced by a new oracle $STAT(f, \mathcal{P})$. The oracle $STAT(f, \mathcal{P})$ takes as input a statistical query of the form (χ, α). Here χ is any mapping of a labeled example to $\{0, 1\}$, and $\alpha \in [0, 1]$. A query (χ, α) is interpreted as a request for the value $P_\chi = \mathbf{Pr}_{\mathbf{x} \in \mathcal{P}}(\chi(\mathbf{x}, f(\mathbf{x})) = 1)$, which can be abbreviated as $\mathbf{Pr}_{EX(f, \mathcal{P})}(\chi = 1)$. Thus, each query is a request for the probability of some event on the distribution generated by $EX(f, \mathcal{P})$. However, the oracle $STAT(f, \mathcal{P})$ will not return the exact value of P_χ but only an approximation, and the role of α is to quantify the amount of error the learning algorithm is willing to tolerate in this approximation.

4.4.1   Query strategy

In the context of support vector machines, the target of the learning algorithm is to learn the set of all support vectors. This is done by incrementally training a SVM on a set of examples consisting of the previous SVs and a new set of points. In the statistical query-based active learning algorithm the new set of points, instead of being randomly generated by $EX(f, \mathcal{P})$, is generated according to $\mathbf{Pr}_\chi$ returned by the oracle $STAT(f, \mathcal{P})$. $\chi(\mathbf{x}, f(\mathbf{x}))$ denotes the event that the example $\mathbf{x}$ is a SV. $f(\mathbf{x})$ is the optimal separating hyperplane. Let $< \mathbf{w}, b >$ be the current separating hyperplane available to the learner. We define the probability $\mathbf{Pr}_\chi$ returned by the oracle $STAT(f, \mathcal{P})$ as follows:

$$P_\chi = \quad c \quad \text{if } y(\mathbf{w} \cdot \mathbf{x} + b) \leq 1 \tag{4.7}$$
$$= 1 - c \text{ otherwise.}$$

Here c is a *confidence parameter* that denotes how close the current hyperplane $< \mathbf{w}, b >$ is to the optimal one, and y is the label of $\mathbf{x}$.

The significance of P_χ is as follows: if c is high, which signifies that the current hyperplane is close to the optimal one, points lying within the margin band of the current hyperplane are highly likely to be the actual SVs. Hence, the probability P_χ returned to the corresponding query is set to a high value c. When the value c is low, the probability of selecting a point lying within the margin decreases, and a high probability value $(1 - c)$ is then assigned to an interior point. Let us now describe a method for estimating the confidence factor c.

4.4.2   Confidence factor of support vector set

Let the current set of support vectors be denoted by $S = \{\mathbf{s}_1, \mathbf{s}_2, \ldots, \mathbf{s}_l\}$. Also, consider a test set $T = \{\mathbf{x}_1', \mathbf{x}_2', \ldots, \mathbf{x}_m'\}$ and an integer k (say, $k = \sqrt{m}$). For every $\mathbf{s}_i \in S$ compute the set of k nearest points in T. Among the k nearest neighbors let k_i^+ and k_i^- number of points have labels $+1$ and -1, respectively. The confidence factor c is then defined as

$$c = \frac{2}{kl} \sum_{i=1}^{l} \min(k_i^+, k_i^-). \tag{4.8}$$

Note that the maximum value of the confidence factor c is unity when $k_i^+ = k_i^- \ \forall i = 1, \ldots, l$, and the minimum value is zero when $\min(k_i^+, k_i^-) = 0$ $\forall i = 1, \ldots, l$. The first case implies that all the support vectors lie near the class boundaries and the set $S = \{s_1, s_2, \ldots, s_l\}$ is close to the actual support vector set. (It may be noted that support vectors are points lying near the class boundaries.) The second case, on the other hand, denotes that the set S consists only of interior points and is far from the actual support vector set. Thus, the confidence factor c measures the degree of closeness of S to the actual support vector set. The higher the value of c is, the closer is the current SV set to the actual SV set.

The use of the factor c can also be justified from the point of view of Bayes classification rule. It is known that for overlapping classes the support vector set consists of the error points and the points lying within a margin band of the decision boundary. Bayes classification rule states that posteriori probabilities of each of the classes are equal along the decision boundary and on the error region. The ratios k_i^+/k and k_i^-/k are nearest neighbor estimates of the posteriori probabilities for the classes $+1$ and -1, respectively. Hence, they attain almost equal values for both error points and points lying near the class boundaries. It may also be mentioned that the support vector set, when used for k nearest neighbor classification, is known to provide high classification accuracy [57].

A version space explanation of the factor c may also be provided. It is evident from the discussion in Section 4.2 that points that split the version space into two equal halves are considered to be the likely candidates for being support vectors. Volumes of the version spaces $\mathcal{V}^+$ and $\mathcal{V}^-$, as obtained after adding those points with labels $+1$ and -1, are equal [272]. Examination of the SVM objective function reveals that, if a neighborhood of a point s_i contains equal number of examples having labels $+1$ and -1, then addition of the point s_i with labels $+1$ and -1 results in version spaces $\mathcal{V}^+$ and $\mathcal{V}^-$, respectively, with equal volumes. Hence, as the value of c (Equation 4.8) increases, the probability that s_i's are the candidate support vectors increases.

4.5 Learning Support Vectors with Statistical Queries

Here we describe a method for active learning of support vectors with statistical queries. The active support vector learning algorithm obtains a new SV set at each step by minimizing the objective function of Equation 4.5 for a set of points consisting of the SVs of the previous step and q new points. These new q points are obtained from the training set using the statistical query strategy, as discussed in the previous section. The algorithm is presented below and the block diagram is shown in Figure 4.3.

Algorithm 2:

Let $A = \{\mathbf{x}_1, \mathbf{x}_2, \ldots, \mathbf{x}_n\}$ denote the entire training set used for SVM design. $SV(B)$ denotes the set of support vectors, of the set B, obtained using the methodology described in Section 4.2. $S_t = \{\mathbf{s}_1, \mathbf{s}_2, \ldots, \mathbf{s}_l\}$ is the support vector set obtained after tth iteration, and $< \mathbf{w}_t, b_t >$ is the corresponding separating hyperplane. $V_t = \{\mathbf{v}_1, \mathbf{v}_2, \ldots, \mathbf{v}_q\}$ is the set of q points actively queried for at step t. c is the confidence factor obtained using Equation 4.8. The learning steps involved are given below:

Initialize: Randomly (without replacement) select an initial starting set V_0 of q instances from the training set A. Set $t = 0$ and $S_0 = SV(V_0)$. Let the parameters of the corresponding hyperplane be $< \mathbf{w}_0, b_0 >$.

While *Stopping Criterion* is not satisfied:

$\quad V_t = \emptyset$.

$\quad$**While** Cardinality$(V_t) \leq q$:

$\quad\quad$ Randomly (without replacement) select an instance $\mathbf{x} \in A$.

$\quad\quad$ Let y be the label of $\mathbf{x}$.

$\quad\quad$**If** $y(\mathbf{w}_t \cdot \mathbf{x} + b) \leq 1$:

$\quad\quad\quad$ Select $\mathbf{x}$ with probability c. Set $V_t = V_t \cup \{\mathbf{x}\}$.

$\quad\quad$**Else:**

$\quad\quad\quad$ Select $\mathbf{x}$ with probability $1 - c$. Set $V_t = V_t \cup \{\mathbf{x}\}$.

$\quad\quad$**End If**

$\quad$**End While**

$\quad S_t = SV(S_t \cup V_t),\ t = t + 1$.

End While

The set S_{t*}, where t^* is the iteration at which the algorithm terminates, contains the final SV set. □

Stopping Criterion: Among the q points actively queried at each step t, let q' points have margin greater than unity $(y(\mathbf{w}_t \cdot \mathbf{x} + b) > 1)$. Learning is stopped if the quantity $\frac{c \cdot q'}{q}$ exceeds a threshold Th (say, $= 0.9$).

Remarks:

1. The selection probability P_χ (Equation 4.7) returned by the statistical query oracle is a two level function of the margin $(y(\mathbf{w} \cdot \mathbf{x} + b))$ of a point $\mathbf{x}$. Continuous functions of margin of $\mathbf{x}$ may also be used. Such an algorithm can be considered to be statistical query-based extensions of the existing methods of active support vector learning that query for the nearest point to the separating hyperplane.

2. The stopping criteria may be interpreted as follows. A high value of the quantity $\frac{q'}{q}$ implies that the query set contains a few points with margin less than unity. No further gain can be thus achieved by the learning

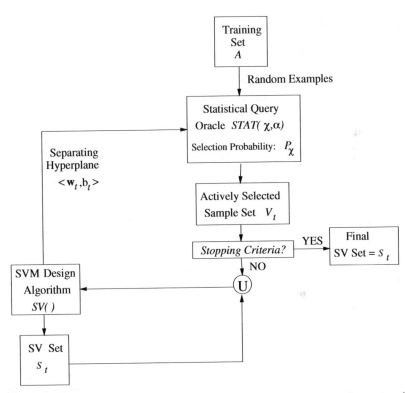

FIGURE 4.3: Active support vector learning with statistical queries (Algorithm 2).

process. The value of q' may also be large when the value of c is low in the initial phase of learning. However, if both c and q' have high values, the current SV set is close to the actual one (i.e., a good classifier is obtained) and also the margin band is empty (i.e., the learning process is saturated); hence, the learning may be terminated.

4.6   Experimental Results and Comparison

Organization of the experimental results is as follows [167]. First, the performance of the two algorithms, presented in Sections 4.3 and 4.5, is compared with two other incremental support vector learning algorithms as well as the batch SVM, in terms of generalization capability, training time and $\mathcal{D}$ (Equation 4.9). The effectiveness of the confidence factor c, used for active querying by the second algorithm, is then studied. Finally, the nature of the margin distribution, obtained by the second algorithm, as compared to those obtained by some other related large margin classifiers is investigated.

Five data sets are used, namely, Wisconsin cancer, Ionosphere, Heart, Twonorm and Forest cover type. They are described in Appendix B. The first four data sets have two overlapping classes. The fifth one (Forest cover type) contains seven classes, but 80% of the points belong to classes one and two. We consider here only the points belonging to those two classes.

4.6.1   Classification accuracy and training time

The algorithms for incremental SV learning with multiple points (Algorithm 1, denoted by IncrSVM in Table 4.1) and active SV learning with statistical queries (Algorithm 2, denoted by StatQSVM in Table 4.1) are compared with (i) incremental SV learning with random chunk selection [35] (denoted by RandSVM in Table 4.1) and (ii) a recently proposed method for active SV learning which queries for the point closest to the current separating hyperplane [36] (denoted by QuerySVM in Table 4.1). Note that the QuerySVM is identical to the 'simple margin' strategy described in [272]. A comparison with the actual batch SVM algorithm (denoted by BatchSVM in Table 4.1) is also provided since this is the ideal one. The batch SVM algorithm could not provide results for the Forest cover type data, due to its large size.

Comparison is made on the basis of the following quantities:

1. Classification accuracy on training set ($a_{training}$): The training set is obtained by sampling 90% of the points from the entire data set. Mean of the accuracy, computed over 10 such random selection, is reported.

2. Classification accuracy on test set (a_{test}): The test set has size 10% of

that of the entire data set and contains points that do not belong to the training set. Here also means over 10 independent runs are reported.

3. Closeness of the SV set: The closeness of the SV set ($\tilde{S}$), obtained by an algorithm, to the actual one (S) which is obtained by the batch SVM algorithm is measured by the distance $\mathcal{D}$ defined as follows [152]:

$$\mathcal{D} = \frac{1}{n_{\tilde{S}}} \sum_{\mathbf{x}_1 \in \tilde{S}} \delta(\mathbf{x}_1, S) + \frac{1}{n_S} \sum_{\mathbf{x}_2 \in S} \delta(\mathbf{x}_2, \tilde{S}) + Dist(\tilde{S}, S), \qquad (4.9)$$

where

$$\delta(\mathbf{x}_1, S) = \min_{\mathbf{x}_2 \in S} d(\mathbf{x}_1, \mathbf{x}_2), \ \ \delta(\mathbf{x}_2, \tilde{S}) = \min_{\mathbf{x}_1 \in \tilde{S}} d(\mathbf{x}_1, \mathbf{x}_2),$$

and

$$Dist(\tilde{S}, S) = \max\{\max_{\mathbf{x}_1 \in \tilde{S}} \delta(\mathbf{x}_1, S), \max_{\mathbf{x}_2 \in S} \delta(\mathbf{x}_2, \tilde{S})\}.$$

$n_{\tilde{S}}$ and n_S are the number of points in $\tilde{S}$ and S, respectively. $Dist(\tilde{S}, S)$ is the Hausdorff distance between sets $\tilde{S}$ and S. $d(\mathbf{x}_1, \mathbf{x}_2)$ is the Euclidean distance between points $\mathbf{x}_1$ and $\mathbf{x}_2$. The distance measure $\mathcal{D}$ has been used for quantifying the errors of set approximation algorithms [152], and is related to the ϵ-cover of a set.

4. CPU time (t_{cpu}) required on a Sun UltraSparc 350MHz workstation.

It is observed from the results shown in Table 4.1 that all the incremental algorithms, as expected, require significantly less training time as compared to the batch SVM with little degradation in classification accuracy. Comparing the three active learning algorithms (namely, QuerySVM, IncrSVM, and StatQSVM) with RandSVM shows that the use of active learning strategy enhances the performance in terms of both classification accuracy and training time, for all the data sets. Again, among the active learning techniques, StatQSVM achieves the highest classification score with minimum $\mathcal{D}$ value in least time for all the cases. This superiority of StatQSVM becomes more apparent for the Forest cover type data, where it significantly outperforms the other three incremental learning methods. When tested for statistical significance (using the methodology described in Section 2.6.2), the classification accuracy of StatQSVM was found to be significantly higher, compared to the other three incremental methods, for all the data sets except the Cancer data, where significance could not be established while comparing with QuerySVM. It may be further noted that QuerySVM provides higher classification accuracy compared to IncrSVM; this is expected since QuerySVM involves complex queries requiring more CPU time.

The nature of convergence of the classification accuracy on test set a_{test} is shown in Figure 4.4 for all the data sets. It is observed that the convergence curve for the StatQSVM algorithm dominates over those of RandSVM,

TABLE 4.1:   Comparison of performance of SVM design algorithms

Data	Algorithm	$a_{training}(\%)$	$a_{test}(\%)$	$\mathcal{D}$	t_{cpu} (sec)
Cancer	BatchSVM	97.44	96.32	*Zero*	1291
	RandSVM	87.19	86.10	10.92	302
	QuerySVM	97.10	96.21	9.91	262
	IncrSVM	92.10	91.01	10.40	221
	StatQSVM	97.40	96.43	7.82	171
Ionosphere	BatchSVM	88.87	84.57	*Zero*	271
	RandSVM	78.10	77.17	8.92	81
	QuerySVM	78.19	77.02	8.01	95
	IncrSVM	79.50	78.22	9.10	78
	StatQSVM	84.09	82.20	7.01	68
Heart	BatchSVM	78.80	77.35	*Zero*	2702
	RandSVM	72.52	70.82	0.37	94
	QuerySVM	75.04	74.01	280	72
	IncrSVM	74.05	72.11	410	55
	StatQSVM	75.82	74.91	168	25
Twonorm	BatchSVM	98.58	97.46	*Zero*	8.01×10^4
	RandSVM	93.40	92.01	12.70	770
	QuerySVM	95.01	93.04	12.75	410
	IncrSVM	95.22	93.10	12.52	520
	StatQSVM	97.02	96.01	12.01	390
Forest cover type	RandSVM	59.22	57.90	-	4.70×10^4
	QuerySVM	66.01	65.77	-	3.20×10^4
	IncrSVM	64.02	61.02	-	2.90×10^4
	StatQSVM	75.44	74.83	-	2.01×10^4

- The value of $\mathcal{D}$ corresponding to BatchSVM is *Zero* by definition.
- Since BatchSVM could not be obtained for the *large* Forest cover type data, $\mathcal{D}$ could not be computed, and is denoted by '-'.

IncrSVM and QuerySVM. Since the RandSVM algorithm selects the chunks randomly, the corresponding curve is smooth and almost monotonic, although its convergence rate is much slower. On the other hand, the QuerySVM algorithm selects only the point closest to the current separating hyperplane and achieves a high classification accuracy in few iterations. However, its convergence curve is oscillatory and the classification accuracy falls significantly after certain iterations. This is expected as querying for points close to the current separating hyperplane may often result in gain in performance if the current hyperplane is close to the optimal one. While querying for interior points reduces the risk of performance degradation, it achieves poor convergence rate. StatQSVM, on the other hand, selects an optimal proportion of low margin and interior points and, hence, maintains a fast convergence rate without oscillatory performance degradation.

4.6.2 Effectiveness of the confidence factor

Figure 4.5 shows the variation of c (Equation 4.8), for the SV sets obtained in StatQSVM, with distance $\mathcal{D}$. It is observed that for all the data sets c is (negatively) correlated with $\mathcal{D}$. As the current SV set approaches the optimal one, the value of $\mathcal{D}$ decreases and the value of confidence factor c increases. Hence, c also provides an effective measure of the closeness of the SV set to the actual one. Variation of c with iteration for the StatQSVM algorithm is shown in Figure 4.6. For all the data sets, the value of the confidence factor c is low in the initial phases of learning, and subsequently it increases to attain a value closer to unity when learning converges.

4.6.3 Margin distribution

Recently it has been shown that the generalization capability of a classifier can be characterized not only by the minimum margin, but also by more general parameters that can be estimated from the margin distribution. Some such parameters were studied in [69]. In the experiments the nature of the margin distribution in terms of the cumulative distribution of the quantity $y(\mathbf{w} \cdot \mathbf{x} + b)$ is also investigated. Figure 4.7 shows the variation of the margin distribution, obtained at different learning iterations of the StatQSVM algorithm, for the Twonorm data set only, as an example. It is seen that with iteration the distribution shifts to the right with more points having high margin. Figure 4.8 presents a comparison among all the four aforesaid SVM learning algorithms, as well as a SVM designed using boosting [212], in terms of their final margin distributions. (Note that boosting SVM is considered in Figure 4.8 because it is well known for providing large margin classifiers, though it is computationally demanding for large data sets. Since it is not an incremental learning method, we did not consider it in Table 4.1 for comparison.) It is observed that for most data points a higher margin value is achieved for both boosting SVM and StatQSVM as compared to batch SVM,

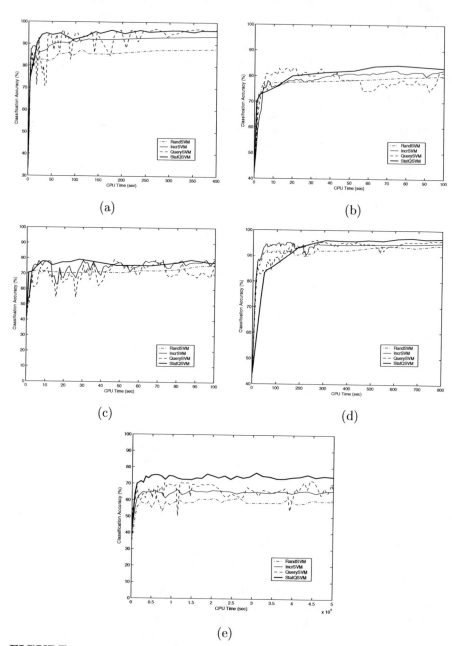

FIGURE 4.4: Variation of a_{test} with CPU time for (a) cancer, (b) ionosphere, (c) heart, (d) twonorm, and (e) forest cover type data.

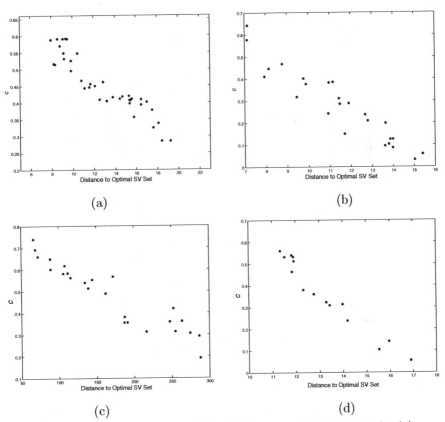

FIGURE 4.5: Variation of confidence factor c and distance $\mathcal{D}$ for (a) cancer, (b) ionosphere, (c) heart, and (d) twonorm data.

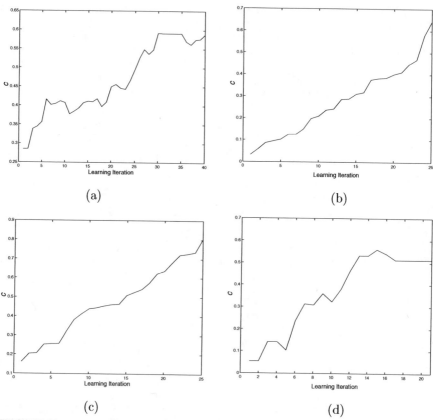

FIGURE 4.6: Variation of confidence factor c with iterations of StatQSVM algorithm for (a) cancer, (b) ionosphere, (c) heart, and (d) twonorm data.

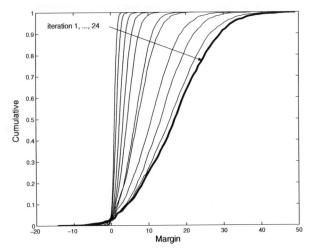

FIGURE 4.7: Margin distribution obtained at each iteration by the StatQSVM algorithm for the Twonorm data. The bold line denotes the final distribution obtained.

RandSVM and QuerySVM. This may be due to the fact that both the former ones incrementally use a set of points that are obtained by sampling from a distribution that varies with iteration. In the case of StatQSVM the statistical query oracle generates this distribution, while for boosting SVM the distribution is obtained from the probability values which are stored for all the points and updated with iteration. Both these distributions drift toward the actual separating hyperplane with iteration.

4.7 Summary

The problem of active learning with SVM is addressed. Two methods for active SVM learning are described to overcome the large QP problem arising in SVM design. The effectiveness of the algorithms is experimentally demonstrated for some real life large data sets. Among the two algorithms presented, the second one, based on statistical query model of learning, provides better performance. This is because of the use of an adaptive query strategy whose novelty is as follows. Most of the algorithms for incremental SV learning either query for points close to the current separating hyperplane or select random chunks consisting mostly of interior points. Both these strategies represent extreme cases; the former one is fast but unstable, while the latter one is robust but slowly converging. The former strategy is useful in the final phase of learning, while the latter one is more suitable in the initial phase. The

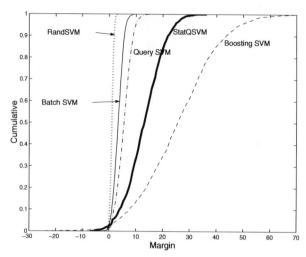

FIGURE 4.8: Margin distribution obtained by some SVM design algorithms for the Twonorm data set.

concept of a statistical query oracle that uses an adaptive confidence factor handles the above trade-off and thereby achieves faster convergence.

In Algorithm 1, an equal number of correctly classified ($n_c = q/2$) and misclassified ($n_m = q/2$) points in the resampling step is selected. One may use other values of n_c/n_m. In that case for data sets having substantial overlap (high sparsity ratio), the choice of n_c and n_m influences the nature of the convergence curve. If more misclassified points, compared to correctly classified points, are chosen (i.e., $n_c/n_m < 1$) the convergence curve is oscillatory in nature. On the other hand, choosing a larger number of correctly classified points compared to misclassified points (*i.e.*, $n_c/n_m > 1$) leads to smoother but slower convergence.

The statistical query-based algorithm involves an adaptation of the query probability. A decision theoretic generalization of the above scheme may provide better active learning strategies. Also, the relationship of the active learning strategies with the mistake bound model of online learning may be investigated. ◇

So far we have used, in Chapters 2–4, the classical approach for developing methodologies for data condensation, feature selection and active learning. The next four chapters (Chapters 5–8) emphasize demonstrating the effectiveness of integrating different soft computing tools, e.g., fuzzy logic, artificial neural networks, rough sets, and genetic algorithms for performing tasks like case (class prototypes) generation, clustering/classification, and rule generation/evaluation for mining and knowledge discovery. Significance of granular computing in a soft paradigm is highlighted.

Chapter 5

Rough-fuzzy Case Generation

5.1 Introduction

Granular computing (GrC) may be regarded as a unified framework for theories, methodologies and techniques that make use of granules in the process of problem solving. A granule is a clump of objects (points), in the universe of discourse, drawn together by indistinguishability, similarity, proximity, or functionality. Granulation leads to information compression/summarization. Therefore computing with granules, rather than points, provides gain in computation time, thereby making the role of granular computing significant in data mining.

Granulation may be crisp or fuzzy, depending on whether the boundaries of granules do or do not lend themselves to precise definition. Fuzzy granulation (*f-granulation*) may be obtained using the concepts of a linguistic variable, fuzzy if-then rule, and fuzzy graph [220, 222, 288]. Recently, rough set theory [213, 214] has become a popular mathematical framework for granular computing. While fuzzy set theory assigns to each object a grade of belongingness to represent an imprecise set, the focus of rough set theory is on the ambiguity caused by limited discernibility of objects in the domain of discourse. The key concepts in rough set theory are those of 'indiscernibility' and 'reducts.' Indiscernibility formalizes the concept of finite precision representation of objects in real life situations, and reducts represent the 'core' of an information system (both in terms of objects and features) in a granular universe. Recently, rough sets and fuzzy sets are being integrated in soft computing framework, the aim being to develop a model of uncertainty stronger than either [209]. In the present chapter we exploit the merits of the aforesaid integration for performing two tasks, namely, case generation and clustering.

A case may be defined as a contextualized piece of knowledge representing an experience that teaches a lesson fundamental to achieving goals of the system [122]. Selection and generation of cases (i.e., representative class prototypes) are two important components of a case-based reasoning (CBR) system. While case selection deals with selecting informative prototypes from the data, case generation concerns construction of 'cases' that need not necessarily include any of the given data points.

Early CBR systems mainly used case selection mechanisms based on the nearest neighbor principle. These algorithms involve case pruning/growing methodologies, as exemplified by the popular IB3 algorithm [7]. A summary of the above approaches may be found in [279]. Recently, fuzzy logic and other soft computing tools have been integrated with CBR for developing efficient methodologies and algorithms [195]. For case selection and retrieval, the role of fuzzy logic has been mainly in providing similarity measures and modeling ambiguous situations [195, 208]. A neuro-fuzzy method for selecting cases has been proposed in [51], where a fuzzy case similarity measure is used, with repeated growing and pruning of cases, until the case base becomes stable. All the operations are performed using a connectionist model with adaptive link structure. Use of fuzzy feature vectors and neural networks for case retrieval has been studied in [150]. It may be noted that cases (class prototypes) represent the informative and irreducible part of a problem. Rough set theory, which also deals with 'information granules' and 'reducts,' is therefore a natural choice for case generation in domains that are data rich, contain uncertainties and allow tolerance for imprecision. Additionally, rough sets have the capability of handling complex objects (e.g., proofs, hierarchies, frames, rule bases), thereby strengthening further the necessity of rough-CBR systems. Some of the attempts made in this regard are available in [228].

In this chapter, we describe a methodology [202] for case generation using the concept of rough-fuzzy hybridization. Each pattern (object) is represented by its fuzzy membership values with respect to three overlapping linguistic property sets, 'low', 'medium' and 'high', thereby generating a fuzzy granulation of the feature space which contains granules with ill-defined boundaries. Discernibility of the granulated objects in terms of attributes is then computed in the form of a discernibility matrix. Using rough set theory a number of decision rules are generated from the discernibility matrix. The rules represent *rough clusters* of points in the original feature space. The fuzzy membership functions corresponding to the region, modeled by a rule, are then stored as a case. A strength factor, representing the a priori probability (size) of the cluster, is associated with each case. In other words, each case has three components, namely, the membership functions of the fuzzy sets appearing in the reducts, the class labels and the strength factor. In the *retrieval* phase, these fuzzy membership functions are utilized to compute the similarity of the stored cases with an unknown pattern.

It may be noted that unlike most case selection schemes, the cases generated here need not be any of the objects (patterns) encountered; rather they represent regions having dimensions equal to or less than that of the input feature space. That is, all the input features (attributes) may not be required to represent a case. This type of variable and reduced length representation of cases results in the decrease in retrieval time. Furthermore, the algorithm deals only with the information granules, not the actual data points. Because of these characteristics its significance to data mining applications is evident.

The methodology performs better in terms of 1-NN accuracy, average number of features per case, case generation time and average case retrieval time when demonstrated on some real life data sets, large both in dimension and size. Comparison is made with the conventional IB3 and IB4 algorithms [7] and random case selection method.

The organization of the chapter is as follows. Section 5.2 describes in brief the concept of granular computing. Section 5.3 presents some of the basic features of rough set theory which are relevant to this chapter. In Section 5.4, the methodology for fuzzy granulation and linguistic representation of patterns is described. The rough-fuzzy case generation methodology is described in Section 5.5, along with experimental results and comparison.

5.2 Soft Granular Computing

Granular computing (GrC) [138, 219] is concerned with the design and processing of information granules. Information granules are collections of entities drawn together by their similarity, functional, spatial or temporal proximity. They are present everywhere in real life problems and can be viewed as a basic vehicle of perception, abstraction and system description. The goal of information granulation is to provide an abstraction of the original problem, in which most of the important relationships still hold true, but fine details are suppressed. One key usage of information granularity is in the modeling of large scale and complex systems. A mathematical model for such a system may be difficult or unattractive to build, due to the high computational cost involved and lack of human comprehensibility of the resulting model. However, it may be possible to reduce the complexity of the system by granulating it, thereby enabling the development of a human comprehensible model with much less computational cost.

Basic issues of granular computing may be studied from two related aspects [284], the construction of granules and computation with granules. The former deals with the formation, representation and interpretation of granules, while the latter deals with the utilization of granules in problem solving.

The interpretation of granules focuses on the semantic side of granule construction. It addresses the question of *why* two objects are put in the same granule. In other words, one must provide the necessary semantic interpretations for notions such as indistinguishability, similarity and proximity. The formation and representation of granules deal with the algorithmic issues of granule construction. They address the problem of *how* to put two objects in the same granule. Algorithms therefore need to be developed for constructing granules efficiently.

Computation with granules can be similarly studied from both semantic and algorithmic perspectives. On one hand, one needs to define and interpret various relationships between granules, such as closeness, dependency and association, and different operations on granules. On the other hand, one needs to design methodologies and tools for computing with granules for tasks such as approximation, reasoning and inference.

The concepts of soft computing and granular computing can be integrated considering both the aforesaid issues, namely, construction of and computation with granules. If soft computing tools are used for construction and representation of granules, the resulting integration may be termed as *soft-granular* computing. Fuzzy granulation [288], using membership function and/or linguistic representation, is an example of soft-granular computing. On the other hand, exploitation of the merits of 'computation with granules' in different soft computing systems or tools like neural networks and fuzzy logic leads to what may be called *granular-soft* computing. Methodologies developed under this paradigm include tools like granular neural networks [292] and granular fuzzy decision trees [221]. While soft-granular computing is used mainly for uncertainty handling, the significance of granular-soft computing is more with respect to computational efficiency.

Most of the research in soft-granular computing is based on the concept of fuzzy-granulation (f-granulation). It is studied in detail in Section 5.4. With rough set as the granular computing tool, f-granulation leads to rough-fuzzy computing [209]. Other soft computing tools used for efficient construction of granules include genetic algorithms [280] and neural networks [207].

Computation with granules is often exploited by different soft computing systems in the framework of granular-soft computing. A prominent example is the use of rough-fuzzy and rough-neuro computing in several data mining and knowledge discovery tasks like classification and rule generation [209]. Granular computing is also used by neuro-rough systems [207] for efficient knowledge encoding [17], rule extraction [56], and information processing [223].

5.3   Rough Sets

Let us present here some preliminaries of rough set theory that are relevant to this chapter. For details one may refer to [214] and [260].

Consider a set U consisting of all students of a school. Each student is described by a single attribute a – that of 'belonging to a class.' Then, U is partitioned by the classes of the school.

Now take a situation when an infectious disease has spread in the school, and the authorities take the two following steps.
(i) If at least one student of a class is infected, all the students of that class are vaccinated. Let $\overline{B}$ denote the union of such classes.
(ii) If every student of a class is infected, the class is temporarily suspended. Let $\underline{B}$ denote the union of such classes.

TABLE 5.1: *Hiring*: An example of a decision table

	Diploma (i)	Experience (e)	French (f)	Reference (r)	Decision
x_1	MBA	Medium	Yes	Excellent	Accept
x_2	MBA	Low	Yes	Neutral	Reject
x_3	MCE	Low	Yes	Good	Reject
x_4	MSc	High	Yes	Neutral	Accept
x_5	MSc	Medium	Yes	Neutral	Reject
x_6	MSc	High	Yes	Excellent	Reject
x_7	MBA	High	No	Good	Accept
x_8	MCE	Low	No	Excellent	Reject

Then, $\underline{B} \subseteq \overline{B}$. Given this information, let the following problem be posed: *Identify the collection of infected students.*

Clearly, this cannot be a unique answer. But any set I that is given as an answer, must contain $\underline{B}$ *and* at least one student from each class comprising $\overline{B}$. In other words, it must have $\underline{B}$ as its *lower approximation* and $\overline{B}$ as its *upper approximation*.

I is then a *rough* concept/set in the information system $< U, \{a\} >$.

Further it may be observed that any set $\prime I$ given as another answer is *roughly equal* to I, in the sense that both are represented (characterized) by $\overline{B}$ and $\underline{B}$.

A formal description of the above principle of rough description of concept/sets is provided below.

5.3.1 Information systems

An *information system* is a pair $S = < U, A >$, where U is a non-empty finite set of *objects* called the *universe* and A a non-empty finite set of *attributes* such that $a : U \to V_a$ for every $a \in A$. The set V_a is called the *value set* of a.

In many situations there is an outcome of classification that is known. This a posteriori knowledge is expressed by one distinguished attribute called decision attribute. Information systems of this kind are called decision systems. A *decision system* is any information system of the form $\mathcal{A} = (U, A \cup \{d\})$, where $d \notin A$ is the *decision attribute*. The elements of A are called *conditional attributes*. An information (decision) system may be represented as an *attribute-value (decision) table*, in which rows are labeled by objects of the universe and columns by the attributes. Table 5.1 is an example of representing a decision system $\mathcal{A}' = (U, \{Diploma, Experience, French, Reference\} \cup \{Decision\})$ for hiring personnel.

5.3.2 Indiscernibility and set approximation

A decision system (i.e., a decision table) expresses all the knowledge available about a system. This table may be unnecessarily large because it could be redundant at least in two ways. The same or indiscernible objects may be represented several times, or some attributes may be superfluous. The notion of equivalence relation is used to tackle this problem.

With every subset of attributes $B \subseteq A$, one can easily associate an *equivalence relation* I_B on U: $I_B = \{(\mathbf{x}_1, \mathbf{x}_2) \in U : \text{for every a} \in B, \text{a}(\mathbf{x}_1) = \text{a}(\mathbf{x}_2)\}$. I_B is called *B-indiscernibility relation*. If $(\mathbf{x}_1, \mathbf{x}_2) \in I_B$, then objects $\mathbf{x}_1$ and $\mathbf{x}_2$ are indiscernible from each other by attributes B. The equivalence classes of the partition induced by the B-indiscernibility relation are denoted by $[\mathbf{x}]_B$. These are also known as *granules*. For example, in the case of the decision system represented by Table 5.1, if we consider the attribute set $B = \{Diploma, Experience\}$, the relation I_B defines the following partition of the universe,

$$I_B = I_{\{Diploma,\ Experience\}} = \{\{\mathbf{x}_3, \mathbf{x}_8\}, \{\mathbf{x}_4, \mathbf{x}_6\}, \{\mathbf{x}_5\}, \{\mathbf{x}_1\}, \{\mathbf{x}_2\}, \{\mathbf{x}_7\}\}.$$

Here $\{\mathbf{x}_3, \mathbf{x}_8\}, \{\mathbf{x}_4, \mathbf{x}_6\}, \{\mathbf{x}_5\}, \{\mathbf{x}_1\}, \{\mathbf{x}_2\}, \{\mathbf{x}_7\}$ are the granules obtained by the relation I_B.

The partition induced by the equivalence relation I_B can be used to build new subsets of the universe. Subsets that are most often of interest have the same value of the outcome attribute, i.e., belong to the same class. It may happen, however, that a concept (e.g., '*Reject*' in Table 1) cannot be defined crisply using the attributes available. It is here that the notion of rough set emerges. Although we cannot delineate the concept crisply, it is possible to delineate the objects that definitely 'belong' to the concept and those that definitely 'do not belong' to the concept. These notions are formally expressed as follows.

Let $\mathcal{A} = (U, A)$ be an information system and let $B \subseteq A$ and $X \subseteq U$. We can approximate X using only the information contained in B by constructing the lower and upper approximations of X. If $X \subseteq U$, the sets $\{\mathbf{x} \in U : [\mathbf{x}]_B \subseteq X\}$ and $\{\mathbf{x} \in U : [\mathbf{x}]_B \cap X \neq \emptyset\}$, where $[\mathbf{x}]_B$ denotes the equivalence class of the object $\mathbf{x} \in U$ relative to I_B, are called the *B-lower* and *B-upper approximation* of X in $\mathcal{S}$ and denoted by $\underline{B}X, \overline{B}X$, respectively. The objects in $\underline{B}X$ can be certainly classified as members of X on the basis of knowledge in B, while objects in $\overline{B}X$ can be classified only as possible members of X on the basis of B. This is illustrated in Figure 5.1. Considering the decision system *Hiring* (Table 5.1), if $B = \{Diploma, Experience\}$ and X is the concept *Reject*, then $\underline{B}X = \{\mathbf{x}_2, \{\mathbf{x}_3, \mathbf{x}_8\}, \mathbf{x}_5\}$ and $\overline{B}X = \{\mathbf{x}_2, \{\mathbf{x}_3, \mathbf{x}_8\}, \{\mathbf{x}_4, \mathbf{x}_6\}, \mathbf{x}_5\}$.

5.3.3 Reducts

Indiscernibility relation reduces the data by identifying equivalence classes, i.e., objects that are indiscernible, using the available attributes. Only one element of the equivalence class is needed to represent the entire class. Reduction can also be done by keeping only those attributes that preserve the

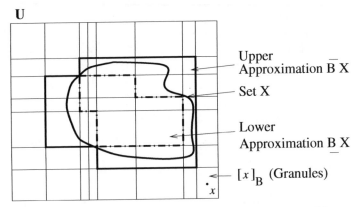

FIGURE 5.1: Rough representation of a set with upper and lower approximations.

indiscernibility relation and, consequently, set approximation. So one is, in effect, looking for *minimal* sets of attributes taken from the initial set A, so that the minimal sets induce the *same* partition on the domain as done by A. In other words, the essence of the information remains intact, and superfluous attributes are removed. The above sets of attributes are called *reducts*. Depending on the nature of information preserved, there may be four important categories of reducts. They are:

1. Reducts not relative to a particular case (or object) and not relative to the decision attribute. The full discernibility relation is preserved. Reducts of this type are minimal attribute subsets that enable us to discern all cases from each other, up to the same degree as the full set of attributes does.

2. Reducts not relative to a particular case (or object) but relative to the decision attribute. All regions with the same value of the generalized decision are preserved. Reducts of this type are minimal conditional attribute subsets $B \subseteq A$ that for all classes enable us to make the same classifications as the full set of attributes does.

3. Reducts relative to case (or object) $\mathbf{x}$ but not relative to the decision attribute. Reducts of this type are minimal conditional attribute subsets that enable us to discern case $\mathbf{x}$ from all other cases up to the same degree as the full set of conditional attributes does.

4. Reducts relative to case (or object) $\mathbf{x}$ and relative to the decision attribute. Our ability to discern case $\mathbf{x}$ from cases with different generalized decision than $\mathbf{x}$ is preserved. Reducts B of this type are minimal conditional attribute subsets that enable us to determine the outcome of case $\mathbf{x}$, up to the same degree as the full set of attributes does.

Reducts have been nicely characterized in [260] by *discernibility matrices* and *discernibility functions*. Consider $U = \{\mathbf{x}_1, \ldots, \mathbf{x}_n\}$ and $A = \{a_1, \ldots, a_p\}$ in the information system $\mathcal{S} = <U, A>$. By the discernibility matrix $\mathbf{M}(\mathcal{S})$ of $\mathcal{S}$ is meant an $n \times n$-matrix (symmetrical with empty diagonal) such that

$$c_{ij} = \{a \in A : a(\mathbf{x}_i) \neq a(\mathbf{x}_j)\}. \tag{5.1}$$

A discernibility function $f_{\mathcal{S}}$ is a function of m boolean variables $\bar{a}_1, \ldots, \bar{a}_p$ corresponding to the attributes $a_1, \ldots, a_p$, respectively, and defined as follows:

$$f_{\mathcal{S}}(\bar{a}_1, \ldots, \bar{a}_p) = \bigwedge \{\bigvee (c_{ij}) : 1 \leq i, j \leq n, \ j < i, \ c_{ij} \neq \emptyset\}, \tag{5.2}$$

where $\bigvee(c_{ij})$ is the disjunction of all variables $\bar{a}$ with $a \in c_{ij}$. It is seen in [260] that $\{a_{i_1}, \ldots, a_{i_r}\}$ is a reduct in $\mathcal{S}$ if and only if $a_{i_1} \wedge \ldots \wedge a_{i_r}$ is a prime implicant (constituent of the disjunctive normal form) of $f_{\mathcal{S}}$.

5.3.4   Dependency rule generation

A principal task in the method of rule generation is to compute reducts relative to a particular kind of information system, the decision system. Relativized versions of discernibility matrices and functions shall be the basic tools used in the computation. d-reducts and d-discernibility matrices are used for this purpose [260]. The methodology is described below.

Let $\mathcal{S} = <U, A>$ be a decision table, with $A = C \cup d$, and d and C its sets of decision and condition attributes respectively. Let the value set of d be of cardinality M, i.e., $V_d = \{d_1, d_2, \ldots, d_M\}$, representing M classes. Divide the decision table $\mathcal{S} = <U, A>$ into M tables $\mathcal{S}_i = <U_i, A_i>$, $i = 1, \ldots, M$, corresponding to the M decision attributes $d_1, \ldots, d_M$, where $U = U_1 \cup \ldots \cup U_M$ and $A_i = C \cup \{d_i\}$.

Let $\{\mathbf{x}_{i1}, \ldots, \mathbf{x}_{ir}\}$ be the set of those objects of U_i that occur in $\mathcal{S}_i, i = 1, \ldots, M$. Now for each d_i-reduct $B = \{b_1, \ldots, b_k\}$ (say), a discernibility matrix (denoted by $\mathbf{M}_{d_i}(B)$) can be derived from the d_i-discernibility matrix as follows:

$$c_{ij} = \{a \in B : a(\mathbf{x}_i) \neq a(\mathbf{x}_j)\}, \tag{5.3}$$

for $i, j = 1, \ldots, n$.

For each object $\mathbf{x}_j \in \mathbf{x}_{i_1}, \ldots, \mathbf{x}_{i_r}$, the discernibility function $f_{d_i}^{\mathbf{x}_j}$ is defined as

$$f_{d_i}^{\mathbf{x}_j} = \bigwedge \{\bigvee (c_{ij}) : 1 \leq i, j \leq n, \ j < i, \ c_{ij} \neq \emptyset\}, \tag{5.4}$$

where $\bigvee(c_{ij})$ is the disjunction of all members of c_{ij}. Then $f_{d_i}^{\mathbf{x}_j}$ is brought to its disjunctive normal form (d.n.f). One thus obtains a dependency rule $\mathbf{r}_i$, viz. $d_i \leftarrow P_i$, where P_i is the disjunctive normal form (d.n.f) of $f_{d_i}^{\mathbf{x}_j}, j \in i_1, \ldots, i_r$.

The dependency factor df_i for $\mathbf{r}_i$ is given by

$$df_i = \frac{card(POS_{B_i}(d_i))}{card(U_i)}, \tag{5.5}$$

where $POS_{B_i}(d_i) = \bigcup_{X \in I_{d_i}} \underline{B}_i(X)$, and $\underline{B}_i(X)$ is the lower approximation of X with respect to B_i. B_i is the set of condition attributes occurring in the rule $\mathbf{r}_i : d_i \leftarrow P_i$. $POS_{B_i}(d_i)$ is the positive region of class d_i with respect to attributes B_i, denoting the region of class d_i that can be surely described by attributes B_i. Thus, df_i measures the information about decision attributes d_i derivable from the condition attributes of a rule B_i. df_i has values in the interval $[0, 1]$, with the maximum and minimum values corresponding to complete dependence and independence of d_i on B_i, respectively.

Example 1:
The methodology for rough set rule generation is illustrated here. Let us consider the *Hiring* decision system $\mathcal{A}' = (U, \{Diploma(i), Experience(e), French(f), Reference(r)\} \cup \{Decision\})$ of Table 5.1. $V_{Decision} = \{Accept, Reject\}$ is the value set of the attribute *Decision*; $V_{Decision}$ is of cardinality two. The original decision table (Table 5.1) is thus split into two decision tables $\mathcal{S}_{Accept}$ (Table 5.2(a)), and $\mathcal{S}_{Reject}$ (Table 5.2(b)). Since all the objects in each table are distinct, they could not be reduced further. Next, for each decision table the discernibility matrices $\mathbf{M}_{Accept}(C)$ and $\mathbf{M}_{Reject}(C)$ are obtained using Equation 5.3. Among them only the matrix $\mathbf{M}_{Accept}(C)$ is shown in Table 5.3, as an illustration. The discernibility function obtained from $\mathbf{M}_{Accept}(C)$ is

$$f_{Accept} = (i \vee e \vee r) \wedge (e \vee f \vee r) \wedge (i \vee f \vee r)$$
$$= (e \wedge i) \vee (e \wedge f) \vee (i \wedge f) \vee r \qquad \text{(disjunctive normal form)}$$

The following dependency rules are obtained from f_{Accept}

$$Accept \leftarrow e \wedge i$$
$$Accept \leftarrow e \wedge f$$
$$Accept \leftarrow i \wedge f$$
$$Accept \leftarrow r$$

5.4 Linguistic Representation of Patterns and Fuzzy Granulation

As is evident from the previous section, rough set theory deals with a set of objects in a granular universe. In the present section we describe a way of obtaining the granular feature space using fuzzy linguistic representation of patterns. Only the case of numeric features is mentioned here. (Features in descriptive and set forms can also be handled in this framework.) The details of the methodologies involved may be found in [203, 204].

TABLE 5.2: Two decision tables obtained by splitting the *Hiring* table S (Table 5.1)

	i	e	f	r	$Decision$
x_1	MBA	Medium	Yes	Excellent	Accept
x_4	MSc	High	Yes	Neutral	Accept
x_7	MBA	High	No	Good	Accept

(a) S_{Accept}

	i	e	f	r	$Decision$
x_2	MBA	Low	Yes	Neutral	Reject
x_3	MCE	Low	Yes	Good	Reject
x_5	MSc	Medium	Yes	Neutral	Reject
x_6	MSc	High	Yes	Excellent	Reject
x_8	MCE	Low	No	Excellent	Reject

(b) S_{Reject}

TABLE 5.3:

Discernibility matrix $\mathbf{M}_{Accept}$ for the split *Hiring* decision table S_{Accept} (Table 5.2(a))

Objects	x_1	x_4	x_7
x_1		i,e,r	e,f,r
x_4			i,f,r
x_7			

Let a pattern (object) $\mathbf{F}$ be represented by p numeric features (attributes), i.e., $\mathbf{F} = [F_1, F_2, \ldots, F_p]$. Note that, $\mathbf{F}$ is equivalent to a p-dimensional feature vector $\mathbf{x}$. Each feature is described in terms of its fuzzy membership values corresponding to three linguistic fuzzy sets, namely, *low* (L), *medium* (M), and *high* (H). Thus a p-dimensional pattern vector is represented as a $3p$-dimensional vector [203, 204]

$$\mathbf{F} = [\mu_{low}^1(F_1), \mu_{medium}^1(F_1), \mu_{high}^1(F_1); \mu_{low}^2(F_2), \mu_{medium}^2(F_2), \mu_{high}^2(F_2);$$
$$\ldots; \mu_{low}^p(F_p), \mu_{medium}^p(F_p), \mu_{high}^p(F_p)] \tag{5.6}$$

where $\mu_{low}^j(.), \mu_{medium}^j(.)$ and $\mu_{high}^j(.)$ indicate the membership values of $(.)$ to the fuzzy sets *low, medium,* and *high* along feature axis j. $\mu(.) \in [0, 1]$.

For each input feature F_j, the fuzzy sets *low, medium* and *high* are characterized individually by a π-membership function whose form is [286]

$$\mu(F_j) = \pi(F_j; c, \lambda) = \begin{cases} 2(1 - \frac{|F_j - c|}{\lambda})^2, & \text{for } \frac{\lambda}{2} \leq |F_j - c| \leq \lambda \\ 1 - 2(\frac{|F_j - c|}{\lambda})^2, & \text{for } 0 \leq |F_j - c| \leq \frac{\lambda}{2} \\ 0, & \text{otherwise}, \end{cases} \tag{5.7}$$

where $\lambda (> 0)$ is the radius of the π-function with c as the central point. For each of the fuzzy sets *low, medium* and *high,* λ and c take different values. These values are chosen so that the membership functions for these three fuzzy sets have overlapping nature (intersecting at membership value 0.5), as shown in Figure 5.2.

Let us now explain the procedure for selecting the centers (c) and radii (λ) of the overlapping π-functions. Let m_j be the mean of the pattern points along j^{th} axis. Then m_{j_l} and m_{j_h} are defined as the mean (along j^{th} axis) of the pattern points having coordinate values in the range $[F_{j_{min}}, m_j)$ and $(m_j, F_{j_{max}}]$, respectively, where $F_{j_{max}}$ and $F_{j_{min}}$ denote the upper and lower bounds of the dynamic range of feature F_j. The centers and the radii of the three π-functions are defined as

$$\begin{aligned} c_{low(F_j)} &= m_{j_l} \\ c_{medium(F_j)} &= m_j \\ c_{high(F_j)} &= m_{j_h} \\ \lambda_{low(F_j)} &= c_{medium(F_j)} - c_{low(F_j)} \\ \lambda_{high(F_j)} &= c_{high(F_j)} - c_{medium(F_j)} \\ \lambda_{medium(F_j)} &= 0.5 \left(c_{high(F_j)} - c_{low(F_j)}\right). \end{aligned} \tag{5.8}$$

Here the distribution of the pattern points along each feature axis is taken into account while choosing the corresponding centers and radii of the linguistic fuzzy sets.

The aforesaid three overlapping functions along each axis generate the fuzzy granulated feature space in p-dimension. The granulated space contains 3^p granules with fuzzy boundaries among them. Here the granules (clumps of similar objects or patterns) are attributed by the three fuzzy linguistic values

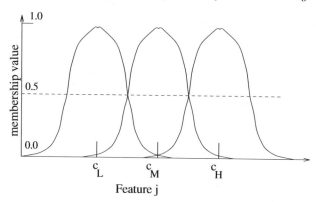

FIGURE 5.2: π−Membership functions for linguistic fuzzy sets *low* (L), *medium* (M) and *high* (H) for each feature axis.

'low,' 'medium' and 'high.' The degree of belongingness of a pattern to a granule (or the degree of possessing a property low, medium, or high by a pattern) is determined by the corresponding membership function.

Furthermore, if one wishes to obtain crisp granules (or crisp subsets), α-cut, $0 < \alpha < 1$, [286] of these fuzzy sets may be used. (α-cut of a fuzzy set is a crisp set of points for which membership value is greater than or equal to α.) Note that three fuzzy property sets 'low,' 'medium' and 'high' are used here. One may consider hedges like 'very,' 'more or less' to generate more granules, i.e., finer granulated space. However, this will enhance the computational requirement for the following tasks of both case generation and retrieval.

5.5   Rough-fuzzy Case Generation Methodology

Here we describe a methodology for case generation on the fuzzy granulated space as obtained in the previous section. This involves two tasks, namely, (a) generation of fuzzy rules using rough set theory, and (b) mapping the rules to cases. Since rough set theory operates on crisp granules (i.e., subsets of the universe) we need to convert the fuzzy membership values of the patterns to binary ones or, to convert the fuzzy membership functions to binary functions in order to represent the crisp granules (subsets) for application of rough set theory. This conversion can be done using an α-cut. This is illustrated in Figure 5.3, where 0.5-cut is used to obtain $3^2 = 9$ crisp granules (subsets) of the 2-dimensional feature space from the linguistic representation of the input features.

The schematic diagram for the generation of case is shown in Figure 5.4. One may note that the inputs to the case generation process are fuzzy mem-

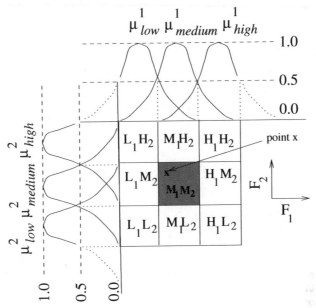

FIGURE 5.3: Generation of crisp granules from linguistic (fuzzy) representation of the features F_1 and F_2. Dark region (M_1, M_2) indicates a crisp granule obtained by 0.5-cuts on the μ^1_{medium} and μ^2_{medium} functions.

bership functions, the output 'cases' are also fuzzy membership functions, but the intermediate rough set theoretic processing is performed on binary functions representing crisp sets (granules). For example, the inputs to Block 2 are fuzzy membership functions. Its outputs are binary membership functions which are used for rough processing in Block 3 and Block 4. Finally, the outputs of Block 4, representing cases, are again fuzzy membership functions. Each task is discussed below.

5.5.1 Thresholding and rule generation

Consider the $3p$ fuzzy membership values of a p dimensional pattern $\mathbf{F}_i$. Then select only those attributes having values greater than or equal to Th (= 0.5, say). In other words, one obtains a 0.5-cut of all the fuzzy sets to obtain binary membership values corresponding to the sets *low, medium* and *high*.

For example, consider the point $\mathbf{x}$ in Figure 5.3. Its $3p$ dimensional fuzzy representation is $\mathbf{F} = [0.4, 0.7, 0.1, 0.2, 0.8, 0.4]$. After binarization it becomes $\mathbf{F}_b = [0, 1, 0, 0, 1, 0]$, which denotes the crisp granule (or subset) at the center of the 3×3 granulated space.

After the binary membership values are obtained for all the patterns, the decision table for rough set rule generation is constituted. As the method

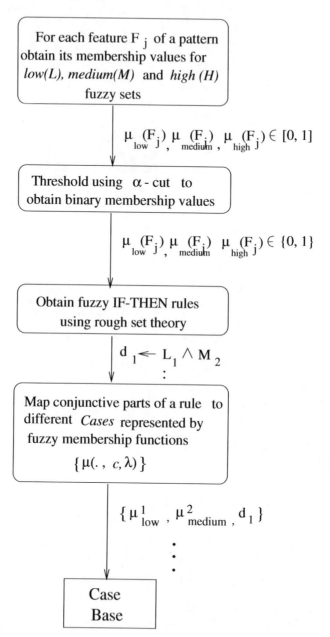

FIGURE 5.4:   Schematic diagram of rough-fuzzy case generation.

considers multiple objects in a class, a separate $n_k \times 3p$-dimensional attribute-value decision table is generated for each class d_k (where n_k indicates the number of objects in d_k). Let there be m sets $O_1, ..., O_m$ of objects in the table having identical attribute values, and $card(O_i) = n_{k_i}, i = 1, ..., m$, such that $n_{k_1} \geq ... \geq n_{k_m}$ and $\sum_{i=1}^{m} n_{k_i} = n_k$. The attribute-value table can now be represented as an $m \times 3p$ array. Let $n_{k_1'}, n_{k_2'}, ..., n_{k_m'}$ denote the distinct elements among $n_{k_1}, ..., n_{k_m}$ such that $n_{k_1'} > n_{k_2'} > ... > n_{k_m'}$. Let a heuristic threshold function be defined as [17]

$$Tr = \left\lceil \frac{\sum_{i=1}^{m} \frac{1}{n_{k_i'} - n_{k_{i+1}'}}}{Th} \right\rceil, \tag{5.9}$$

so that all entries having frequency less than Tr are eliminated from the table, resulting in the reduced attribute-value table. The main motive of introducing this threshold function lies in reducing the size of the case base and in eliminating the noisy patterns. From the reduced attribute-value table, thus obtained, rough dependency rules are generated using the methodology described in Section 5.3.4.

5.5.2 Mapping dependency rules to cases

We now describe the technique for mapping rough dependency rules to cases. The algorithm is based on the observation that each dependency rule (having frequency above some threshold) represents a cluster in the feature space. It may be noted that only a subset of features appears in each of the rules; this indicates the fact that the entire feature set is not always necessary to characterize a cluster. A *case* is constructed out of a *dependency rule* in the following manner:

1. Consider the antecedent part of a rule; split it into atomic formulas containing only conjunction of literals.

2. For each atomic formula, generate a case – containing the centers and radii of the fuzzy linguistic variables ('low', 'medium', and 'high'), which are present in the formula. (Thus, multiple cases may be generated from a rule.)

3. Associate with each such case generated the precedent part of the rule and the case strength equal to the dependency factor of the rule (Equation 5.5). The strength factor reflects the size of the corresponding cluster and the significance of the case.

Thus a case has the following structure:
case{
Feature i: $fuzzset_i$: center, radius;
. . . . . .

Class k

Strength }

where $fuzzset$ denotes the fuzzy sets 'low,' 'medium' or 'high.' The method is explained below with the help of an example.

One may note that while 0.5-cut is used to convert the $3n$ fuzzy membership functions of a pattern to binary ones for rough set rule generation (Section 5.5.1), the original fuzzy functions are retained in order to use them in for representing the generated cases (Section 5.5.2). These are also illustrated in Figure 5.4, where the outputs μ^1_{low}, μ^2_{medium} are fuzzy sets (membership functions).

Example 2:

Consider data set having two features F_1, F_2 and two classes as shown in Figure 5.5. The granulated feature space has $3^2 = 9$ granules. These granules are characterized by three membership functions along each axis and have ill-defined boundaries. Let the following two dependency rules be obtained from the reduced attribute table:

$$class_1 \leftarrow L_1 \wedge H_2, \ df = 0.5$$

$$class_2 \leftarrow H_1 \wedge L_2, \ df = 0.4$$

Let the parameters of the fuzzy sets 'low,' 'medium' and 'high' be as follows:
Feature 1: c_L=0.1, λ_L=0.5, c_M=0.5, λ_M=0.7, c_H=0.7, λ_H=0.4.
Feature 2: c_L=0.2, λ_L=0.5, c_M=0.4, λ_M=0.7, c_H=0.9, λ_H=0.5.

Therefore, we have the following two cases:

case 1{

Feature No: 1, $fuzzset$(L): center=0.1, radius=0.5
Feature No: 2, $fuzzset$ (H): center=0.9, radius=0.5
Class=1
Strength=0.5 }

case 2{

Feature No: 1, $fuzzset$ (H): center=0.7, radius=0.4
Feature No: 2, $fuzzset$ (L): center=0.2, radius=0.5
Class=2
Strength=0.4 }

5.5.3 Case retrieval

Each case thus obtained in the previous section is a collection of fuzzy sets $\{fuzzsets\}$ described by a set of 1-dimensional π-membership functions with different c and λ values. To compute the similarity of an unknown pattern **F**

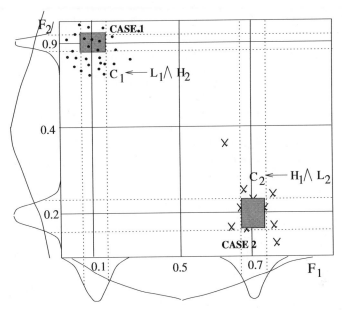

FIGURE 5.5: Rough-fuzzy case generation for a two-dimensional data.

(of dimension p) to a case $\mathbf{p}$ (of variable dimension p_m, $p_m \leq p$), we use

$$sim(\mathbf{F}, \mathbf{p}) = \sqrt{\frac{1}{p_m} \sum_{j=1}^{p_m} \left(\mu^j_{fuzzset}(F_j) \right)^2} \qquad (5.10)$$

where $\mu^j_{fuzzset}(F_j)$ is the degree of belongingness of the jth component of $\mathbf{F}$ to $fuzzset$ representing the case $\mathbf{p}$. When $\mu^j = 1$ for all j, $sim(\mathbf{F}, \mathbf{p}) = 1$ (maximum) and when $\mu^j = 0$ for all j, $sim(\mathbf{F}, \mathbf{p}) = 0$ (minimum). Therefore Equation 5.10 provides a collective measure computed over the degree of similarity of each component of the unknown pattern with the corresponding one of a stored case. The higher the value of the similarity, the closer is the pattern $\mathbf{F}$ to the case $\mathbf{p}$. Note that fuzzy membership functions in Equation 5.10 take care of the distribution of points within a granule thereby providing a better similarity measure between $\mathbf{F}$ and $\mathbf{p}$ than the conventional Euclidean distance between two points.

For classifying (or to provide a label to) an unknown pattern, the case closest to the pattern, in terms of $sim(\mathbf{F}, \mathbf{p})$ measure, is retrieved and its class label is assigned to that pattern. Ties are resolved using the parameter *Case Strength*.

5.6   Experimental Results and Comparison

Some experimental results [202] on three real life data sets, namely, Iris data, Forest cover type data and Multiple features data sets (Appendix B), are presented here. The last two data sets have a large number of samples and features.

The cases generated using the rough-fuzzy methodology are compared with those obtained using the following three case selection methodologies:

(i) Instance-based learning algorithm, IB3 [7],

(ii) Instance-based learning algorithm with reduced number of features, IB4 [4]. The feature weighting is learned by random hill climbing in IB4. A specified number of features having high weights is selected, and

(iii) Random case selection.

Comparison is made on the basis of the following:

(a) 1-NN classification accuracy using the generated/selected cases. For all the data 10% of the samples are used as a training set for case generation and 90% of the samples are used as a test set. Mean of the accuracy computed over 10 such random split is reported.

(b) Number of cases stored in the case base.

(c) Total CPU time required (on a DEC Alpha 400 MHz workstation) for case generation.

(d) Average CPU time required (on a DEC Alpha 400 MHz workstation) to retrieve a case for the patterns in test set.

For the purpose of illustration, the rough dependency rules and the corresponding generated cases are provided in Tables 5.4 and 5.5, respectively, for the Iris data, as an example. Comparative results of the rough-fuzzy case generation methodology with other case selection algorithms are presented in Tables 5.6, 5.7 and 5.8 for the Iris, Forest cover type and Multiple features data, respectively, in terms of number of cases, 1-NN classification accuracy, average number of features per case (p_{avg}), and case generation (t_{gen}) and retrieval (t_{ret}) times. It can be seen from the tables that the cases obtained using the rough-fuzzy methodology are much superior to random selection method and IB4, and close to IB3 in terms of classification accuracy. (The superiority over random selection and IB4 is statistically significant, in terms of the test statistics described in Section 2.6.2.) The method requires significantly less time compared to IB3 and IB4 for case generation. As is seen from the tables, the average number of features stored per case (p_{avg}) by the rough-fuzzy technique is much less than the original data dimension (p). As a consequence, the average retrieval time required is very low. IB4 also stores cases with a reduced number of features and has a low retrieval time, but its accuracy is much less compared to the method described. Moreover, all the cases involve an equal number of features, unlike the rough-fuzzy case generation.

TABLE 5.4: Rough dependency rules for the Iris data

C_1	$\leftarrow$	$L_1 \wedge H_2 \wedge L_3$	$df = 0.81$
C_2	$\leftarrow$	$M_1 \wedge L_2 \wedge M_4$	$df = 0.81$
C_3	$\leftarrow$	$H_1 \wedge H_4$	$df = 0.77$

TABLE 5.5: Cases generated for the Iris data

case 1{
Feature No: 1, $fuzzset$(L): center=5.19, radius=0.65
Feature No: 2, $fuzzset$ (H): center=3.43, radius=0.37
Feature No: 3, $fuzzset$ (L): center=0.37, radius=0.82
Class=1
Strength=0.81
}
case 2{
Feature No: 1, $fuzzset$(M): center=3.05, radius=0.34
Feature No: 2, $fuzzset$ (L): center=1.70, radius=2.05
Feature No: 4, $fuzzset$ (M): center=1.20, radius=0.68
Class=2
Strength=0.81
}
case 3{
Feature No: 1, $fuzzset$(H): center=6.58, radius=0.74
Feature No: 4, $fuzzset$ (H): center=1.74, radius=0.54
Class=3
Strength=0.77
}

TABLE 5.6: Comparison of case selection algorithms for Iris data

Algorithm	No. of Cases	p_{avg}	Classification accuracy (%)	t_{gen} (sec)	t_{ret} (sec)
Rough-fuzzy	3	2.67	98.17	0.2	0.005
IB3	3	4	98.00	2.50	0.01
IB4	3	4	90.01	4.01	0.01
Random	3	4	87.19	0.01	0.01

5.7 Summary

After explaining the concept of granular computing and its relevance to data mining, a methodology for case generation by exploiting the merits of

TABLE 5.7: Comparison of case selection algorithms for Forest cover type data

Algorithm	No. of Cases	p_{avg}	Classification accuracy (%)	t_{gen} (sec)	t_{ret} (sec)
Rough-fuzzy	542	4.10	67.01	244	4.4
IB3	545	10	66.88	4055	52.0
IB4	545	4	50.05	7021	4.5
Random	545	10	41.02	17	52.0

TABLE 5.8: Comparison of case selection algorithms for Multiple features data

Algorithm	No. of Cases	p_{avg}	Classification accuracy (%)	t_{gen} (sec)	t_{ret} (sec)
Rough-fuzzy	50	20.87	77.01	1096	10.05
IB3	52	649	78.99	4112	507
IB4	52	21	41.00	8009	20.02
Random	50	649	50.02	8.01	507

rough-fuzzy hybridization is presented. Fuzzy set theory is used to represent a pattern in terms of its membership to linguistic variables. This gives rise to efficient fuzzy granulation of the feature space. On the granular universe thus obtained, rough sets are used to form reducts which contain *informative* and *irreducible* information both in terms of features and patterns. The fuzzy linguistic rules obtained from the reducts represent different clusters in the granular feature space. Granular clusters (regions), modeled by the rules, are mapped to different cases, represented by different fuzzy membership functions.

Since rough set theory is used to obtain cases through crude rules (i.e., it deals with information granules, and not the original data), case generation time is reduced. Also, since only the informative regions and the relevant subset of features are stored (i.e., the generated cases are represented by different reduced number of features), case retrieval time decreases significantly. Therefore, the case generation algorithm is suitable for mining data sets, large both in dimension and size.

In this chapter a simple rough set rule generation strategy is adopted along with fuzzy granulation to demonstrate the power of granular computing. Other general rough set models such as tolerance relations and rough mereology may yield better performance. Also, the capability of rough mereology for handling heterogeneous, symbolic and relational data may be utilized for problems like multimedia mining and genomic data analysis.

Chapter 6

Rough-fuzzy Clustering

6.1 Introduction

The clustering problem has broad appeal and usefulness as one of the steps in exploratory data analysis [238]. It is an important task in several data mining applications including document retrieval, image/spatial data segmentation, and market analysis [238]. Data mining applications place the following two primary requirements on clustering algorithms: scalability to large data sets (or, the issue of computation time) [29] and non-presumption of any canonical data properties like convexity.

Clustering algorithms are often based on (a) iterative refinement of cluster parameters by optimizing some criterion function or likelihood of some probabilistic model (e.g., k-means [238], mixture of Gaussians [53]), or (b) graph theoretic techniques, where each cluster represents a subgraph of a graph of the entire data. One of the well-known graph theoretic clustering is based on the construction of the minimal spanning tree (MST) of the data [290]. Both the clustering approaches, iterative and graph-theoretic, have their advantages and disadvantages and cannot directly be applied for data mining. While the iterative refinement schemes like k-means and expectation maximization (EM) are fast and easily scalable to large databases [29], they can produce only convex clusters and are sensitive to initialization of the parameters. The graph-theoretic methods can model arbitrary shaped clusters but are slow and sensitive to noise. It may be noted that the advantages of one are complementary in overcoming the limitations of the other, and vice versa.

In this chapter we describe a rough-fuzzy clustering algorithm, which can be considered as an integration of iterative (using the EM algorithm), grid/granule based (using rough set theory), and graph theoretic (using minimal spanning tree) methods. The algorithm has the capability of generating arbitrary shaped clusters and is scalable to large data sets. In the clustering algorithm rough set theoretic logical rules are used to obtain initial approximate mixture model parameters. As in the previous chapter, linguistic representation of patterns is used for fuzzy granulation. The crude mixture model, after refinement through EM, leads to accurate clusters. Here, rough set theory offers a fast and robust (noise insensitive) solution to the initialization and local minima problem of iterative refinement clustering. Also, the problem of choosing the number of mixtures is circumvented, since the number of Gaussian components to be used is automatically decided by rough set theory.

The problem of modeling non-convex clusters is addressed by constructing a minimal spanning tree (MST) with each Gaussian as nodes and Mahalanobis distance between them as edge weights. Since graph-theoretic clustering is performed on the Gaussian models rather than the individual data points and the number of models is much fewer than that of the data points, the computational time requirement is significantly small. A (non-convex) cluster obtained from the graph is a particular subset of all the Gaussians used to model the data.

Experimental results are presented for some real life and artificially generated non-convex data sets. It is found that rough set with fuzzy discretization enhances the performance of EM algorithm both in terms of cluster quality and computational time. Integration of minimal spanning tree with rough-fuzzy initialized EM results in further improvement of performance with a slight increase in computational time. The merits of the integrations algorithm are also demonstrated, in another part of the experiment, for the problem of segmentation of multispectral satellite images.

The organization of the chapter is as follows. Section 6.2 describes some of the major approaches adopted for clustering along with their merits/demerits. Four commonly used algorithms for large data sets, namely, CLARANS, BIRCH, DBSCAN, and STING, are described in brief in Section 6.3. The CEMMiSTRI algorithm integrating EM algorithm, minimal spanning tree, and rough sets is described in detail in Section 6.4, and its experimental results are provided in Section 6.5 along with comparisons. An application of the method for segmentation of multispectral images is shown in Section 6.6. Section 6.7 provides the summary.

6.2   Clustering Methodologies

Major clustering methods can be classified into the following categories [88].

Partitioning methods: Given a data set of n objects and k, the number of clusters to form, a partitioning algorithm organizes the objects into k partitions, where each partition represents a cluster. The clusters are formed to optimize an objective partitioning criterion, often called a *similarity function*, such as distance, so that the objects within a cluster are 'similar,' whereas the objects of different clusters are 'dissimilar.' A partitioning method starts with an initial partition and uses an iterative refinement technique that attempts to improve the partitioning by moving objects from one group to another. The most well-known and commonly used partitioning methods are k-means, k-medoids and their variations. Probabilistic methods, often based on the mixture modeling and expectation maximization (EM) algorithm, are also popular. Partitional methods work well for finding spherical shaped clusters in small to medium-sized data sets. For clustering very large data sets and to find clusters with complex shapes, these methods need to be extended.

Hierarchical and graph theoretic methods: A hierarchical method can be classified as either agglomerative or divisive, based on how the hierarchical decomposition is formed. The agglomerative approach, also called the bottom-up approach, starts with each object forming a separate group. It successfully merges the objects or groups close to one another, until all the groups are merged to one, or the required number of clusters are obtained. The divisive approach, also called the top-down approach, starts with all the objects in the same cluster. In each successive iteration, a cluster is split into smaller clusters, until eventually each object represents one cluster, or until a required number of clusters are obtained. Hierarchical methods suffer from the fact that once a step (merge or split) is done, it can never be undone. This rigidity leads to sensitivity to noise in the data. In graph-theoretic clustering, a graph is constructed with each data point as a node, and each cluster represents a subgraph of a graph of the entire data. One of the well-known graph-theoretic clustering called the complete linkage algorithm is based on the construction of the minimal spanning tree (MST) of the data [290].

Both the partitioning and graph theoretic approaches have their advantages and disadvantages and cannot directly be applied for data mining. While the partitioning schemes are fast and easily scalable to large databases [29], they can produce only convex clusters and are sensitive to initialization of the parameters. The graph-theoretic methods can model arbitrary shaped clusters but are slow and sensitive to noise. It may be noted that the advantages of one are complementary in overcoming the limitations of the other.

Density-based methods: Besides partitioning and hierarchical methods other clustering algorithm have been developed based on the notion of density. The general idea is to continue growing the given cluster as long as the density (number of data points) in the 'neighborhood' exceeds some threshold. Such a method can be used to filter out noise and discover clusters of aribitrary shape.

Grid-based methods: Grid-based methods quantize the object space into a finite number of cells (granules) that form a grid structure. The clustering operations are performed on the grid structure (i.e., on the granulated space). The main advantage of this approach is its fast processing time, which is typically independent of the number of data objects.

6.3   Algorithms for Clustering Large Data Sets

Traditional clustering algorithms are often suitable only for small and medium sized data sets. Over the past five years many of them have been extended in several ways to achieve scalability to data sets with large size and dimensions, and containing noisy patterns. We describe below four clustering methods of different categories, suitable for large data sets. They are CLARANS (partitional), BIRCH (hierarchical), DBSCAN (density based), and STING (grid based) algorithms.

6.3.1   CLARANS: Clustering large applications based upon randomized search

CLARANS [184] is a k-medoids type algorithm which combines sampling techniques with the PAM (partitioning around medoid) method. PAM selects an initial random sample of k medoids, from which it repeatedly tries to make a better choice of medoids. All possible pairs of objects are analyzed, where one object in each pair is considered a medoid and the other is not. The quality of the resulting clustering, measured by squared error, is calculated for each such combination. An object o_j is replaced with the object causing greatest reduction in squared error. The set of best objects for each cluster in one iteration forms the medoids for the next iteration. In CLARA, which is a modified version of PAM, instead of taking the whole set of data into consideration, a small portion of the actual data is chosen as its representative. Medoids are then chosen from this sample using the PAM algorithm.

CLARANS does not confine itself to any particular sample over all the iterations. It draws a sample with some randomness in each step of the search of the PAM algorithm. The clustering process can thus be considered as searching a graph where every node is a potential solution, that is a set of medoids. The clustering obtained after replacing a single medoid is called the *neighbor* of the current clustering. If a better neighbor is found CLARANS moves to the neighbor's node and the process starts again; otherwise, the current node produces a local optimum accepted as a solution.

CLARANS has been experimentally found to be more effective than both PAM and CLARA. It can be used to find the most natural clusters in data and it also enables detection of the outliers.

6.3.2   BIRCH: Balanced iterative reducing and clustering using hierarchies

BIRCH [291] is an integrated hierarchical clustering method. It introduces two concepts, *clustering feature* and *clustering feature tree (CF tree)*. These are used to summarize cluster representations and help achieve scalability to large data sets. A clustering feature (CF) is a triplet (n, LS, SS) summarizing the information about the subcluster of objects. Here, n is the number of points in the subcluster, LS is the linear sum of n points, and SS is the squared sum of the points. In other words, CF contains the zeroth, first and second moments of the subcluster. A CF tree is a height balanced tree that stores cluster features for a hierarchical clustering. The nonleaf nodes store sums of CFs of their children and thus summarize the clustering information about their children. A CF tree has two parameters: branching factor, B, and threshold, T. The branching factor specifies the maximum number of children per nonleaf node. The threshold parameter specifies the maximum diameter of subclusters stored at the leaf nodes of the tree. These two factors influence the size of the resulting tree.

The BIRCH clustering algorithm consists of two phases:

- Scanning the data set to buid an initial CF tree.

- Application of a partitional clustering algorithm (e.g., k-means) to cluster the leaf nodes of the CF tree.

In the first phase the CF tree is built dynamically as objects are inserted. An object is inserted to the closest leaf entry (subcluster). If the diameter of the subcluster stored in the leaf node after insertion is larger than the threshold value, then the leaf node and possibly other nodes are split. After insertion of the new object, information about it is passed toward the root of the tree. Thus iterative balancing and reducing is performed.

Experiments have shown the linear scalability of the algorithm with respect to the number of objects, and good quality of clustering. However, since each node in a CF tree can hold only a limited number of points due to its size, a CF tree node does not always correspond to what a user may consider a natural cluster. Moreover, if the clusters are not spherical in shape, BIRCH does not perform well because it uses the notion of radius or diameter to control the boundary of a cluster.

6.3.3 DBSCAN: Density-based spatial clustering of applications with noise

DBSCAN [61] is a density-based clustering algorithm. The algorithm grows different regions with sufficiently high density into clusters of arbitrary shapes. It defines a cluster as a maximal set of density connected points. The following concepts are used in the process.

- The neighborhood within a radius ϵ of a given object is called the 'ϵ-neighborhood' of the object.

- If the ϵ-neighborhood of an object contains at least a minimum number, *MinPts*, of objects, then the object is called a 'core object.'

- Given a set of objects, D, we say that an object p is 'directly density reachable' from object q if p is within ϵ-neighborhood of q, and q is a core object.

- An object p is 'density reachable' from object q with respect to ϵ and *MinPts* in a set of objects, D, if there is a chain pf objects $p_1, \ldots, p_n$, $p_1 = q$ and $p_n = p$ such that p_{i+1} is directly density reachable from p_i with respect to ϵ and *MinPts*, for $1 \leq i \leq n, p_i \in D$.

- An object p is 'density connected' to object q with respect to ϵ and *MinPts* in a set of objects, D, if there is an object $o \in D$ such that both p and q are density reachable from o with respect to ϵ and *MinPts*.

A *density-based cluster* is a set of density connected objects that is maximal with respect to density reachibility. Objects not connected to any cluster are considered to be 'noise.' DBSCAN searches for clusters by checking the ϵ-neighborhood of each point in the data set. If the ϵ-neighborhood of a point p contains more than *MinPts* points, a new cluster with p as a core object is created. DBSCAN then iteratively collects directly density reachable objects from these core objects, which may involve the merging of a few density reachable clusters. The process terminates when no new point can be added to any cluster.

If a spatial index is used, the computational complexity is $O(n\log n)$, where n is the number of objects. Otherwise it is $O(n^2)$.

6.3.4 STING: Statistical information grid

STING [277] is a grid-based multiresolution clustering technique in which the feature space is divided into rectangular cells. There are usually several levels of such rectangular cells corresponding to different levels of resolution, and these cells form a hierarchical structure: each cell at a high level is partitioned to form a number of cells at the next lower level. Statistical information regarding the attributes in each grid cell (such as the mean, maximum, and minimum values) is precomputed and stored. Statistical parameters corresponding to the higher level cells can easily be computed from those of the lower level cells. These parameters include the following: the attribute independent parameter, *count*, and the attribute dependent parameters like m (mean), s (standard deviation), *min* (minimum), *max* (maximum), and the type of *distribution* that the attribute value in the cell follows, such as normal, uniform, exponential, or none (if the distribution is unknown). Initially, the parameters are calculated from the data. The distribution is provided by users.

If the cluster membership of a point is queried, the statistical parameters can be used to obtain it in a top-down grid-based method as follows. First, a layer within the hierarchical structure is determined from which the query answering process starts. This layer typically contains a small number of cells.

For each cell in the current layer, the confidence interval reflecting the cell's relevancy to the given query is computed. The irrelevant cells are removed from further consideration. Processing of the next lower level examines only the remaining relevant cells. This process is repeated until the bottom layer is reached. At this time, if the query specification is met, the regions of the relevant cells that satisfy the query are returned. Otherwise, the data that fall into the relevant cells are retrieved and further processed until they meet the requirements of the query.

STING scans the data set only once to calculate the statistical parameters of the cells, and hence the time complexity of generating the clusters is $O(n)$, where n is the number of data points. After generating the hierarchical structure, the query processing time is $O(g)$, where g is the total number of grid cells at the lowest level, which is usually much smaller than n. ◇

There are several clustering algorithms which integrate the merits of some of the above methods depending on the applications. For example, CURE [84] is an intermediate between hierarchical and partitional approaches, CLIQUE [1] is grid as well as density based, and COBWEB [67] uses concepts from both statistical and hierarchical clustering.

In the next section we describe CEMMiSTRI [168], a rough-fuzzy clustering algorithm, which can be considered as an integration of partitional (using the EM algorithm), grid/granule based (using rough set theory), and graph theoretic (using minimal spanning tree) methods.

6.4 CEMMiSTRI: Clustering using EM, Minimal Spanning Tree and Rough-fuzzy Initialization

A general method of partitional clustering using statistical principles is to represent the probability density function of the data as a *mixture model*, which asserts that the data is a combination of k individual component densities (commonly Gaussians), corresponding to k clusters. The task is to identify, given the data, a set of k populations in the data and provide a model (density distribution) for each of the populations. The EM algorithm is an effective and popular technique for estimating the mixture model parameters [53]. It iteratively refines an initial cluster model to better fit the data and terminates at a solution which is locally optimal for the underlying clustering criterion [53]. Log-likelihood is used as the objective function which measures how well the model fits the data. Like other iterative refinement clustering methods, including the popular k-means algorithm, the EM algorithm is fast and its scalable versions are available [29]. An advantage of EM over k-means is that it provides a statistical model of the data and is capable of handling the associated uncertainties. However, a problem arising due to its iterative nature is convergence to a local rather than the global optima. It is sensitive to initial conditions and is not robust. To overcome the initialization problem, several methods for determining 'good' initial parameters for EM have been suggested, mainly based on subsampling, voting and two-stage clustering [159]. However, most of these methods have heavy computational requirement and/or are sensitive to noise.

In Section 5.5 we have shown how fuzzy granulation along with rough set theoretic rule generation can be used to efficiently generate cases (class prototypes). Note that these logical rules correspond to different important regions of the feature space and represent crude clusters. The above capability of rough-fuzzy computing is exploited here for fast clustering via the expectation maximization (EM) algorithm and minimal spanning tree (MST).

6.4.1   Mixture model estimation via EM algorithm

The mixture model approximates the data distribution by fitting k component density functions f_h, $h = 1, \ldots, k$ to a data set D having n patterns and p features. Let $\mathbf{x} \in D$ be a pattern, the mixture model probability density function evaluated at $\mathbf{x}$ is:

$$p(\mathbf{x}) = \sum_{h=1}^{k} w_h f_h(\mathbf{x}|\phi_h). \tag{6.1}$$

The weights w_h represent the fraction of data points belonging to model h, and they sum to one ($\sum_{h=1}^{k} w_h = 1$). The functions $f_h(\mathbf{x}|\phi_h)$, $h = 1, \ldots, k$ are the component density functions modeling the points of the hth cluster. ϕ_h represents the specific parameters used to compute the value of f_h (e.g., for a Gaussian component density function, ϕ_h is the mean and covariance matrix).

For continuous data, Gaussian distribution is the most common choice for component density function. This is motivated by a result from density estimation theory stating that any distribution can be effectively approximated by a mixture of Gaussians with weights w_h. The multivariate Gaussian with p-dimensional mean vector μ_h and $p \times p$ covariance matrix Σ_h is:

$$f_h(\mathbf{x}|\mu_h, \Sigma_h) = \frac{1}{\sqrt{(2\pi)^p|\Sigma_h|}} exp\left(-\frac{1}{2}(\mathbf{x} - \mu_h)^T(\Sigma_h)^{-1}(\mathbf{x} - \mu_h)\right) \tag{6.2}$$

The quality of a given set of parameters $\mathbf{\Phi} = \{(w_h, \mu_h, \Sigma_h), h = 1, \ldots, k\}$ is determined by how well the corresponding mixture model fits the data. This is quantified by the log-likelihood of the data, given the mixture model:

$$L(\mathbf{\Phi}) = \sum_{\mathbf{x} \in D} \log\left(\sum_{h=1}^{k} w_h f_h(\mathbf{x}|\mu_h, \Sigma_h)\right). \tag{6.3}$$

The EM begins with an initial estimation of $\mathbf{\Phi}$ and iteratively updates it such that $L(\mathbf{\Phi})$ is non-decreasing. We next outline the EM algorithm.

EM Algorithm:

Given a data set D with n patterns and p continuous features, a stopping tolerance $\epsilon > 0$ and mixture parameters $\mathbf{\Phi}^j$ at iteration j, compute $\mathbf{\Phi}^{j+1}$ at iteration $j+1$ as follows:

Step 1. *(E-Step)* For pattern $\mathbf{x} \in D$:

Compute the membership probability $w_h(\mathbf{x})$ of $\mathbf{x}$ in each cluster $h = 1, \ldots, k$:

$$w_h^j(\mathbf{x}) = \frac{w_h^j f_h(\mathbf{x}|\mu_h^j, \Sigma_h^j)}{\sum_i w_i^j f_i(\mathbf{x}|\mu_i^j, \Sigma_i^j)}.$$

Step 2. *(M-Step)* Update mixture model parameters:

$$w_h^{j+1} = \sum_{\mathbf{x} \in D} w_h^j(\mathbf{x}),$$

$$\mu_h^{j+1} = \frac{\sum_{\mathbf{x} \in D} w_h^j(\mathbf{x})\mathbf{x}}{\sum_{\mathbf{x} \in D} w_h^j(\mathbf{x})},$$

$$\Sigma_h^{j+1} = \frac{\sum_{\mathbf{x} \in D} w_h^j(\mathbf{x}) \left(\mathbf{x} - \mu_h^{j+1}\right) \left(\mathbf{x} - \mu_h^{j+1}\right)^T}{\sum_{\mathbf{x} \in D} w_h^j(\mathbf{x})}, \quad h = 1, \ldots, k.$$

Stopping Criterion: If $|L(\mathbf{\Phi}^j) - L(\mathbf{\Phi}^{j+1})| \leq \epsilon$, Stop. Otherwise, set $j \leftarrow j+1$ and Go To Step 1. $L(\mathbf{\Phi})$ is as given in Equation 6.3.

6.4.2 Rough set initialization of mixture parameters

In this section we describe the methodology for obtaining crude initial values of the parameters ($\mathbf{\Phi}$) of the mixture of Gaussians used to model the data. The parameters are refined further using EM algorithm described in the previous section. The methodology is based on the observation that 'reducts' obtained using rough set theory represent crude clusters in the feature space.

Reducts are computed using the methodology for fuzzy granulation and rule generation described in Sections 5.3.4 and 5.4. Note that, case generation (studied in Section 5.5) is a supervised task while clustering involves unsupervised data analysis. Hence, unlike Section 5.5.1, where decision relative reducts are used, here we use reducts that are not relative to decision attributes. In addition a 'support factor' is defined to measure the strength of a reduct.

Support factor sf_i for the rule $\mathbf{r}_i$ is defined as

$$sf_i = \frac{n_{k_i}}{\sum_{i=1}^r n_{k_i}}, \tag{6.4}$$

where $n_{k_i}, i = 1, \ldots, r$ are the cardinality of the sets O_i of identical objects belonging to the reduced attribute value table.

6.4.3 Mapping reducts to mixture parameters

The mixture model parameters consist of the number of component Gaussian density functions (k) and weights (w_h), means (μ_h) and variances (Σ_h) of the components. We describe below the methodology for obtaining them.

1. Number of Gaussians (k): Consider the antecedent part of a rule $\mathbf{r}_i$; split it into atomic formulas containing only conjunction of literals. For each such atomic formula, assign a component Gaussian. Let the number of such formula be k.

2. Component weights (w_h): Weight of each Gaussian is set equal to the normalized support factor sf_i (obtained using Equation 6.4) of the rule $(\mathbf{r}_i)$ from which it is derived, $w_h = \frac{sf_i}{\sum_{i=1}^{k} sf_i}$.

3. Means (μ_h): An atomic formula consists of the conjunction of a number of literals. The literals are linguistic fuzzy sets 'low,' 'medium' and 'high' along some feature axes. The component of the mean vector along that feature is set equal to the center (c) of the π-membership function of the corresponding fuzzy linguistic set. Note that all features do not appear in a formula, implying those features are not necessary to characterize the corresponding cluster. The component of the mean vector along those features which do not appear are set to the mean of the entire data along those features.

4. Variances (Σ_h): A diagonal covariance matrix is considered for each component Gaussian. As in the case of means, the variance for feature j is set equal to radius λ of the corresponding fuzzy linguistic set. For those features not appearing in a formula the variance is set to a small random value.

Example:

Consider the following two reducts obtained from a reduced attribute value table of data having two dimensions F_1 and F_2. The example is illustrated in Figure 6.1.

$$cluster_1 \leftarrow L_1 \wedge H_2, \ sf_1 = 0.50$$

$$cluster_2 \leftarrow H_1 \wedge L_2, \ sf_2 = 0.40$$

Let the parameters of the fuzzy linguistic sets 'low,' 'medium' and 'high' be as follows:

Feature 1: $c_L=0.1$, $\lambda_L=0.5$, $c_M=0.5$, $\lambda_M=0.7$, $c_H=0.7$, $\lambda_H=0.4$.
Feature 2: $c_L=0.2$, $\lambda_L=0.5$, $c_M=0.4$, $\lambda_M=0.7$, $c_H=0.9$, $\lambda_H=0.5$.

Then we have two component Gaussians with parameters as follows:

$$w_1 = 0.56, \ \mu_1 = [0.1, 0.9] \text{ and } \Sigma_1 = \begin{bmatrix} 0.5 & 0 \\ 0 & 0.5 \end{bmatrix}$$

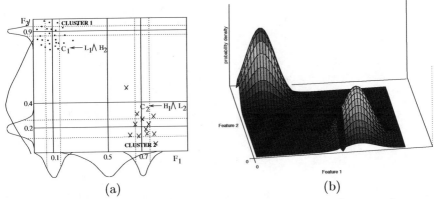

FIGURE 6.1: Rough-fuzzy generation of crude clusters for two-dimensional data (a) data distribution and rough set rules, (b) probability density function for the initial mixture model.

$$w_2 = 0.44, \; \mu_2 = [0.7, 0.2] \text{ and } \Sigma_2 = \begin{bmatrix} 0.5 & 0 \\ 0 & 0.5 \end{bmatrix} \qquad \diamond$$

We summarize below all the steps for rough set initialization of mixture models.

1. Represent each pattern in terms of its membership to fuzzy linguistic sets *low*, *medium* and *high* along each axis. Thus a p-dimensional pattern is now represented by a $3p$-dimensional vector.

2. Threshold each $3p$-dimensional vector containing fuzzy membership values to obtain $3p$-dimensional binary vector. Retain only those vectors that are distinct and appear with frequency above a threshold.

3. Construct an attribute-value table from the reduced set of binary vectors.

4. Construct discernibility matrix from the attribute value table. Generate discernibility functions (rules) for each object in the matrix. Consider atomic formula of the rules which are conjunction of literals (linguistic variables 'low,' 'medium' and 'high,' in this case).

5. Map each atomic formula to parameters w_h, μ_h and Σ_h of corresponding component Gaussian density functions.

6.4.4 Graph-theoretic clustering of Gaussian components

In this section we describe the methodology for obtaining the final clusters from the Gaussian components used to represent the data. A minimal spanning tree (MST) based approach is adopted for this purpose. The MST

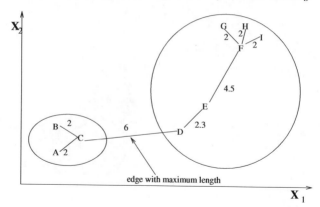

FIGURE 6.2:   Using minimal spanning tree to form clusters.

is a graph that connects a data set of n points so that a complete 'tree' of n-1 edges is built. (A tree is a connected graph without cycles.) The tree is 'minimal' when the total length of the edges is the minimum necessary to connect all the points. A MST may be constructed using either Kruskal's or Prim's algorithm. The Kruskal's algorithm is described in Section 6.4.4.1.

The desired number of clusters of points may be obtained from a MST by deleting the edges having highest weights. For example for the set of 9 points {A, B, C, D. E, F, G, H, I} illustrated in Figure 6.2, two clusters can be obtained by deleting the edge CD having highest weight 6. The two subgraphs represent the clusters. It may be mentioned that arbitrary shaped clusters may be obtained using the above algorithm.

Instead of using individual points, we construct a MST whose vertices are the Gaussian components of the mixture model and the edge weights are the Mahalanobis distance (D_M) between them defined as:

$$D_M^2 = (\mu_1 - \mu_2)^T (\Sigma_1 + \Sigma_2)^{-1} (\mu_1 - \mu_2) \tag{6.5}$$

where μ_1, μ_2, and Σ_1, Σ_2 are the means and variances of the pair of Gaussians. To obtain k clusters, $k - 1$ edges having the highest weights are deleted, and components belonging to a single connected subgraph after deletion are considered to represent a single cluster.

Note that each cluster obtained as above is a mixture model in itself. The number of its component Gaussians is equal to the number of vertices of the corresponding subgraph. For assigning a point ($\mathbf{x}$) to a cluster, probability of belongingness of $\mathbf{x}$ to each of the clusters (sub-mixture models) is computed using Equation 6.1, and the cluster giving the highest probability p($\mathbf{x}$) is assigned to $\mathbf{x}$, i.e., we follow the Bayesian classification rule.

6.4.4.1 Kruskal's algorithm for constructing MST

In Kruskal's algorithm, the nodes of the graph, with n data points as nodes, are initially considered as n distinct partial trees with one node each. At each step of the algorithm, two distinct partial trees are connected into a single partial tree by an edge of the graph. When only one partial tree exists (after $n-1$ such steps), it is a minimal spanning tree.

The issue of course is what connecting edge/arc to use at each step. The answer is to use the arc of minimum cost that connects two distinct trees. To do this, the arcs can be placed in a priority queue based on weight. The arc of lowest weight is then examined to see if it connects two distinct trees. To determine if an edge (x, y) connects distinct trees, we can implement the trees with a *father* field in each node. Then we can traverse all ancestors of x and y to obtain the roots of the trees containing them. If the roots of the two trees are the same node, x and y are already in the same tree, arc (x, y) is discarded, and the arc of the next lowest weight is examined. Combining two trees simply involves setting the father of the root of one to the root of the other.

Forming the initial priority queue is $O(e \log e)$, where e is the number of edges. Removing the minimum weight arc and adjusting the priority queue is $O(\log e)$. Locating the root of a tree is $O(\log n)$. Initial formation of n trees is $O(n)$. Thus, assuming that $n < e$, as is true in most graphs, Kruskal's algorithm is $O(e \log e)$.

6.5 Experimental Results and Comparison

Experiments are performed on two real life data sets (Forest cover type and Multiple features) with a large number of samples and dimension. An artificial non-convex data set (Pat) is also considered for the convenience of demonstrating some features of the algorithm along with visualization of the performance. The data sets are described in Appendix B.

The clustering results of the CEMMiSTRI algorithm, described in the previous section, are compared with those obtained using

1. k-means algorithm with random initialization (KM).

2. k-means algorithm with rough set initialization (of centers) and graph-theoretic clustering (RKMG).

3. EM algorithm with random initialization and graph-theoretic clustering (EMG).

4. EM algorithm with means initialized with the output of k-means algorithm and with graph-theoretic clustering (KEMG).

5. BIRCH [291].

Among the algorithms mentioned above, methods 2, 3, and 4 have the capability for obtaining non-convex clusters, while method 1 can obtain convex clusters only. It may be mentioned that the hybrid algorithm uses EM algorithm with rough set initialization and graph-theoretic clustering. For the purpose of comparison, in addition to rough set theoretic initialization, we have also considered EM algorithms with random initialization (method 3) and another popular method for initialization (method 4). Besides these, to demonstrate the effect of rough set theoretic initialization on another hybrid iterative refinement-graph theoretic clustering method, we consider method 2, which is the k-means algorithm with graph theoretic clustering. We could not present the comparisons with purely graph-theoretic techniques (i.e., on the original data) as they require an infeasibly long time for the data sets used.

Comparison is performed on the basis of cluster quality index β [198] and CPU time. CPU time is obtained on an Alpha 400 MHz workstation. β is defined as [198]:

$$\beta = \frac{\sum_{i=1}^{k} \sum_{j=1}^{n_i} (X_{ij} - \bar{X})^T (X_{ij} - \bar{X})}{\sum_{i=1}^{k} \sum_{j=1}^{n_i} (X_{ij} - \bar{X}_i)^T (X_{ij} - \bar{X}_i)} \tag{6.6}$$

where n_i is the number of points in the ith ($i = 1, \ldots, k$) cluster, X_{ij} is the feature vector of the jth pattern ($j = 1, \ldots, n_i$) in cluster i, $\bar{X}_i$ the mean of n_i patterns of the ith cluster, n is the total number of patterns, and $\bar{X}$ is the mean value of the entire set of patterns. Note that β is nothing but the ratio of the total variation and within-cluster variation. This type of measure is widely used for feature selection and cluster analysis [198]. For a given data and k (number of clusters) value, the higher the homogeneity within the clustered regions, the higher would be the β value.

For the purpose of visualization of the partitioning, and illustration of several characteristics of the algorithm, we first present the results on the artificial Pat data set which is of smaller dimension (=2). The non-convex character of the data is shown in Figure 6.3. The reducts obtained using rough set theory, and the parameters of the corresponding four Gaussians are as follows:

$$cluster_1 \leftarrow L_1 \wedge M_2; \quad w_1 = 0.15, \mu_1 = [0.223, 0.511], \Sigma_1 = \begin{bmatrix} 0.276 & 0 \\ 0 & 0.240 \end{bmatrix}$$

$$cluster_2 \leftarrow H_1 \wedge M_2; \quad w_2 = 0.16, \mu_2 = [0.753, 0.511], \Sigma_2 = \begin{bmatrix} 0.233 & 0 \\ 0 & 0.240 \end{bmatrix}$$

$$cluster_3 \leftarrow M_1 \wedge H_2; \quad w_3 = 0.35, \mu_3 = [0.499, 0.744], \Sigma_3 = \begin{bmatrix} 0.265 & 0 \\ 0 & 0.233 \end{bmatrix}$$

$$cluster_4 \leftarrow M_1 \wedge L_2; \quad w_4 = 0.34, \mu_4 = [0.499, 0.263], \Sigma_4 = \begin{bmatrix} 0.265 & 0 \\ 0 & 0.248 \end{bmatrix}$$

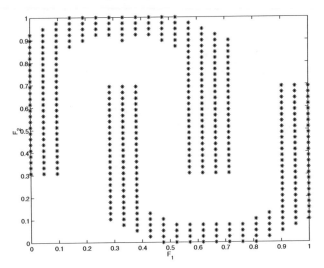

FIGURE 6.3: Scatter plot of the artificial data Pat.

The distribution of points belonging to each component Gaussian, obtained after refining the parameters using EM, is plotted in Figure 6.4. These are indicated by symbols: $+$, o, $\diamond$, and $\triangle$. The variation of log-likelihood with EM iteration is presented in Figure 6.5 for both random initialization and rough set initialization. It is seen that for rough set initialization log-likelihood attains a higher value at the start of EM. The final clusters (two in number) obtained by the integrated CEMMiSTRI after graph-theoretic partitioning of the Gaussians are shown in Figure 6.6(a). The algorithm is seen to produce the same natural non-convex partitions, as in the original data. It may be noted that the conventional k-means algorithm, which is capable of generating convex clusters efficiently, fails to do so (Figure 6.6(b)), as expected.

Table 6.1 provides comparative results (in terms of β and CPU time) of the CEMMiSTRI algorithm with other four, as mentioned before, for three different data sets. It is seen that the CEMMiSTRI algorithm produces clusters having the highest β value for all the cases. Note that, since no training/test set selection is involved, the concept of statistical significance is not applicable here. The CPU time required is less than that of the other two EM-based algorithms (EMG and KEMG). For the k-means algorithm (KM), although the CPU time requirement is very low, its performance is significantly poorer. The BIRCH algorithm requires the least CPU time but has performance poorer than the integrated algorithm, KEMG, EMG, and RKMG.

Rough set theoretic initialization is found to improve the β value as well as reduce the time requirement of both EM and k-means. It is also observed that k-means with rough set theoretic initialization (RKMG) performs better than EM with random initialization (EMG), although it is well known that EM is usually superior to k-means in partitioning.

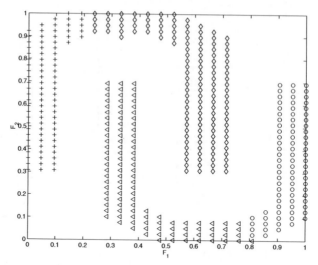

FIGURE 6.4: Scatter plot of points belonging to four different component Gaussians for the Pat data. Each Gaussian is represented by a separate symbol ($+$, o, $\diamond$, and $\triangle$).

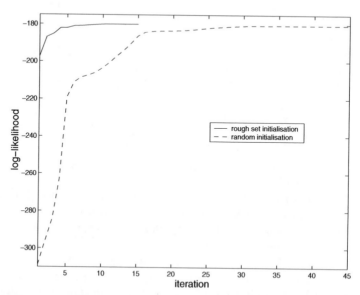

FIGURE 6.5: Variation of log-likelihood with EM iterations for the Pat data.

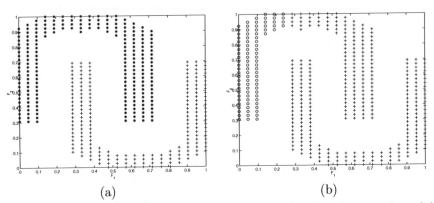

(a) (b)

FIGURE 6.6: Final clusters obtained using (a) hybrid algorithm (b) *k*-means algorithm for the Pat data (clusters are marked by '+' and 'o').

TABLE 6.1: Comparative performance of clustering algorithms

Algorithm	Cluster quality (β)	CPU time (sec)
Forest cover type data		
CEMMiSTRI	7.10	1021
KEMG	6.21	2075
EMG	5.11	1555
RKMG	5.90	590
KM	3.88	550
BIRCH	4.21	104
Multiple features data		
CEMMiSTRI	11.20	721
KEMG	10.90	881
EMG	10.40	810
RKMG	10.81	478
KM	7.02	404
BIRCH	8.91	32
Pat data		
CEMMiSTRI	18.10	1.04
KEMG	15.40	2.10
EMG	10.90	1.80
RKMG	15.30	0.91
KM	8.10	0.80
BIRCH	9.02	0.55

6.6 Multispectral Image Segmentation

In the present section, we describe an application of the CEMMiSTRI algorithm to another real life problem, namely, segmentation of multispectral satellite images into different land cover types. Merits of the methodology as depicted in the previous section are also found to hold good. Before we provide the results of investigations, we describe, in brief, the relevance of the methodology for multispectral image segmentation and the implementation procedure. Note that the process of fuzzy discretization used here is different from that used in the previous section.

Segmentation is a process of partitioning an image space into some nonoverlapping meaningful homogeneous regions. The success of an image analysis system depends on the quality of segmentation. Two broad approaches to segmentation of remotely sensed images are gray level thresholding and pixel classification. In thresholding [198] one tries to get a set of thresholds $\{T_1, T_2, \ldots, T_k\}$ such that all pixels with gray values in the range $[T_i, T_{i+1})$ constitute the ith region type. On the other hand in pixel classification, homogeneous regions are determined by clustering the feature space of multiple image bands. Both thresholding and pixel classification algorithms may be either local, i.e., context dependent, or global, i.e., blind to the position of a pixel. The multispectral nature of most remote sensing images make pixel classification the natural choice for segmentation.

Statistical methods are widely used in an unsupervised pixel classification framework because of their capability of handling uncertainties arising from both measurement error and the presence of mixed pixels. In most statistical approaches, an image is modeled as a 'random field' consisting of collections of two random variables $Y = (Y_s)_{s \in S}, X = (X_s)_{s \in S}$. The first one takes values in the field of 'classes,' while the second one deals with the field of 'measurements' or 'observations.' The problem of segmentation is to estimate Y from X. A general method of statistical clustering is to represent the probability density function of the data as a *mixture model*, which asserts that the data is a combination of k individual component densities (commonly Gaussians), corresponding to k clusters. The task is to identify, given the data, a set of k populations in it and provide a model (density distribution) for each of the populations. The EM algorithm is an effective and popular technique for estimating the mixture model parameters. It iteratively refines an initial cluster model to better fit the data and terminates at a solution which is locally optimal for the underlying clustering criterion [53]. An advantage of EM is that it is capable for handling uncertainties due to mixed pixels and helps in designing multivalued recognition systems. The EM algorithm has following limitations: (i) the number of clusters needs to be known, (ii) the solution depends strongly on initial conditions, and (iii) it can model only convex clusters.

The first limitation is a serious handicap in satellite image processing since in real images the number of classes is frequently difficult to determine a priori. To overcome the second, several methods for determining 'good' initial parameters for EM have been suggested, mainly based on subsampling, voting and two-stage clustering [159]. However, most of these methods have high computational requirements and/or are sensitive to noise. The stochastic EM

(SEM) algorithm [155] for segmentation of images is another attempt in this direction which provides an upper bound on the number of classes, robustness to initialization and fast convergence.

The clustering algorithm, described in Section 6.4, circumvents many of the above problems.

6.6.1 Discretization of image bands

Discretization of the feature space, for the purpose of rough set rule generation, is performed by gray level thresholding of the image bands individually. Thus, each attribute (band) now takes on values in $\{1, 2, ., k + 1\}$, where k is the number of threshold levels for that band. The fuzzy correlation $(C(\mu_1, \mu_2))$ between a fuzzy representation of an image (μ_1) and its nearest two-tone version (μ_2) is used. Fuzzy correlation $C(\mu_1, \mu_2)$ is defined as [196]

$$C(\mu_1, \mu_2) = 1 - \frac{4}{X_1 + X_2} \left(\sum_{i=0}^{T} \{[\mu_1(i)]^2 h(i)\} + \sum_{i=T+1}^{L-1} \{[1 - \mu_1(i)]^2 h(i)\} \right)$$

(6.7)

with $X_1 = \sum_{i=0}^{L-1} [2\mu_1(i) - 1]^2 h(i)$ and $X_2 = \sum_{i=0}^{L-1} [2\mu_2(i) - 1]^2 h(i) = \text{constant}$, $L - 1$ is the maximum grey level and $h(i)$ is the frequency of the ith grey level. The *maximas* of the $C(\mu_1, \mu_2)$ represent the threshold levels. For details of the above method one may refer to [196]. We have considered correlation as a measure of thresholding, since it is found recently to provide good segmentation in less computational time compared to similar methods [198]. However, any other gray level thresholding technique may be used. Note that we have not used fuzzy linguistic granulation of the feature space here since histogram-based thresholding provides a natural mean of discretization of images.

6.6.2 Integration of EM, MST and rough sets

Block diagram of the integrated segmentation methodology is shown in Figure 6.7.

6.6.3 Index for segmentation quality

Quality of the segmentation results is evaluated using the index β (Equation 6.6).

6.6.4 Experimental results and comparison

Results are presented on two IRS-1A (4 bands) images. The images were taken using LISS-II scanner in the wavelength range $0.77-0.86\mu m$ with a spatial resolution of $36.25m \times 36.25m$. The images are of size 512×512. They cover areas around the cities of Calcutta and Bombay.

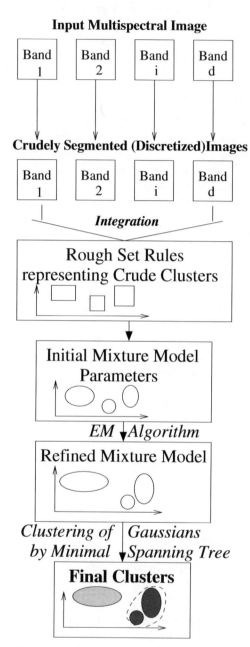

FIGURE 6.7:   Block diagram of the image segmentation algorithm.

For the Calcutta image the gray level thresholds obtained using the correlation based methodology are band 1: {34,47}, band 2: {20,29}, band 3: {24,30} and band 4: {31,36}. For the Bombay image the corresponding values are {36,60}, {22,51}, {23,68} and {11,25}. After discretization, the attribute value table is constructed. Eight rough set rules (for Calcutta image) and seven rules (for Bombay image), each representing a crude cluster, are obtained. The rules are then mapped to initial parameters of the component Gaussians and refined using EM algorithm. The Gaussians are then merged using the minimal spanning tree based technique discussed in Section 6.4.4, thereby resulting in five clusters (from original eight and seven Gaussians). For both the images, progressive improvement was observed from the initial gray level thresholding of the individual bands, clustering using crude mixture model obtained from rough set rules, clustering using refined mixture model obtained by EM, and finally to graph theoretic clustering of the component Gaussians.

The performance of the hybrid CEMMiSTRI algorithm is compared extensively with that of various other related ones, as mentioned in Section **??**. These involve different combinations of the individual components of the hybrid scheme, namely, rough set initialization, EM and MST, with other related schemes, e.g., random initialization and k-means algorithm. The algorithms compared are (a) randomly initialized EM and k-means algorithm (EM, KM) (best of 5 independent random initializations), (b) rough set initialized EM and k-means (centers) algorithm (REM, RKM), (c) EM initialized with the output of k-means algorithm (KMEM), (d) EM with random initialization and MST clustering (EMMST), and (e) fuzzy k-means (FKM) algorithm.

For the purpose of qualitative comparison of the segmentation results we have considered the index β (Equation 6.6). We also present the total CPU time required by these algorithms on a DEC Alpha 400 MHz workstation. It may be noted that except for the algorithms involving rough set, the number of clusters is not automatically determined.

Comparative results are presented in Tables 6.2 and 6.3. Segmented images of the city of Calcutta obtained by these algorithms are also presented in Figure 6.8, for visual inspection. For the Bombay image we show the segmented versions only for the CEMMiSTRI and the KM algorithm having the highest and lowest β values, respectively. The following conclusions can be arrived at from the results:

1. *EM vs k-means*: It is observed that EM is superior to k-means (KM) both with random and rough set initialization. However, k-means requires considerably less time compared to EM. The performance of fuzzy k-means (FKM) is intermediate between k-means and EM, though its time requirement is more than EM.

2. *Effect of rough set initialization*: Rough set theoretic initialization (REM, RKM) is found to improve the β value as well as reduce the time require-

TABLE 6.2: Comparative performance of different clustering methods for the Calcutta image

Algorithm	No. of clusters	Index β	Time (sec)
EM	5	5.91	1720
KM	5	5.25	801
REM	8	6.97	470
RKM	8	5.41	301
KMEM	8	6.21	1040
EMMST	5	6.44	1915
FKM	5	5.90	2011
CEMMiSTRI	5	7.37	505

ment substantially for both EM and k-means. Rough set initialization is also superior to k-means initialization (KMEM).

3. *Contribution of MST*: Use of MST adds a small computational load to the EM algorithms (EM, REM); however, the corresponding integrated methods (EMMST and the CEMMiSTRI algorithm) show a definite increase in β value.

4. Integration of all three components, EM, rough set and MST, in the hybrid CEMMiSTRI algorithm produces the best segmentation in terms of β value in the least computation time. This is also supported visually if we consider Figures 6.10 and 6.11 which demonstrate the zoomed image of two man-made structures, viz., river bridge and airport strips of the Calcutta image corresponding to the integrated method and KM algorithm providing the highest and lowest β values, respectively.

5. *Computation time*: It is observed that the CEMMiSTRI algorithm requires significantly less time compared to other algorithms having comparable performance. Reduction in time is achieved due to two factors. Rough set initialization reduces the convergence time of the EM algorithm considerably compared to random initialization. Also, since the MST is designed on component Gaussians rather than individual data points it adds very little load to the overall time requirement while improving the performance significantly.

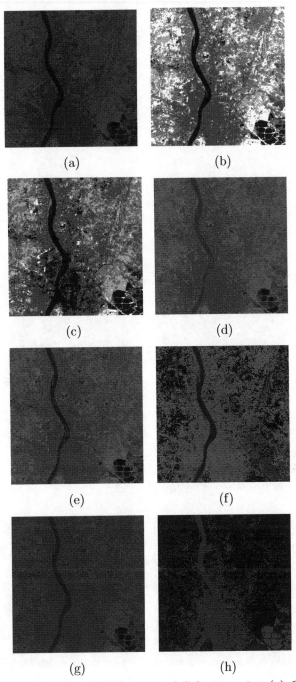

(a) (b)

(c) (d)

(e) (f)

(g) (h)

FIGURE 6.8: Segmented IRS image of Calcutta using (a) CEMMiSTRI, (b) EM with MST (EMMST), (c) fuzzy k-means algorithm (FKM), (d) rough set initialized EM (REM), (e) EM with k-means initialization (KMEM), (f) rough set initialized k-means (RKM), (g) EM with random initialization (EM), (h) k-means with random initialization (KM).

TABLE 6.3: Comparative performance of different clustering methods for the Bombay image

Algorithm	No. of clusters	Index β	Time (sec)
EM	5	9.11	1455
KM	5	8.45	701
REM	7	10.12	381
RKM	7	10.00	277
KMEM	7	12.71	908
EMMST	5	14.04	1750
FKM	5	9.20	1970
CEMMiSTRI	5	17.10	395

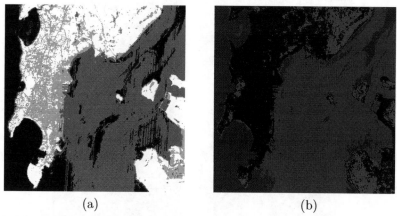

(a)   (b)

FIGURE 6.9: Segmented IRS image of Bombay using (a) CEMMiSTRI, (b) k-means with random initialization (KM).

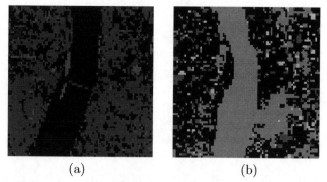

(a)   (b)

FIGURE 6.10: Zoomed images of a bridge on the river Ganges in Calcutta for (a) CEMMiSTRI, (b) k-means with random initialization (KM).

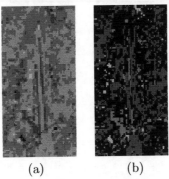

(a) (b)

FIGURE 6.11: Zoomed images of two parallel airstrips of Calcutta airport for (a) CEMMiSTRI, (b) k-means with random initialization (KM).

6.7 Summary

First we have provided a brief review on different clustering approaches, followed by some commonly used algorithms, e.g., CLARANS, BIRCH, DB-SCAN, and STING, applicable to large data sets. Then the CEMMiSTRI method integrating EM algorithm, MST and rough sets is described in detail which provides efficient clustering of intractable pattern classes and is scalable to large data sets.

Rough-fuzzy granular computing is found to be successful in effectively circumventing the initialization and local minima problems of iterative refinement clustering algorithms (like EM and k-means). In addition, this improves the clustering performance, as measured by β value.

The merits of integrating graph-theoretic clustering (e.g., capability of generating non-convex clusters) and iterative refinement clustering (such as low computational time requirement) are also demonstrated. At the local level the data is modeled by Gaussians, i.e., as combination of convex sets, while globally these Gaussians are partitioned using graph-theoretic technique, thereby enabling the efficient detection of the non-convex clusters present in the original data. Since the number of Gaussians is much less than the total number of data points, the computational time requirement for this integrated method is much less than that required by a conventional graph theoretic clustering.

Chapter 7

Rough Self-Organizing Map

7.1   Introduction

In the previous two chapters we have demostrated how rough sets and the concept of granular computing can be integrated with fuzzy sets to design efficient algorithms for performing data mining tasks like case generation and clustering. In this chapter we describe how the said concept can be embedded into a self-organizing map (SOM) for clustering, thereby generating a rough-SOM.

In the framework of rough-neuro computing, research has been done mainly in the following three directions: (a) use of rough sets for encoding weights of knowledge-based networks, (b) incorporating roughness in the neuronal level, and (c) rough set theoretic interpretation of network outputs. It may be noted that most of the integrations are made in supervised framework using layered networks [17, 264]. Therefore, the uniqueness of the rough-SOM is evident.

The self-organizing map [119] is an unsupervised network which has recently become popular for unsupervised mining of large data sets. The process of self-organization generates a network whose weights represent prototypes of the input data. Performance of the SOM can be further enhanced by appropriate selection of the initial parameters of the map. This circumvents, to a certain extent, the problems of slow convergence and local minima. Three main approaches to SOM initialization [119] are (a) random initialization, (b) initialization using data samples, and (c) linear initialization. Random initialization simply means that random values are assigned to parameters. In case of initialization with data samples, the initial parameters (code book vectors) automatically lie in the same part of the feature space as that of the input data. The linear initialization method takes advantage of the principal component (PCA) analysis of the input data. The parameters here are initialized to lie in the same subspace that is spanned by two eigenvectors corresponding to the largest eigenvalues of the input data. This has the effect of stretching the self-organizing map in a direction along which the data contains the most significant amount of energy. The linear initialization method provides superior performance compared to the first two but has substantial computational overhead for large data sets. It also performs poorly when the data is spherically distributed over all the dimensions.

The significance of this chapter is twofold. First, it demonstrates how rough set theory can be integrated with SOM, thereby designing the rough self-organizing map (RSOM). Second, it shows how the RSOM can offer a fast and robust solution to the initialization and local minima problems of SOM. In RSOM, rough set theoretic knowledge is used to encode the weights as well as to determine the network size. Fuzzy set theory is used for discretization of the feature space. Information granules in the discretized feature space are then used for rule generation using rough set theory. The rules are mapped to the parameters of the SOM. Since the computation is performed on the granules rather than the data points, the time required is small and therefore the RSOM is suitable for large data sets. Also, the rough set rules used for encoding correspond to different cluster centers of the data and thus provide a good initialization of the parameters. The trained RSOM is then used for generating linguistic rules. The methodology considers only the strong link weights of the networks, thereby providing only those rules that are superior in terms of coverage, reachability and fidelity.

Self-organizing performance of the RSOM is measured in terms of learning time, representation error, cluster quality and network compactness. All these characteristics have been demonstrated on four different data sets and compared with those of the randomly and linearly initialized SOMs. Since the rules produced by RSOM are linguistic, comparison is made here with a fuzzy self-organizing map (FSOM) [172], which is also capable of generating linguistic rules.

The organization of the chapter is as follows: A brief description of the conventional SOM is presented in Section 7.2 for convenience. This is followed by the methodology for designing the RSOM in Section 7.3. The algorithm for rule extraction and their evaluation indices are also described in Section 7.4. Experimental results and comparisons are provided in Section 7.5 followed by concluding remarks in Section 7.6.

7.2 Self-Organizing Maps (SOM)

The self-organizing map or the Kohonen feature map is a two-layered network. The first layer of the network is the input layer. The second layer, called the competitive layer, is usually organized as a two-dimensional grid. All interconnections go from the first layer to the second (Figure 7.1).

All the nodes in the competitive layer compare the inputs with their weights and compete with each other to become the winning unit having the lowest difference. The basic idea underlying what is called competitive learning is roughly as follows: Assume a sequence of input vectors $\{\mathbf{x} = \mathbf{x}(t) \in R^n\}$, where t is the time coordinate, and a set of variable reference vectors $\{\mathbf{m}_i(t) :$

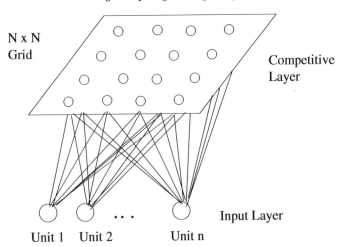

FIGURE 7.1: The basic network structure for the Kohonen feature map.

$\mathbf{m}_i \in R^n$, $i = 1, 2, \ldots, k\}$ where k is the number of units in the competitive layer. Initially the values of the reference vectors (also called weight vectors) are set randomly. At each successive instant of time t, an input pattern $\mathbf{x}(t)$ is presented to the network. The input pattern $\mathbf{x}(t)$ is then compared with each $\mathbf{m}_i(t)$ and the best matching $\mathbf{m}_i(t)$ is updated to match even more closely the current $\mathbf{x}(t)$.

If the comparison is based on some distance measure $d(\mathbf{x}, m_i)$, altering $\mathbf{m}_i$ must be such that, if $i = c$ the index of the best-matching reference vector, then $d(\mathbf{x}, \mathbf{m}_c)$ is reduced, and all the other reference vectors $\mathbf{m}_i$, with $i \neq c$, are left intact. In this way the different reference vectors tend to become specifically "tuned" to different domains of the input variable $\mathbf{x}$.

7.2.1 Learning

The first step in the operation of a Kohonen network is to compute a matching value for each unit in the competitive layer. This value measures the extent to which the weights or reference vectors of each unit match the corresponding values of the input pattern. The matching value for each unit i is $||x_j - m_{ij}||$ which is the distance between vectors $\mathbf{x}$ and $\mathbf{m}_i$ and is computed by

$$\sqrt{\sum_j (x_j - m_{ij})^2} \quad \text{for} \quad j = 1, 2, \ldots, n \tag{7.1}$$

The unit with the lowest matching value (the best match) wins the competition. In other words, the unit c is said to be the best matched unit if

$$||\mathbf{x} - \mathbf{m}_c|| = \min_i \left\{ ||\mathbf{x} - \mathbf{m}_i|| \right\}, \tag{7.2}$$

where the minimum is taken over all units i in the competitive layer. If two units have the same matching value, then by convention, the unit with the lower index value i is chosen.

The next step is to self-organize a two-dimensional map that reflects the distribution of input patterns. In biophysically inspired neural network models, correlated learning by spatially neighboring cells can be implemented using various kinds of lateral feedback connections and other lateral interactions. Here the lateral interaction is enforced directly in a general form, for arbitrary underlying network structures, by defining a neighborhood set N_c around the winning cell. At each learning step, all the cells within N_c are updated, whereas cells outside N_c are left intact. The update equation is:

$$\Delta m_{ij} = \begin{cases} \alpha(x_j - m_{ij}) & \text{if unit } i \text{ is in the neighborhood } N_c, \\ 0 & \text{otherwise,} \end{cases} \qquad (7.3)$$

and

$$m_{ij}^{\text{new}} = m_{ij}^{\text{old}} + \Delta m_{ij} \qquad (7.4)$$

Here α is the learning parameter. This adjustment results in both the winning unit and its neighbors, having their weights modified, becoming more like the input pattern. The winner then becomes more likely to win the competition should the same or a similar input pattern be presented subsequently.

7.2.2   Effect of neighborhood

The width or radius of N_c can be time-variable; in fact, for good global ordering, it has experimentally turned out to be advantageous to let N_c be very wide in the beginning and shrink monotonically with time (Figure 7.2). This is because a wide initial N_c, corresponding to a coarse spatial resolution in the learning process, first induces a rough global order in the m_i values, after which narrowing of N_c improves the spatial resolution of the map; the acquired global order, however, is not destroyed later on. This allows the topological order of the map to be formed.

7.3   Incorporation of Rough Sets in SOM (RSOM)

As described in the previous chapter, the dependency rules generated using rough set theory from an information system are used to discern objects with respect to their attributes. However the dependency rules generated by rough set are coarse and therefore need to be fine-tuned. Here the dependency rules are used to get a crude knowledge of the cluster boundaries of the input patterns to be fed to a self-organizing map [193]. This crude knowledge is used to encode the initial weights of the nodes of the map, which is then trained

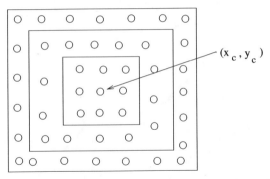

FIGURE 7.2:   Neighborhood N_c, centered on unit c (x_c, y_c). Three different neighborhoods are shown at distance $d = 1, 2,$ and 3.

using the usual learning process (Section 7.2). Since an initial knowledge about the cluster boundaries is encoded into the network, the learning time reduces greatly with improved performance.

The steps involved in the process are described in the next two sections.

7.3.1   Unsupervised rough set rule generation

Fuzzy discretization: From the initial data set, use fuzzy discretization process to create the information system.

Rough set rule generation: For each object in the information table, generate the discernibility function

$$f_A (\bar{a}_1, \bar{a}_2, \ldots, \bar{a}_{3n}) = \wedge \{\vee c_{ij} | 1 \le j \le i \le 3n, c_{ij} \ne \phi\} \qquad (7.5)$$

where $\bar{a}_1, \bar{a}_2, \ldots, \bar{a}_{3n}$ are the $3n$ Boolean variables corresponding to the attributes $a_1, a_2, \ldots, a_{3n}$ of each object in the information system. The expression f_A is reduced to its set of prime implicants, which generates the set of all reducts of A.

7.3.2   Mapping rough set rules to network weights

Determination of network topology: The self-organizing map is created with $3n$ inputs (Section 7.2), which correspond to the attributes of the information table, and a competitive layer of $P \times P$ grid of units where P is the total number of implicants present in discernibility functions of all the objects of the information table.

Determination of network parameters: Each implicant of the function f_A is mapped to one unit per row in the competitive layer of the network (i.e., for P implicants the size of the competitive layer is $P \times P$). High weights are given to those links that come from the attributes which occur in the implicant expression. The idea behind this is that when an input pattern belonging to

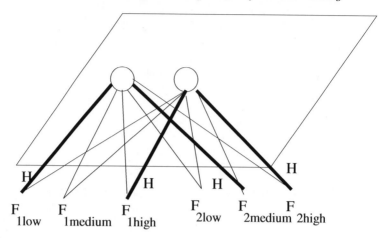

FIGURE 7.3:   Mapping of reducts in the competitive layer of RSOM.

an object, say O_i, is applied to the inputs of the network, one of the implicants of the discernibility function of O_i will be satisfied and the corresponding unit in the competitive layer will fire and emerge as the winning unit. In this way the initial knowledge obtained with rough set methodology is used to train the SOM. This is explained with the following example.

Let the reduct of an object O_i be

$$O_i : (F_{1low} \wedge F_{2medium}) \vee (F_{1high} \wedge F_{2high})$$

where $F_{(\cdot)low}, F_{(\cdot)medium}$ and $F_{(\cdot)high}$ represent the low, medium, and high values of the corresponding features.

Then the implicants are mapped to the nodes of the layer in the following manner. Here high weights (H) are given only to those links which come from the features present in the implicant expression. Other links are given low weights as in Figure 7.3.

After the network is trained, linguistic rules are generated from the network and are quantitatively evaluated in terms of strength of the rules, and coverage, reachability and fidelity of the rule base.

7.4   Rule Generation and Evaluation

7.4.1   Extraction methodology

The steps involved in extraction of rules from the trained RSOM are given below:

1. Let f_{th} be a frequency threshold having value equal to 0.5 times the frequency of the highest winning node.

2. Consider only those nodes $(n_i,\ i = 1, \ldots, w)$ of the competitive layer for which the number of times the node has won during training is greater than f_{th}.

3. For such a node n_i, take into account only those links whose weight values are greater than 0.5. All other links of the node are ignored during rule generation. Thus if the links F_{1low} and $F_{2medium}$ of the node n_i have weight values greater than 0.5, then the rule extracted from the node will be $(F_{1low} \wedge F_{2medium})$.

4. The disjunction of all such rules extracted from the nodes belonging to the same cluster gives rise to a combined rule for that cluster.

7.4.2 Evaluation indices

Here we provide some measures in order to evaluate the performance of the rules extracted from the network.

i) Strength

Let m_{ij} be weight of the jth link of a node i having winning frequency greater than f_{th}. Then the strength (s) of the rules extracted from the node i is given by

$$s = \frac{\sum_j m_{ij} \geq 0.5}{\sum_j m_{ij}} \tag{7.6}$$

where $j = 1, \ldots, 3n$, $3n$ being the number of input features to the net. Thus, higher the strength of the rule, greater is the value of the link weights of the node whose features appear in the rule.

ii) Cover

Ideally the rules extracted should cover all the cluster regions of the pattern space. One may use the percentage of samples from the input data set for which no rules have fired as a measure of the uncovered region. A rule base having a smaller uncovered region is superior.

iii) Reachability

Reachability (R) of a rule base represents the number of rules that each sample of the input data set can alone fire or can alone reach. If r_i is the number of rules that the ith sample of the input data set can fire then reachability of the rule base is given by

$$R = \frac{\sum_{i=1}^{l} r_i}{l} \tag{7.7}$$

where l is the total number of samples in the input data set. Ideally, each input sample should be reached by one and only one rule and there should not be any uncovered region. Under this condition R equals to 1. A value of

R less than 1 implies that the rule base is incomplete and provides uncovered region. On the other hand, a value of R greater than 1 implies the presence of ambiguous and/or redundant rules.

iv) Fidelity

Fidelity represents how closely the rule base approximates the parent neural network model. It is defined as the percentage of the input data set for which the network and the rule base output agree.

v) Size of the rule base

The size of the rule base is measured by the number of rules extracted from the network.

7.5 Experimental Results and Comparison

Some experimental results [193] for four different data, namely, Pat, Vowel, Forest cover type and Satellite image are presented here. All these data sets are described in Appendix B.

The Pat data has non-convex clusters, while the vowel classes are overlapping. Since the problems of slow convergence and local minima are acute for such data sets, they have been considered here to demonstrate the effectiveness of RSOM. Moreover, since the Pat data set is two dimensional the results relating to it can be visually verified. The other data sets, namely, Forest cover data and Satellite image data have large sizes typical of data mining applications.

As an illustration of the parameters of the fuzzy membership functions and the rough set reducts, we mention them below only for the Pat data.

$$
\begin{aligned}
c_{low}(F_1) &= 0.223095 \\
c_{medium}(F_1) &= 0.499258 \\
c_{high}(F_1) &= 0.753786 \\
\lambda_{low}(F_1) &= 0.276163 \\
\lambda_{medium}(F_1) &= 0.254528 \\
\lambda_{high}(F_1) &= 0.265345
\end{aligned}
$$

$$
\begin{aligned}
c_{low}(F_2) &= 0.263265 \\
c_{medium}(F_2) &= 0.511283 \\
c_{high}(F_2) &= 0.744306 \\
\lambda_{low}(F_2) &= 0.248019 \\
\lambda_{medium}(F_2) &= 0.233022 \\
\lambda_{high}(F_2) &= 0.240521
\end{aligned}
$$

$$O_1 : (F_{1low} \wedge F_{2high}) \vee (F_{1medium} \wedge F_{2high})$$
$$O_2 : (F_{1low} \wedge F_{2medium})$$
$$O_3 : (F_{1high} \wedge F_{2medium})$$
$$O_4 : (F_{1high} \wedge F_{2low}) \vee (F_{1medium} \wedge F_{2low})$$

7.5.1 Clustering and quantization error

To demonstrate the effectiveness of the RSOM, its performance is compared with those of the randomly initialized self-organizing map and the linearly initialized self-organizing map. The following measures are considered for comparison.

i. Initialization time t_{init}

This measures the time required to generate the initial parameters of the self-organizing maps.

ii. Quantization Error

The quantization error (q_E) measures how fast the weight vectors of the winning nodes in the competitive layer are aligning themselves with the input vectors presented during training. It is defined as:

$$q_E = \frac{\sum_{p=1}^{l} \left(\sum_{\text{all winning nodes}} \sqrt{\left(\sum_j (x_{pj} - m_j)^2 \right)} \right)}{l}, \quad (7.8)$$

where $j = 1, \ldots, 3n$, $3n$ represents the number of input features to the network, x_{pj} is the jth component of pth pattern and l is the total number of patterns. Hence, higher the quantization error (q_E), larger is the difference between the reference vectors and the input vectors of the nodes in the competitive layer.

iii. Entropy and β-index

For measuring the quality of cluster structure two indices, namely, an entropy measure [198] and β-index [198] are used. These are defined below.

Entropy:

Let the distance between two weight vectors p, q be

$$D_{pq} = \left[\sum_j \left(\frac{x_{pj} - x_{qj}}{\max_j - \min_j} \right)^2 \right]^{\frac{1}{2}} \quad j = 1, 2, \ldots, 3n \quad (7.9)$$

where x_{pj} and x_{qj} denote the weight values for p and q respectively along the jth direction. $\max_j$ and $\min_j$ are, respectively, the maximum and minimum values computed over all the samples along jth axis.

Let the similarity between p, q be defined as

$$\text{sim}(p, q) = e^{-\gamma D_{pq}}, \quad (7.10)$$

where $\gamma = \frac{-\ln 0.5}{\bar{D}}$, a positive constant, is such that

$$\text{sim}(p, q) = \begin{cases} 1 & \text{if } D_{pq} = 0 \\ 0 & \text{if } D_{pq} = \infty \\ 0.5 & \text{if } D_{pq} = \bar{D}. \end{cases} \tag{7.11}$$

$\bar{D}$ is the average distance between points computed over the entire data set. Entropy is defined as

$$E = -\sum_{p=1}^{l}\sum_{q=1}^{l}\left(\text{sim}(p, q) \times \log \text{sim}(p, q) + (1 - sim(p, q)) \times \log(1 - \text{sim}(p, q))\right).$$

$$\tag{7.12}$$

If the data is uniformly distributed in the feature space entropy is maximum. When the data has well-formed clusters, uncertainty is low and so is entropy.

β-index :

β-index [198] is defined as:

$$\beta = \frac{\sum_{i=1}^{k}\sum_{p=1}^{l_i}\left(\mathbf{x}_p^i - \bar{\mathbf{x}}\right)^T\left(\mathbf{x}_p^i - \bar{\mathbf{x}}\right)}{\sum_{i=1}^{k}\sum_{p=1}^{l_i}\left(\mathbf{x}_p^i - \bar{\mathbf{x}}^i\right)^T\left(\mathbf{x}_p^i - \bar{\mathbf{x}}^i\right)} \tag{7.13}$$

where l_i is the number of points in the ith ($i = 1, \ldots, k$) cluster, $\mathbf{x}_p^i$ is the pth pattern ($p = 1, \ldots, l_i$) in cluster i, $\bar{\mathbf{x}}^i$ is the mean of l_i patterns of the ith cluster, and $\bar{\mathbf{x}}$ is the mean value of the entire set of patterns. Note that β is nothing but the ratio of the total variation and within-cluster variation. This type of measure is widely used for feature selection and cluster analysis. For a given data set and k (number of clusters) value, as the homogeneity within the clustered regions increases, the value of β increases. It may be mentioned here that β-index is used in Chapter 6 for measuring segmentation quality of images.

iv. Frequency of Winning Nodes (f_k)

Let k be the number of rules (characterizing the clusters) obtained using rough sets. For example $k = 4$ for Pat data, $k = 14$ for vowel data, $k = 2955$ for forest cover data, and $k = 789$ for satellite image data. Then f_k denotes the number of wins of the top k nodes in the competitive layer. f_k reflects the error if all but k nodes would have been pruned. In other words, it measures the number of sample points correctly represented by these nodes.

v. Number of Iterations for Convergence

This means the number of iterations after which the error does not vary more than 1% in successive iterations.

The comparative results for the four data sets are presented in Table 7.1. The following conclusions can be made from the obtained results:

1. *Less initialization time:* The initialization time (t_{init}) required for RSOM is least compared to others for all the data sets. This is due to the fact that,

TABLE 7.1: Comparison of RSOM with randomly and linearly initialized SOM

Data	Initialization method	t_{init} (sec)	Quant. error	Iteration	Entropy	f_k	β-index
	Random	0	0.038	5000	0.7557	83	0.99
Pat	Linear	2.71	0.027	450	0.6802	87	0.99
	Rough	2.52	0.022	50	0.6255	112	0.99
	Random	0	32.58	8830	0.6717	245	0.06
Vowel	Linear	2.82	0.090	90	0.6020	250	1.02
	Rough	2.75	0.081	95	0.6141	316	0.96
	Random	0	5.950	220	0.9897	1.02×10^4	2.52
Forest Cover	Linear	4096	0.405	25	0.9590	1.07×10^5	4.82
	Rough	253	0.205	22	0.9020	4.04×10^5	8.97
	Random	0	2.90	1080	0.4230	1.04×10^3	2.12
Satellite Image	Linear	1045	0.702	455	0.3520	7.12×10^3	7.97
	Rough	121	0.505	28	0.2897	2.02×10^4	2.02

in rough set framework, computation is performed on information granules rather than the individual data points, thereby requiring less time.

2. *Better cluster quality:* RSOM has lowest value of entropy for all the data sets except vowel, thus implying lower intracluster distance and higher intercluster distance in the clustered space. Since PCA is better applicable to vowel data, linear initialization is more effective here. Similar is the case with β-index, indicating that RSOM provides more homogeneity within its clustered regions. The quantization error of RSOM is least compared to other methods for all the data sets.

3. *Less learning time:* The number of iterations required by RSOM to achieve the least error level is seen to be least for all the cases, except the vowel data where linear SOM has a slight edge. The convergence curves of the quantization errors are presented, for convenience, in Figures 7.4–7.5 only for the Pat and vowel data sets. It is seen that RSOM starts from a very low value of quantization error compared to the other two methods.

4. *Compact representation of data:* It is seen from f_k values that in the case of RSOM fewer nodes in the competitive layer dominate; i.e., they win for most of the samples in the training set. On the other hand, in random and linear SOM this number is larger. This means RSOM should have the least errors if all but k nodes would have been pruned. In other words, RSOM achieves a more compact representation of the data.

As a demonstration of the nature of distribution of the frequency of winning nodes, the results corresponding to random SOM and RSOM are shown in Figures 7.6 and 7.7, respectively, only for the two-dimensional Pat data. Separation between the clusters is seen to be more prominent in Figure 7.7. These winning nodes may be viewed as the prototype points (cases) representing the two classes. Unlike the random SOM, here the prototypes selected are not just a subset of the original data points; rather they represent, like linear SOM, some collective information generated by the network after learning the entire data set.

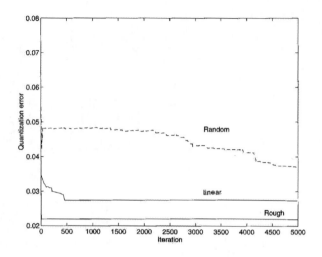

FIGURE 7.4:   Variation of quantization error with iteration for Pat data.

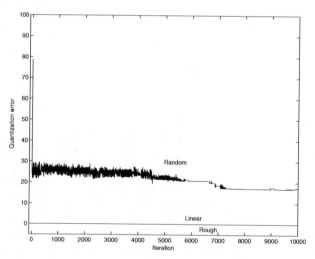

FIGURE 7.5:   Variation of quantization error with iteration for vowel data.

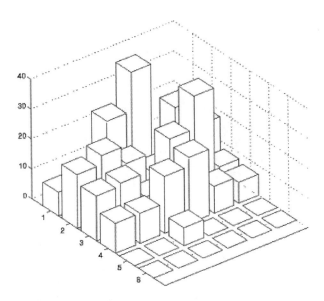

FIGURE 7.6:   Plot showing the frequency of winning nodes using random weights for the Pat data.

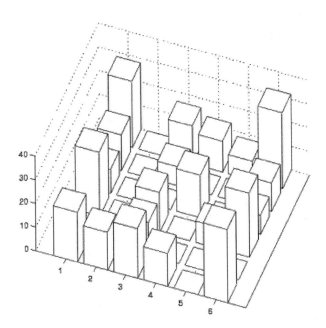

FIGURE 7.7:   Plot showing the frequency of winning nodes using rough set knowledge for the Pat data.

TABLE 7.2:   Comparison of rules extracted from RSOM and FSOM

Data	Method	Uncovered region	Fidelity	Reachability	No. of rules
Pat	RSOM	5.25%	14.6%	1.6	10
	FSOM	7.67%	23.0%	1.4	14
Vowel	RSOM	5.25%	14.6%	1.6	10
	FSOM	7.67%	23.0%	1.4	14
Forest	RSOM	23.12%	17.20%	1.2	509
Cover	FSOM	41.04%	27.00%	1.1	2537
Satellite	RSOM	11.02%	11.27%	2.2	112
Image	FSOM	17.19%	19.02%	2.5	205

7.5.2 Performance of rules

The linguistic rules obtained from RSOM are compared with those extracted from fuzzy self-organizing map (FSOM) [172] in terms of uncovered region, fidelity and reachability of the rule base (Table 7.2). As mentioned earlier since the rules produced by RSOM are linguistic, comparison is made here with a fuzzy self-organizing map (FSOM) [172] which is also capable of generating linguistic rules.

The rules extracted from RSOM for the Pat and vowel data sets are given below as an example. The rules are seen to model well the class distribution of the data sets. The subscripts denote the strength of the individual rules.

Pat data:

Cluster 1: $(F_{1low} \wedge F_{2medium})_{0.80} \vee F_{1low_{0.67}} \vee F_{2high_{0.59}} \vee F_{2medium_{0}}.58 \vee (F_{1high} \wedge F_{2medium})_{0.79}$

Cluster 2: $(F_{1high} \wedge F_{2high})_{0.75} \vee F_{1high_{0.52}} \vee F_{1medium_{0.70}} \vee F_{2low_{0.63}} \vee (F_{1low} \wedge F_{2low})_{0.78}$

Vowel data:

Cluster 1: $(F_{1low} \wedge F_{2high} \wedge F_{3medium})_{0.86} \vee (F_{1medium} \wedge F_{2low} \wedge F_{2low})_{0.93} \vee (F_{1low} \wedge F_{2low} \wedge F_{3low})_{0.92}$

Cluster 2: $F_{2high_{0.75}} \vee (F_{2high} \wedge F_{3medium})_{0.82}$

Cluster 3: $(F_{1medium} \wedge F_{2high} F_{3medium})_{0.88} \vee (F_{1medium} \wedge F_{2high} \wedge F_{3high})_{0.90}$

Cluster 4: $(F_{1low} \wedge F_{2high} \wedge F_{3high})_{0.92}$

Cluster 5: $(F_{2high} \wedge F_{3high})_{0.82} \vee (F_{1medium} \wedge F_{2low} \wedge F_{3medium})_{0.86}$

Cluster 6: $(F_{1medium} \wedge F_{2low} \wedge F_{3high})_{0.90} \vee (F_{1low} \wedge F_{2low} \wedge F_{3medium})_{0.88} \vee (F_{1low} \wedge F_{2medium})_{0.77}$

The rule base extracted from RSOM is much smaller in size and yet it yields better fidelity, i.e., provides more accurate representation of the parent network compared to that of FSOM. In spite of the smaller size of the rule base, the coverage of RSOM is better than that of FSOM, keeping comparable reachability.

7.6 Summary

A method of designing a self-organizing map incorporating the theory of rough sets with fuzzy discretization is described. Rough set theory is used to encode domain knowledge in the form of crude rules, which are mapped for initialization of the weights of SOM. It offers a fast and robust solution through granular computation. The aforesaid integration [193] of rough sets with SOM is the first of its kind. Besides it helps in reducing the local minima and convergence problems of SOM learning, as an application specific merit.

Superiority of the model (RSOM), compared to both random and linear initialization of weights of SOM, is demonstrated in terms of learning time, quality of clusters and quantization error. Here the clusters obtained by RSOM are mostly found to be more compact with prominent boundaries; i.e., the resulting SOM is sparse with fewer separated winning nodes. This observation is more prominent for the large data sets, thereby signifying the importance of RSOM for data mining applications.

Since RSOM achieves compact clusters, it enables one to generate a rule base which contains fewer number of linguistic rules, yet provides better representation of the network as compared to fuzzy SOM (FSOM) in terms of fidelity and coverage. The concept of rough knowledge encoding, described here, may also be applied in enhancing the performance of Batch-SOM [120], which is widely used in data mining problems.

Chapter 8

Classification, Rule Generation and Evaluation using Modular Rough-fuzzy MLP

8.1 Introduction

So far we have described various data mining tasks such as condensation, feature selection, learning, case generation and clustering. The present chapter deals with the tasks of classification, rule generation and rule evaluation. Here we describe a synergistic integration of four soft computing components, namely, fuzzy sets, rough sets, neural networks and genetic algorithms along with modular decomposition strategy, for generating a modular rough-fuzzy multilayer perceptron (MLP). The resulting connectionist system achieves gain in terms of performance, learning time and network compactness for classification and linguistic rule generation. Different quantitative indices are used for evaluating the linguistic rules, and to reflect the knowledge discovery aspect.

There are ongoing efforts during the past decade to integrate fuzzy logic, artificial neural networks (ANN) and genetic algorithms (GAs) to build efficient systems in soft computing paradigm. Recently, the theory of rough sets [213, 214], as explained before, is also being used in soft computing [209]. The rough-fuzzy MLP [17], developed in 1998 for pattern classification, is such an example for building an efficient connectionist system. In this hybridization, fuzzy sets help in handling linguistic input information and ambiguity in output decision, while rough sets extract the domain knowledge for determining the network parameters. Some other attempts in using rough sets (either individually or in combination with fuzzy set) for designing supervised neural network systems are available in [264] where rough sets are used mainly for generating the network parameters, and in [223] where roughness at the neuronal level has been incorporated. One may also note the utility of GAs in determining the network parameters as well as the topology (growing/pruning of links), as has been noticed during the past decade [192]. Several algorithms have been developed for extracting embedded knowledge, in the form of symbolic rules, from these hybrid networks [110, 268, 270].

Two important issues which have not been adequately addressed by the above methodologies are those of lengthy training time and poor interpretability of the networks. A major disadvantage in neural networks learning of large scale tasks is the high computational time required (due to local minima and slow convergence). Use of knowledge-based networks offers only a partial solution to the problem. Also, in most of the above methodologies the link weights of the network are rather uniformly distributed and the network is not suitable for extracting crisp (certain) rules. Compact networks with structure imposed on the weight values are more desirable in this respect for network interpretation. The concept of modular learning (in an evolutionary framework) is considered to deal with these problems.

A recent trend in neural network design for large scale problems is to split the original task into simpler subtasks, and to co-evolve the subnetwork modules for each of the subtasks [90]. The modules are then combined to obtain the final solution. Some of the advantages of this modular approach include decomplexification of the task, and its meaningful and clear neural representation. The *divide and conquer* strategy leads to super-linear speed-up in training. It also avoids the 'temporal crosstalk problem' and interference while learning. In addition, the number of parameters (i.e., weights) can be reduced using modularity, thereby leading to a better generalization performance of the network [235], compactness in size and crispness in extracted rules. It may be mentioned here that the said modular approach provides a way of ensemble learning, which has recently become popular for large-scale learning problems.

In the present chapter a modular evolutionary approach is adopted for designing a hybrid connectionist system in soft computing framework for both classification and classificatory rule generation. The basic building block used is the rough-fuzzy MLP [17], mentioned earlier. The original classification task is split into several subtasks and a number of rough-fuzzy MLPs are obtained for each subtask. The subnetwork modules are integrated in a particular manner so as to preserve the crude domain knowledge which was encoded in them using rough sets. The pool of integrated networks is then evolved using a GA with a restricted (adaptive/variable) mutation operator that utilizes the domain knowledge to accelerate training and preserves the localized rule structure as potential solutions. The parameters for input and output fuzzy membership functions of the network are also tuned using GA together with the link weights. A procedure for generation of rough set dependency rules for handling directly the real valued attribute table containing fuzzy membership values is used. This helps in preserving all the class representative points in the dependency rules by adaptively applying a threshold that automatically takes care of the shape of membership functions. Unlike other attempts of knowledge-based network design [17, 273], here all possible inference rules, and not only the best rule, contribute to the final solution. The use of GAs in this context is beneficial for modeling multi-modal distributions, since all major representatives in the population are given fair chance during network synthesis. Superiority of the integrated model, over some related ones, is experimentally demonstrated in terms of classification accuracy, network size and training time when both real life (speech and medical) and artificially generated data sets, with dimension ranging from two to twenty-one and class boundaries overlapping as well as nonlinear, are considered as input.

In the second part of the chapter, an algorithm for extracting linguistic rules, based on this hybrid model, is presented. The performance of the rules is evaluated quantitatively using some measures such as *accuracy, certainty, fidelity, coverage, compactness, computational time* and *confusion* to evaluate the quality of the rules. A quantitative comparison of the rule extraction algorithm is made with some existing ones such as *Subset* [73], *M of N* [273] and X2R [143]. It is observed that the methodology extracts rules which are fewer in number, yet accurate, and have high certainty factor and low confusion with less computation time.

Note that the rules generated here are classificatory ones. These are useful for predicting the class labels of new instances/patterns. There is another class of rules, called association rules, which are important for predicting the co-occurence of item sets in a database.

The organization of the chapter is as follows: Some ensemble methods for neural network learning are first described in Section 8.2. Different algorithms for discovering association and classification rules are then provided in Sections 8.3 and 8.4, for convenience. Section 8.5 explains, in brief, the rough-fuzzy MLP [17]. The design procedure of the modular evolutionary algorithm is described in Section 8.6. The rule extraction method and the quantitative performance measures are presented in Section 8.7. The effectiveness of the modular rough-fuzzy model and its comparison with some related ones are provided in Section 8.8. Finally, Section 8.9 concludes the chapter.

8.2   Ensemble Classifiers

An ensemble is a set/team of individually trained classifiers (such as neural networks and decision trees) whose predictions are combined while classifying new instances. Previous research has shown that an ensemble classifier is often more accurate than any of the single classifiers in the ensemble. In the past few years, several investigations have been done toward developing a rigorous theoretical background of ensemble methods. *Ensemble* is called different names in the literature [127] including classifier combination, mixture of experts, committees machines, voting pool of classifiers, bagging, boosting, arcing, wagging, and stacked generalization. There are four basic approaches to ensemble learning [127]. They are mentioned below:

Approach A. Here, the individual classifiers are given (trained in advance), and the problem is to pick a combination scheme and train it if necessary.

Approach B. The individual classifiers are trained simultaneously in the process of ensemble learning. The set of classifiers can be homogeneous, i.e., formed using identical classifier models (e.g., multilayer perceptron) with different structures, parameters, initialization protocols, etc. Alternatively, a heterogeneous set can be designed.

Approach C. Here each classifier is built on an individual subset of features. This is useful when the input dimension is large (e.g., a few hundreds), and groups of features come from different sources or different data preprocessing systems.

Approach D. This is based on the principle that alteration of the training set can lead to a team of diverse classifiers, which is not possible to be produced by the above three approaches. Diversity among the classifiers in the team means that the individual classifiers, although having high accuracy rate, may contradict with respect to missclassified objects. This property alone can guarantee to produce a good team even with the simplest combination scheme. Three popular algorithms in this approach, namely, boosting [250], bagging [31] and ARCing [31], are described below.

Let there be L classifiers C_1, C_2, C_i, ..., C_L. Then partition the data randomly into L parts and use a different part to train each classifier. These classifiers are subsequently refined in the following ways:

1. Boosting: Test a classifier C_1 on the entire data set, filter out the misclassified objects and then retrain C_2 on them. Continue with the cascade until C_L is built.

2. Bagging: Design bootstrap samples by resampling from the entire data set with a uniform distribution and retrain a classifier C_i on each sample.

3. Adaptive resampling (ARCing): Design bootstrap samples by resampling from the training set with a nonuniform distribution. Update the distribution with respect to previous successes. Thus, the misclassified data points will appear more often in the subsequent training samples.

The indivdual classifiers in an ensemble may be obtained using any of the above four approaches. These classifiers are then combined. Some methods for combining them in an ensemble are described next. There are generally two types of combinations: *classifier selection* and *classifier fusion*. The presumption in classifier selection is that each classifier is "an expert" in some local area of the feature space. When a feature vector **x** is submitted for classification, the classifier responsible for the vicinity of **x** is given the highest credit to label **x**. We can nominate exactly one classifier to make the decision or use more than one "local expert" for this purpose. Classifier fusion assumes that all the classifiers are trained over the whole feature space and are thereby considered as *competitive* rather than *complementary*.

Fusion and selection are often merged. Instead of nominating one "expert," a small group of them can be nominated. We can then take their judgments and weight them by the level of expertise that they have on **x**. Thus, the classifier with the highest individual accuracy could be made the "leading expert" in the team.

Neural networks (NNs) are the most popular choice for the individual classifiers in the team. This choice, initially made by intuition, has now been justified theoretically [127]. The classification error of an ensemble can be decomposed by algebraic manipulation into two terms: bias and variance with respect to individual classifier outputs. Ideally, both terms should be small which is hardly possible for a single classifier model. Simple classifiers such as linear discriminant analysis have low variance and high bias. This means that these models are not very sensitive to small changes in the training data set (the calculation of the discriminant functions will not be much affected by small alterations in the training data) but at the same time are unable to reach low error rates. Conversely, neural networks have been shown to be ultimately versatile; i.e., they can approximate any classification boundary with an arbitrary precision. The price to pay for the low error rate is that neural classifiers may get overtrained. Thus, neural classifiers have low bias (any classification boundary can be modeled) and high variance (small changes in the data set might lead to a very different neural network). Assume that we combine different classifiers of the same bias and the same variance V by averaging the classifier outputs, e.g.,

$$\mu_i(\mathbf{x}) = \frac{1}{L} \sum_{k=1,L} d_{k,i}(\mathbf{x}).$$

Then the combination bias will be the same as that of the individual classifiers but the variance can be smaller than V, thereby reducing the total error of the combination.

If the ensemble consists of *identical* classifiers, then no improvement will be gained by the combination as the variance of the team estimate will be V. If the ensemble consists of *statistically independent* classifiers, then the combination variance is $\frac{V}{L}$ and the error is subsequently reduced. An even better team can be constituted if the classifiers are *negatively dependent*; i.e., they misclassify different object sets. To construct *diverse* classifiers of high accuracy, we need a versatile model. Neural networks are therefore an ideal choice to be individual members of the team. Their high variance should not be a concern as there are combination mechanisms that will reduce it.

Typically, MLP and radial basis function (RBF) networks are used, but variants thereof are also considered [186]. Training of the individual neural classifiers in the ensemble may be done using the aforesaid A, B, C, or D approaches.

8.3   Association Rules

An association rule is an expression $A \Rightarrow B$, where A and B represent two different sets of items. The meaning of such rules is quite intuitive: Given a database $\mathcal{D}$ of transactions, where each transaction $T \in \mathcal{D}$ is a set of items, $A \Rightarrow B$ expresses that whenever a transaction T contains A than T probably contains B also. The probability or rule confidence c is defined as the percentage of transactions containing B in addition to A with regard to the overall number of transactions containing A. The support of a rule is the number of transactions containing A (irrespective of presence of B) with respect to the total number of transactions in a database. The idea of association rules originated from the analysis of market-basket data where rules like "A customer who buys products x_1 and x_2 also buys product y with probability $c\%$" are found. Their direct applicability to a wide range of business problems together with their inherent understandability made the association rules discovery a popular mining method. Many generalizations of association rules have been proposed, e.g., frequent itemsets, query flocks, multilevel and multidimensional rules, and sequential rules.

When mining association rules there are mainly two problems to deal with. First of all there is algorithmic complexity. The time requirement grows quickly as the number of transactions and items grow. Second, interesting rules must be picked up from the set of generated rules. Several interestingness measures have been proposed in the literature for this purpose. In the next section we discuss some popular rule generation algorithms, followed by some rule interestingness measures in Section 8.3.2.

8.3.1   Rule generation algorithms

The most influential algorithm for mining Boolean association rules is the Apriori algorithm. Many variations of the Apriori algorithm has been proposed for improving its efficiency. These include partitioning, sampling, dynamic itemset counting and hashing. Here we describe the Apriori algorithm and some of its variations as follows. For details one may refer to [3, 88].

8.3.1.1   Apriori

The name of the algorithm is based on the fact that the algorithm uses prior knowledge of frequent itemset properties. Apriori employs an iterative approach known as level-wise search, where k-itemsets are used to explore k+1-itemsets. First the set of frequent 1-itemsets is found. Let this set be denoted by L_1. Then L_1 is used to find L_2, the set of frequent 2-itemsets, which is used to find L_3, and so on, until no more frequent k-itemsets are found. The finding of each L_k requires one full scan of the database.

To improve the efficiency of level-wise generation of frequent itemsets, an important property called the *Apriori property* is used to reduce the search space. In order to use the Apriori property, all the nonempty subsets of a frequent itemset must also be frequent. This property is based on the following observation. By definition, if an itemset I does not possess a minimum support min_sup it is not frequent. If an item A is added to the itemset I, then the resulting itemset (*i.e.*, $I \cup A$) cannot occur more frequently than I; therefore $I \cup A$ is not frequent either. This property belongs to a special category of properties called *anti-monotone* in the sense that "if a set cannot pass a test, all of its supersets will fail the same test as well."

Apriori algorithm uses the above property to find L_k from L_{k-1}. A two-step process is followed, consisting of *join* and *prune* actions.

1. *Join step*: To find L_k; a set of candidate k-itemsets is generated by joining L_{k-1} with itself. This set of candidates is denoted as C_k. Joining is performed by considering different combinations of the joinable members of L_{k-1}, where members of L_{k-1} are joinable if their first $(k-2)$ items are in common.

2. *Prune step*: C_k is a superset of L_k; that is, its members may or may not be frequent, but all of the frequent k-itemsets are included in C_k. A scan of the database to determine the count of each candidate in C_k would result in the determination of L_k. C_k, however, can be huge. To reduce the size of C_k, the Apriori property is used as follows. Any $(k-1)$-itemset that is not frequent cannot be a subset of a frequent k-itemset. Hence, if any $(k-1)$-subset of a candidate k-itemset is not in L_{k-1}, then the candidate cannot be frequent either and so can be removed from C_k.

Once the frequent itemsets from the transactions in a database have been found, it is straightforward to generate the strong association rules from them (where the *strong* association rules satisfy both minimum support and minimum confidence). This can be done using the following equation for confidence.

$$confidence(A \Rightarrow B) = \frac{support\_count(A \cup B)}{support\_count(A)} \tag{8.1}$$

where $support\_count(A \cup B)$ is the number of transactions containing the itemsets $A \cup B$, and $support\_count(A)$ is the number of transactions containing itemsets A. Based on this equation, association rules can be generated as follows:

- For each frequent itemset l, generate all nonempty subsets of l.

- For every nonempty subset s of l, output the rule "$s \Rightarrow (l - s)$" if $\frac{support\_count(l)}{support\_count(s)} \geq min\_conf$, where min_conf is the minimum pre-assigned confidence threshold.

Since the rules are generated from frequent itemsets, each one automatically satisfies the minimum support criterion. Next we discuss some of the strategies for improving the efficiency of the Apriori algorithm.

8.3.1.2   Partitioning

A partitioning technique [248] can be used that requires just two database scans to mine the frequent itemsets. It consists of two phases. In Phase I, the algorithm subdivides the transactions of database D into p nonoverlapping partitions. If the minimum support threshold for transactions in D is *min_sup*, then minimum itemset support count for a partition is *min_sup* × *the number of transactions in that partition*. For each partition, all frequent itemsets within the partition are found. These are referred to as local frequent itemsets.

A local frequent itemset may or may not be frequent with respect to the entire database, D. Any itemset that is potentially frequent with respect to D must occur as a frequent itemset in at least one of the partitions. Therefore all the local frequent itemsets are candidate itemsets with respect to D. The collection of frequent itemsets from all these partitions forms the global candidate itemsets. In Phase II, a second scan of D is conducted in which the actual support of each candidate is assessed in order to determine the global frequent itemsets.

8.3.1.3   Sampling

The basic idea of the sampling approach [271] is to pick a random sample S from the given data D, and then search for the frequent itemsets in S instead of D. In this way, we trade-off some degree of accuracy with computation time. The sample size of S is such that the search for frequent itemsets in S can be done in the main memory, and so only one scan of transactions in S is required overall. Since we are searching for the frequent itemsets in S rather than in D, we may miss some of the global frequent itemsets. To lessen this possibility, a support threshold lower than the minimum support value is used to find the frequent itemsets local to S.

8.3.1.4   Dynamic itemset counting

Dynamic itemset counting technique [33] involves partitioning the database into some blocks marked by their start points. Here, new candidate itemsets can be added at any start point, unlike in the Apriori algorithm, which determines new candidate itemsets only immediately prior to each complete database scan. The technique is dynamic in the sense that it estimates the support of all the itemsets that have been counted so far by adding new candidate itemsets, provided all of their subsets are estimated to be frequent. The resulting algorithm requires fewer database scans than the Apriori algorithm.

8.3.2 Rule interestingness

Typically the number of rules generated is very large, but only a few of these are of interest to the domain expert anlyzing the data. Therefore, one needs to threshold the huge number of discovered patterns and report only those that may be of some use. Interestingness measures, representing the novelty, utility and significance of a rule, are used in this regard.

Interestingness measures can be classified based on three criteria – foundation principle, scope, and class of the measure. *Foundation principle* describes the general nature of the methodology used for computing the measure. It may be probabilistic, syntactic, distance-based or utilitarian. *Scope* describes the number of rules covered by each interestingness value generated by each measure (i.e., a single rule or the whole rule set). The measure *class* may be either objective or subjective. Objective measures are based upon the structure of the discovered rules, while subjective measures are based upon the user beliefs or biases regarding reltionships in the data.

Some measures commonly used for scoring association rules are mentioned below along with their category.

- Itemset measures of Agrawal and Srikant [267] (probabilistic, single rule, objective)

- Rule templates of Klemettinen et al. [115] (syntactic, single rule, subjective)

- Interestingness of Silbershatz and Tuzhilin [257] (probabilistic, rule set, subjective)

- Interestingness of Gray and Orlowska [81] (probabilistic, single rule, objective)

- Interestingness of Dong and Li [58] (distance based, single rule, subjective)

- Reliable exceptions of Liu et al. [140] (probabilistic, single rule, objective)

- Peculiarity of Zhong et al. [294] (distance based, single rule, objective)

8.4 Classification Rules

Algorithms for classification-rule mining aim to discover a small set of rules from the data set to form an accurate classifier. They are mainly used in predictive data mining tasks such as financial forecasting, fraud detection and customer retention. The challenges to classification rule mining include scaling up to data sets with large number of points and attributes, and handling of heterogeneous data with missing attribute values, and dynamic/time varying data sets.

Major classification-rule mining algorithms are based on (a) decision trees, (b) neural networks, (c) genetic algorithms, and (d) inductive logic programming. Among them, decision trees are most widely used. Each leaf node of a decision tree represents a classification rule. Bottom-up traversal of the tree, from a leaf to the root, and conjuncting the attributes corresponding to the nodes traversed, generate a classification rule. Different indices mainly based on minimum description length, entropy and probabilistic distance measures are used for tree construction. The earliest rule mining algorithms based on decision trees are the ID3 and C4.5 [232]. Both are based on entropy measures. Some scalable decision-tree induction algorithms include SLIQ [158], RainForest [75] and SPRINT [254].

Neural network-based rule generation algorithms mainly use layered networks in supervised framework. A recent survey on neuro-fuzzy rule generation algorithms is available in [170]. Some of these are described in details in Section 8.7.

Genetic algorithms (GA) have been used for evolving rule-based systems for high dimensional pattern classification problems. The GA-based rule mining methods vary with respect to both chromosomal representation of rules and the rule evaluation measure used as objective function. GA-based machine learning techniques, namely, the Michigan and Pittsburgh approach [100], are often used for evolving the rules. Some other notable GA-based rule generation systems are MASSON [245] and PANIC [78].

Inductive logic programming (ILP) [179] is a machine learning technique used for construction of first-order clausal theories from examples and background knowledge. The aim is to discover, from a given set of preclassified examples, a set of classification rules with high predictive power. The PRO-GOL [180] and FOIL [233] classification algorithms, based on this method, were successfully applied in many domains. However, a limitation of these algorithms is their high computational complexity. Recently, several ILP-based scalable rule induction algorithms, e.g., TILDE [26] and GOLEM [181], are developed.

Evaluating the quality of rules for classification is an important problem in data mining. Quality can be measured using indices like accuracy, coverage, certainty, comprehensibility, compactness and confusion. These are discussed in details in Section 8.7.2.

The design procedure of an evolutionary rough-fuzzy MLP for classification, rule generation and rule evaluation is discussed in Section 8.6. This is based on a basic module, called rough-fuzzy MLP [17], which is discussed in short in the next section for convenience.

8.5 Rough-fuzzy MLP

The rough-fuzzy MLP [17] is described briefly in this section. First we explain the fuzzy MLP, for convenience. This is followed by the knowledge encoding algorithm for mapping the rules to the parameters of a fuzzy MLP.

8.5.1 Fuzzy MLP

The fuzzy MLP model [203] incorporates fuzziness at the input and output levels of the MLP and is capable of handling exact (numerical) and/or inexact (linguistic) forms of input data. Any input feature value is described in terms of some combination of membership values to the linguistic property sets *low* (L), *medium* (M) and *high* (H). Class membership values (μ) of patterns are represented at the output layer of the fuzzy MLP. During training, the weights are updated by backpropagating errors with respect to these membership values such that the contribution of uncertain vectors is automatically reduced.

A three-layered feedforward MLP is used. The output of a neuron in any layer (h) other than the input layer ($h = 0$) is given as

$$y_j^h = \frac{1}{1 + exp(-\sum_i y_i^{h-1} w_{ji}^{h-1})} \ , \qquad (8.2)$$

where y_i^{h-1} is the state of the ith neuron in the preceding $(h-1)$th layer and w_{ji}^{h-1} is the weight of the connection from the ith neuron in layer $h-1$ to the jth neuron in layer h. For nodes in the input layer, y_j^0 corresponds to the jth component of the input vector. Note that $x_j^h = \sum_i y_i^{h-1} w_{ji}^{h-1}$.

8.5.1.1 Input vector

A p-dimensional pattern $\mathbf{F_i} = [F_{i1}, F_{i2}, \ldots, F_{ip}]$ is represented as a $3p$-dimensional vector

$$\mathbf{F_i} = [\mu_{low(F_{i1})}(\mathbf{F_i}), \ldots, \mu_{high(F_{ip})}(\mathbf{F_i})] = [y_1^0, y_2^0, \ldots, y_{3p}^0] \ , \qquad (8.3)$$

where the μ values indicate the membership functions of the corresponding linguistic π-sets *low*, *medium* and *high* along each feature axis and $y_1^0, \ldots, y_{3p}^0$ refer to the activations of the $3p$ neurons in the input layer.

When the input feature is numerical, one may use $\pi-$fuzzy sets (in the one-dimensional form), with range [0,1], as represented by Equation 5.7. Note that features in linguistic and set forms can also be handled in this framework [203].

8.5.1.2 Output representation

Consider an M-class problem domain such that we have M nodes in the output layer. Let the p-dimensional vectors $\mathbf{o}_k = [o_{k1}...o_{kp}]$ and $\mathbf{v}_k = [v_{k1}, ..., v_{kp}]$

denote the mean and standard deviation respectively of the numerical training data for the kth class c_k. The weighted distance of the training pattern $\mathbf{F}_i$ from kth class c_k is defined as

$$z_{ik} = \sqrt{\sum_{j=1}^{p} \left[\frac{F_{ij} - o_{kj}}{v_{kj}} \right]^2} \quad for \quad k = 1, \ldots, M \ , \tag{8.4}$$

where F_{ij} is the value of the jth component of the ith pattern point.

The membership of the ith pattern in class k, lying in the range $[0, 1]$ is defined as [200]

$$\mu_k(\mathbf{F}_i) = \frac{1}{1 + \left(\frac{z_{ik}}{f_d} \right)^{f_e}} \ , \tag{8.5}$$

where positive constants f_d and f_e are the denominational and exponential fuzzy generators controlling the amount of fuzziness in the class membership set.

8.5.2 Rough set knowledge encoding

Rough set knowledge encoding involves two steps: generating rough set dependency rules, and mapping the rules to initial network parameters. The basic principle of rough set rule generation is already discussed in Section 5.3. The following paragraphs describe, in brief, the steps used here to obtain the dependency rules, and the methodology for mapping the rules to the weights of a fuzzy MLP.

Consider the case of feature F_j for class c_k in the M-class problem domain. The inputs for the ith representative sample $\mathbf{F}_i$ are mapped to the corresponding three-dimensional feature space of $\mu_{low(F_{ij})}(\mathbf{F}_i)$, $\mu_{medium(F_{ij})}(\mathbf{F}_i)$ and $\mu_{high(F_{ij})}(\mathbf{F}_i)$. Let these be represented by L_j, M_j and H_j, respectively. These values are then used to construct the attribute value table. As the method considers multiple objects in a class, a separate $n_k \times 3p$-dimensional attribute-value decision table is generated for each class c_k (where n_k indicates the number of objects in c_k).

For constructing the discernibility matrix, the absolute distance between each pair of objects is computed along each attribute L_j, M_j, H_j for all j. Equation 5.3 is then modified to directly handle a real-valued attribute table consisting of fuzzy membership values. Define

$$c_{ij} = \{ a \in B : \ | a(\mathbf{x}_i) - a(\mathbf{x}_j) | > Th \} \tag{8.6}$$

for $i, j = 1, \ldots, n_k$, where Th is an adaptive threshold. Note that the adaptivity of this threshold is in-built, depending on the inherent shape of the membership function. Dependency rules are generated from the discernibility matrix using the methodology described in Section 5.3.4.

Consider Figure 8.1. Let a_1, a_2 correspond to two membership functions (attributes) with a_2 being steeper as compared to a_1. It is observed that

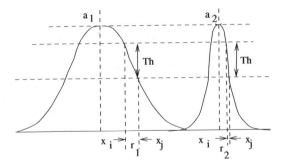

FIGURE 8.1: Illustration of adaptive thresholding of membership functions.

$r_1 > r_2$. This results in an implicit adaptivity of Th while computing c_{ij} in the discernibility matrix directly from the real-valued attributes. Here lies the novelty of the method. Moreover, this type of thresholding also enables the discernibility matrix to contain all the representative points/clusters present in a class. This is particularly useful in modeling multimodal class distributions. Note that the above notion of adaptive thresholding, for constructing the discernibility matrix, is similar to that used in [218] related to *shadowed sets*. Dependency rules are generated from the discernibility matrix, obtained as above, using the methodology described in Section 5.3.4.

While designing the initial structure of the rough-fuzzy MLP, the union of the rules of the M classes is considered. The input layer consists of $3p$ attribute values while the output layer is represented by M classes. The hidden layer nodes model the first level (innermost) operator in the antecedent part of a rule, which can be either a conjunct or a disjunct. The output layer nodes model the outer level operands, which can again be either a conjunct or a disjunct. For each inner level operator, corresponding to one output class (one dependency rule), one hidden node is dedicated. Only those input attributes that appear in this conjunct/disjunct are connected to the appropriate hidden node, which in turn is connected to the corresponding output node. Each outer level operator is modeled at the output layer by joining the corresponding hidden nodes. Note that a single attribute (involving no inner level operators) is directly connected to the appropriate output node via a hidden node, to maintain uniformity in rule mapping.

Let the dependency factor for a particular dependency rule for class c_k be $df = \alpha = 1$ by Equation 5.5. The weight w_{ki}^1 between a hidden node i and output node k is set at $\frac{\alpha}{fac} + \varepsilon$, where fac refers to the number of outer level operands in the antecedent of the rule and ε is a small random number taken to destroy any symmetry among the weights. Note that $fac \geq 1$ and each hidden node is connected to only one output node. Let the initial weight so clamped at a hidden node be denoted as β. The weight $w_{ia_j}^0$ between an attribute a_j (where a corresponds to *low* (L), *medium* (M) or *high* (H)) and hidden node i is set to $\frac{\beta}{facd} + \varepsilon$, such that $facd$ is the number of attributes connected by the corresponding inner level operator. Again $facd \geq 1$. Thus for an M-class problem domain there are at least M hidden nodes. It is to be mentioned that the number of hidden nodes is determined directly from the dependency rules based on the form in which the antecedents are present in the rules.

8.6 Modular Evolution of Rough-fuzzy MLP

The design procedure of modular neural networks (MNN) involves two broad steps – effective decomposition of the problem such that the subproblems can be solved with compact networks, and efficient combination and training of the networks such that there is gain in terms of training time, network size and accuracy. These are described in detail in the following section along with the steps involved and the characteristic features [162, 171, 205].

8.6.1 Algorithm

The methodology has two phases. First an M-class classification problem is split into M two-class problems. Let there be M sets of subnetworks, with $3p$ inputs and one output node each. Rough set theoretic concepts are used to encode domain knowledge into each of the subnetworks, using Equations 5.4 and 8.6. As explained in Section 8.5.2 the number of hidden nodes and connectivity of the knowledge-based subnetworks is automatically determined. Each two-class problem leads to the generation of one or more crude subnetworks, each encoding a particular decision rule. Let each of these constitute a pool. So one obtains $m \geq M$ pools of knowledge-based modules. Each pool k is perturbed to generate a total of n_k subnetworks, such that $n_1 = \ldots = n_k = \ldots = n_m$. These pools constitute the initial population of subnetworks, which are then evolved independently using genetic algorithms.

At the end of the above phase, the modules/subnetworks corresponding to each two-class problem are concatenated to form an initial network for the second phase. The inter module links are initialized to small random values as depicted in Figure 8.2. A set of such concatenated networks forms the initial population of the GA. The mutation probability for the inter-module links is now set to a high value, while that of intra-module links is set to a relatively lower value. This sort of *restricted* mutation helps preserve some of the localized rule structures, already extracted and evolved, as potential solutions. The initial population for the GA of the entire network is formed from all possible combinations of these individual network modules and random perturbations about them. This ensures that for complex multimodal pattern

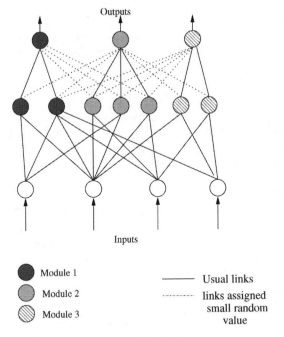

FIGURE 8.2: Intra- and inter-module links.

distributions all the different representative points remain in the population. The algorithm then searches through the reduced space of possible network topologies. The steps are summarized below followed by an example.

8.6.1.1   Steps

Step 1: For each class generate rough set dependency rules using the methodology described in Section 5.3.4.

Step 2: Map each of the dependency rules to a separate subnetwork modules (fuzzy MLPs) using the methodology described in Section 8.5.2.

Step 3: Partially evolve each of the subnetworks using conventional GA.

Step 4: Concatenate the subnetwork modules to obtain the complete network. For concatenation the intra-module links are left unchanged while the inter-module links are initialized to low random values (Figure 8.2). Note that each of the subnetworks solves a 2-class classification problem, while the concatenated network solve the actual M-class problem. Every possible combination of subnetwork modules is generated to form a pool of networks.

Step 5: The pool of networks is evolved using a *modified* GA with an adaptive/variable mutation operator. The mutation probability is set to a low value for the intra-module links and to a high value for the inter-module links.

Example:

Consider a problem of classifying a two-dimensional data into two classes. The input fuzzifier maps the features into a six-dimensional feature space. Let a sample set of rules obtained from rough set theory be

$$c_1 \leftarrow (L_1 \wedge M_2) \vee (H_2 \wedge M_1), \ c_2 \leftarrow M_2 \vee H_1, \ c_2 \leftarrow L_2 \vee L_1,$$

where L_j, M_j, H_j correspond to $\mu_{low(F_j)}$, $\mu_{medium(F_j)}$, $\mu_{high(F_j)}$, respectively. For the first phase of the GA three different pools are formed, using one crude subnetwork for class 1 and two crude subnetworks for class 2, respectively. Three partially trained subnetworks result from each of these pools. They are then concatenated to form $(1 \times 2) = 2$ networks. The population for the final phase of the GA is formed with these networks and perturbations about them. The steps followed in obtaining the final network are illustrated in Figure 8.3.

Remarks:

(i) The use of rough sets for knowledge encoding provides an established mathematical framework for network decomposition. Knowledge encoding not only produces an initial network close to the optimal one, it also reduces the search space. The initial network topology is automatically determined and provides good *building blocks* for the GA.

(ii) In earlier concurrent algorithms for neural network learning, there exist no guidelines for the decomposition of network modules [293]. Arbitrary subnetworks are assigned to each of the classes. Use of networks with the same number of hidden nodes for all classes leads to overlearning in the case of simple classes and poor learning in complex classes. Use of rough set theory circumvents the above problem.

(iii) Sufficient reduction in training time is obtained, as the above approach parallelizes the GA to an extent. The search string of the GA for subnetworks being smaller, more than linear decrease in searching time is obtained. Also a very small number of training cycles are required in the refinement phase, as the network is already very close to the solution. Note that the modular aspect of the algorithm is similar to the co-evolutionary algorithm (CEA) used for solving large scale problems with EAs [293].

(iv) The splitting of an M-class problem into M two-class problems bears an analogy to the well-known *divide and conquer* strategy and speeds up the search procedure significantly. Here one can use a smaller chromosome and/or population size, thereby alleviating to some extent the space-time complexity problem.

(v) The algorithm indirectly constrains the solution in such a manner that a structure is imposed on the connection weights. This is helpful for subsequent rule-extraction from the weights, as the resultant network obtained has sparse but strong interconnection among the nodes. Although in the above process some amount of optimality is sacrificed, and often for many-class problems the number of nodes required may be higher than optimal, yet the network is less redundant. However the nature of the objective function considered and the modular knowledge based methodology used enables sufficient amount of

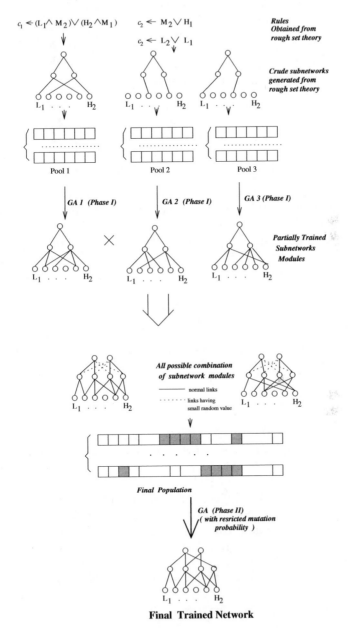

FIGURE 8.3: Steps for designing a sample modular rough-fuzzy MLP.

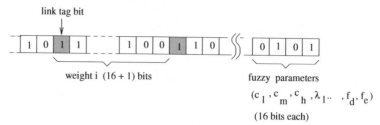

FIGURE 8.4:   Chromosome representation.

link pruning, and the total number of links are found to be significantly less. The use of *restricted* mutation (as defined in Section 8.6.2.3) minimizes the destruction of encoded rule structures in the knowledge-based networks.

(vi) For each two-class (sub)problem a set of subnetworks encoding separate decision rules is available. Since all possible combinations of these subnetworks are considered for the final evolutionary training, greater diversity within the population is possible. This results in faster convergence of the GA which utilizes multiple theories about a domain. This also ensures that all the clusters in the feature space are adequately represented in the final solution.

8.6.2   Evolutionary design

Here we discuss different features of genetic algorithms [80] with relevance to the modular training algorithm.

8.6.2.1   Chromosomal representation

The problem variables consist of the weight values and the input/output fuzzification parameters. Each of the weights is encoded into a binary word of 16 bit length, where [000...0] decodes to -128 and [111...1] decodes to 128. An additional bit is assigned to each weight to indicate the presence or absence of the link. The fuzzification parameters tuned are the center (c) and radius (λ) for each of the linguistic attributes *low*, *medium* and *high* of each feature, and the output fuzzifiers f_d and f_e [203]. These are also coded as 16 bit strings in the range $[0, 2]$. For the input parameters, [000...0] decodes to 0 and [111...1] decodes to 1.2 times the maximum value attained by the corresponding feature in the training set. The chromosome is obtained by concatenating all the above strings (Figure 8.4). Sample values of the string length are around 2000 bits for reasonably sized networks.

Initial population is generated by coding the networks obtained by rough set based knowledge encoding and by random perturbations about them. A population size of 64 was considered.

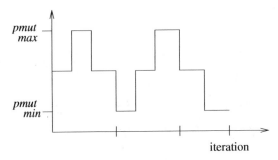

FIGURE 8.5: Variation of mutation probability with iteration.

8.6.2.2 Crossover

It is obvious that due to the large string length, single point crossover would have little effectiveness. Multiple point crossover is adopted, with the distance between two crossover points being a random variable between 8 and 24 bits. This is done to ensure a high probability for only one crossover point occurring within a word encoding a single weight. The crossover probability is fixed at 0.7.

8.6.2.3 Mutation

The search string being very large, the influence of mutation is more on the search compared to crossover. Each of the bits in the string is chosen to have some mutation probability ($pmut$). The mutation probability has a spatio-temporal variation. The variation of $pmut$ with iteration is shown in Figure 8.5. The maximum value of $pmut$ is chosen to be 0.4 and the minimum value as 0.01. The mutation probabilities also vary along the encoded string, the bits corresponding to inter-module links being assigned a probability $pmut$ (i.e., the value of $pmut$ at that iteration) and intra-module links assigned a probability $pmut/10$. This is done to ensure least alterations in the structure of the individual modules already evolved. Hence, the mutation operator indirectly incorporates the domain knowledge extracted through rough set theory.

8.6.2.4 Choice of fitness function

An objective function of the form described below is chosen.

$$F_{\text{obj}} = \alpha_1 f_1 + \alpha_2 f_2 \, , \tag{8.7}$$

where
$$f_1 = \frac{No. \ of \ Correctly \ Classified \ Sample \ in \ Training \ Set}{Total \ No. \ of \ Samples \ in \ Training \ Set}$$

$$f_2 = 1 - \frac{No. \ of \ links \ present}{Total \ No. \ of \ links \ possible}.$$

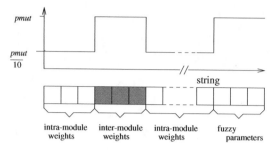

FIGURE 8.6: Variation of mutation probability along the encoded string (chromosome).

Here α_1 and α_2 determine the relative weight of each of the factors. α_1 is taken to be 0.9 and α_2 is taken as 0.1, to give more importance to the classification score compared to the network size in terms of number of links. Note that we optimize the network connectivity, weights and input/output fuzzification parameters simultaneously.

8.6.2.5   Selection

Selection is done by the *roulette wheel* method. The probabilities are calculated on the basis of ranking of the individuals in terms of the objective function, instead of the objective function itself. *Elitism* is incorporated in the selection process to prevent oscillation of the fitness function with generation. The fitness of the best individual of a new generation is compared with that of the current generation. If the latter has a higher value the corresponding individual replaces a randomly selected individual in the new population.

8.7   Rule Extraction and Quantitative Evaluation

8.7.1   Rule extraction methodology

Algorithms for rule generation from neural networks mainly fall in two categories – pedagogical and decompositional [270]. Pedagogical methods generate rules by presenting input patterns to the network and considering the outputs obtained. Decompositional methods, on the other hand, consider the structure of the trained network for extracting logical rules. Although the pedagogical methods have smaller computational complexity, they provide relatively poor noise tolerance and inability to model complex multimodal patterns. Decompositional methods often produce rules having good generalization properties, but also require greater computational complexity specially in large networks.

The algorithm used for the modular rough-fuzzy MLP [205] can be categorized as decompositional. It is explained below.

1. Compute the following quantities:
   $PMean=$ Mean of all positive weights, $PThres_1=$ Mean of all positive weights less than $PMean$, $PThres_2=$ Mean of all weights greater than $PMean$. Similarly calculate $NThres_1$ and $NThres_2$ for negative weights.

2. For each hidden and output unit

   (a) for all weights greater than $PThres_1$ search for positive rules only, and for all weights less than $NThres_1$ search for negated rules only by *Subset* method.

   (b) search for combinations of positive weights above $Pthres_2$ and negative weights greater than $NThres_1$ that exceed the bias. Similarly search for negative weights less than $NThres_2$ and positive weights below $PThres_1$ to find out rules.

3. Associate with each rule j a confidence factor

$$cf_j = \inf_{j:\ all\ nodes\ in\ the\ path} \frac{(\Sigma_i w_{ji} - \theta_j)}{\Sigma_i w_{ji}}, \tag{8.8}$$

where w_{ji} is the ith incoming link weight to node j.

Since the modular training algorithm imposes a structure on the network, resulting in a sparse network having few strong links, the $PThres$ and $NThres$ values are well separated. Hence the above rule extraction algorithm generates most of the embedded rules over a small number of computational steps.

The computational complexity of the algorithm is as follows. Let the network have i, h, o numbers of input, hidden and output nodes, respectively. Let us make the assumption that $i = h = o = k$. Let the fraction of weights having value in $[0, PThres_1)$, $[PThres_1, PThres_2)$, $[PThres_2, \infty)$, be p_1, p_2, p_3 respectively. Similarly let the corresponding fractions for negative weights be n_1, n_2, n_3. Then the computational complexity ($\mathcal{C}$) becomes
$$\mathcal{C} = k.(\ 2^{(p_2+p_3)k+1} + 2^{(n_2+n_3)k+1} + 2^{(p_3+n_1)k+1} + 2^{(p_1+n_3)k+1}\ ).$$
If n_1, n_2, p_1, $p_2 \ll p_3$, n_3,
$$\mathcal{C} \approx 4k.\ (2^{p_3 k} + 2^{n_3 k}) = 4k.\ (e^{\ln 2.p_3 k} + e^{\ln 2.n_3 k}).$$
Also if p_3, $n_3 \ll 1$,
$$\mathcal{C} \approx 4k.(1 + \ln 2.(p_3 + n_3)k + 0.5.(\ln 2.(p_3 + n_3))^2 k^2,\ i.e.,\ \mathcal{C} \approx \mathcal{O}(k^3).$$

An important consideration is the order of application of rules in a rule base. Since most of the real life patterns are noisy and overlapping, rule bases obtained are often not totally consistent. Hence multiple rules may fire for a single example. Several existing approaches apply the rules sequentially, often leading to degraded performance. The rules extracted by the above method have confidence factors associated with them. Therefore if multiple rules are fired, one uses the strongest rule having the highest confidence.

Some other popular rule extraction algorithms are described below. The first two among them are decompositional methods and the third one a pedagogical method.

1. *Subset:* The *Subset* method [73] conducts a breadth-first search for all the hidden and output nodes over the input links. The algorithm starts by determining whether any sets containing a single link are sufficient to guarantee that the bias is exceeded. If yes, then these sets are rewritten as rules in disjunctive normal form. The search proceeds by increasing the size of the subsets until all possible subsets have been explored. Finally the algorithm removes subsumed and overly general rules. The algorithm is described below [73]:

   For each hidden and output unit

   (a) Extract up to β_p subsets of the positively weighted incoming links whose summed weight is greater than the bias of the unit.

   (b) For each subset $\mathcal{P}$ of β_p subsets found in step 1

       i. Extract up to β_n minimal subsets of negatively weighted links whose summed weight is greater than the bias of the unit *minus* the sum of $\mathcal{P}$.

       ii. Let $\mathcal{Z}$ be a new predicate used nowhere else.

       iii. With each subset $\mathcal{N}$ of β_n subsets found in step 2(a) form the rule "IF $\mathcal{N}$ THEN $\mathcal{Z}$."

       iv. Form the rule "IF $\mathcal{P}$ and NOT $\mathcal{Z}$ THEN *name of unit*."

   The major problem with the *Subset* algorithm is that the cost of finding all subsets grows as the size of the power set of the links to each unit. It requires lengthy, exhaustive searches of size $\mathcal{O}(2^k)$ for a hidden/output node with a fan-in of k and extracts a large set of rules, upto $\beta_p*(1+\beta_n)$. Some of the generated rules may be repetitive, as permutations of rule antecedents are not taken care of automatically. Moreover, there is no guarantee that all useful knowledge embedded in the trained network will be extracted. To avoid the otherwise prohibitive combinatorics, all implementations of *Subset* algorithm use heuristics.

2. *M of N:* To overcome the combinatorial problem of *Subset* algorithm, Opitz and Shavlik [187] developed the *M of N* method which searches for rules of the form:
   IF (M of the following N antecedents are true) THEN ...
   The algorithm is described below [273].

   (a) For each hidden and output unit form groups/clusters of similarly weighted links.

   (b) Set link weights of all group members to the average of the group, creating equivalence classes.

(c) Eliminate groups that have no significant effect on the sign of the total activation.

(d) Freeze all link weights and optimize biases of all hidden and output unit using backpropagation algorithm.

(e) Form a single rule for each hidden and output unit. The rule consists of a threshold given by the bias and weighted antecedents specified by the remaining links.

(f) When possible simplify rules to eliminate superfluous weights and thresholds.

Computational complexity of the *M of N* algorithm is $\mathcal{O}(k^3 + (k^2.j))$, where j is the number of examples. Additionally, the rule extraction procedure involves a back-propagation step requiring significant computational time. The algorithm has good generalization (accuracy) but can have degraded comprehensibilty [9]. Note that one considers groups of links as equivalence classes, thereby generating a bound on the number of rules rather than establishing a ceiling on the number of antecedents.

3. *X2R:* The X2R algorithm [143] uses discretization, feature selection, and concept learning to generate rules from raw data. Instead of analyzing the link weights of a neural network it generates the rule from the input output decision table of a trained neural network. The discretization algorithm usually used by X2R is the *Chi_2* algorithm. It is based on χ^2 statistics and helps to filter out noisy patterns. Feature merging is also performed in the discretization process. After discretization of the raw data following three steps are performed:

(a) Rule generation: It chooses the most frequently occurred pattern as the base to generate a rule, then the next frequently occurred, etc. The core of this step is a greedy algorithm that finds the shortest rule based on the first-order information, which can differentiate the patterns under consideration from the patterns of other classes. It then iteratively generates rules and removes the patterns covered by each rule until all patterns are covered by the rules.

(b) Rule clustering: Rules generated in the above step are grouped in terms of their class labels for further processing.

(c) Rule pruning: In each rule cluster, redundant rules are eliminated, specific rules are replaced by more general rules. A default rule is chosen in cases when no rule can be applied to a pattern.

The worst case computational complexity for X2R is $O(j^2, d^2)$, where j is the number of patterns and d is the number of features. The rules generated by X2R are shorter and the number of rules is smaller. The error rate of the rules is no worse than the inconsistency rate found in the original data. The rules generated by X2R, however, are order sensitive; i.e., the rules should be fired in sequence. Although the rules of this type are normally short, the ordering hinders human's understanding of the rules.

Among the above three rule extraction techniques, the ones similar in spirit to the algorithm used for the modular rough-fuzzy method are the *Subset* method [73] and *M of N* method [273]. The major problem with the *Subset* algorithm is that the cost of finding all subsets grows as the size of the power set of the links to each unit. It requires lengthy, exhaustive searches of size $\mathcal{O}(2^k)$ for a hidden/output node with a fan-in of k and extracts a large set of rules, up to $\beta_p * (1 + \beta_n)$, where β_p and β_n are the number of subsets of positively and negatively weighted links, respectively. Some of the generated rules may be repetitive, as permutations of rule antecedents are not taken care of automatically. Moreover, there is no guarantee that all useful knowledge embedded in the trained network will be extracted. Computational complexity of the *M of N* algorithm is $\mathcal{O}(k^3 + (k^2.j))$, where j is the number of examples. Additionally, the rule extraction procedure involves a back-propagation step requiring significant computation time. The algorithm has good generalization (accuracy) but can have degraded comprehensibility [270]. Note that one considers groups of links as equivalence classes, thereby generating a bound on the number of rules rather than establishing a ceiling on the number of antecedents.

8.7.2 Quantitative measures

Here we present some measures in order to evaluate the performance of the rules. Among them, *Certainty* and *Confusion*, reflecting the confidence and ambiguity in a decision, were defined recently [202].

Let N be an $M \times M$ matrix whose (i, j)th element n_{ij} indicate the number of patterns actually belonging to class i, but classified as class j.

   i. *Accuracy:* It is the correct classification percentage, provided by the rules on a test set defined as $\frac{n_{ic}}{n_i}.100$, where n_i is equal to the number of points in class i, and n_{ic} of these points are correctly classified.

  ii. *User's Accuracy* [240]: If n'_i points are found to be classified into class i, then the user's accuracy (U) is defined as $\quad U = n_{ic}/n'_i$. This gives a measure of the confidence that a classifier assigns to a region as belonging to a class. In other words, it denotes the level of purity associated with a region.

 iii. *Kappa* [240]: The coefficient of agreement called "kappa" measures the relationship of beyond-chance agreement to expected disagreement. It uses all the cells in the confusion matrix, not just the diagonal elements. The estimate of kappa (K) is the proportion of agreement after chance agreement is removed from consideration. The kappa value for class i (K_i) is defined as

$$K_i = \frac{n.n_{ic} - n_i.n_i'}{n.n_i' - n_i.n_i'}.$$

(8.9)

The numerator and denominator of overall kappa are obtained by summing the respective numerators and denominators of K_i separately over all classes.

iv. *Fidelity* [270]: This represents how closely the rule base approximates the parent neural network model [270]. One can measure this as the percentage of the test set for which network and the rule base output agree. Note that fidelity may or may not be greater than accuracy.

v. *Confusion:* This measure quantifies the goal that the "*Confusion should be restricted within minimum number of classes.*" This property is helpful in higher level decision making. Let $\hat{n}_{ij}$ be the mean of all n_{ij} for $i \neq j$. Then we define

$$Conf = \frac{Card\{n_{ij} : n_{ij} \geq \hat{n}_{ij}, i \neq j\}}{M}$$

(8.10)

for an M class problem. The lower the value of $Conf$, the fewer the number of classes between which confusion occurs.

vi. *Cover:* Ideally the rules extracted should cover all the cluster regions of the pattern space. One may use the percentage of examples from a test set for which no rules are invoked as a measure of the uncovered region. A rule base having a smaller uncovered region is superior.

vii. *Rule base size:* It is measured in terms of the number of rules. The lower the value is, the more compact is the rule base.

viii. *Computational complexity:* This may be represented by the CPU time required.

ix. *Certainty:* By the certainty of a rule base one quantifies the confidence of the rules as defined by the certainty factor cf (Equation 8.8).

8.8 Experimental Results and Comparison

The modular rough-fuzzy MLP [205], described in Sections 8.6 and 8.7, has been implemented on both real life (Vowel, Hepatobiliary and Cervical cancer) and artificially generated (Pat) data. These data sets have overlapping and nonlinear class boundaries. The details of the data are provided in Appendix B.

Let the modular rough-fuzzy methodology be termed Model S. Other models compared include:

Model O: An ordinary MLP trained using back-propagation (BP) with weight decay.

Model F: A fuzzy MLP trained using BP [203] (with weight decay).

Model R: A fuzzy MLP trained using BP (with weight decay), with initial knowledge encoding using rough sets [17].

Model FM: A modular fuzzy MLP trained with GAs along with tuning of the fuzzification parameters. Here the term *modular* refers to the use of subnetworks corresponding to each class that are later concatenated using GAs.

8.8.1   Classification

Recognition scores obtained for Vowel, Hepatobiliary and Pat data by the soft modular network (Model S) are presented in Table 8.2. It also shows a comparison with other related MLP-based classification methods (Models O, F, R and FM). In all cases, 10% of the samples are used as a training set, and the remaining samples are used as a test set. Ten such independent runs are performed and the mean value and standard deviation of the classification accuracy, computed over them, are presented in Table 8.2.

The dependency rules, as generated via rough set theory and used in the encoding scheme, are shown in Table 8.1 only for Vowel data, as an example. The values of input fuzzification parameters used are also presented in Table 8.1. The corresponding π-functions are shown in Figure 8.7 only for feature F_1, as an illustration. In Table 8.1, F_i, where F stands for *low, medium* or *high*, denotes a property F of the ith feature [203]. The integrated networks contain 18, 15 and 10 hidden nodes in a single layer for Vowel, Pat, and Hepatobiliary data, respectively. After combination 96, 61 and 16 networks were obtained, respectively. The initial population of the GA was formed using 64 networks in each of these cases. In the first phase of the GA (for models FM and S), each of the subnetworks are partially trained for 10 sweeps.

The classification accuracies obtained by the models are analyzed for statistical significance. Tests of significance (as described in Section 2.6.2) are performed for the inequality of means (of accuracies) obtained using the modular rough-fuzzy algorithm and the other methods compared. In Table 8.2, we present the mean and standard deviation (SD) of the accuracies. Using the means and SDs, the value of the test statistics is computed. If the value exceeds the corresponding tabled value, the means are unequal with statistical significance (an algorithm having higher mean accuracy is significantly superior to the one having lower value).

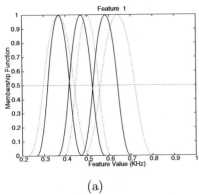
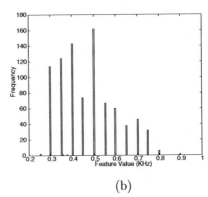

(a)   (b)

FIGURE 8.7: (a) Input π-functions and (b) data distribution along F_1 axis for the Vowel data. Solid lines represent the initial functions and dashed lines represent the functions obtained finally after tuning with GAs. The horizontal dotted lines represent the threshold level.

TABLE 8.1: Rough set dependency rules for Vowel data along with the input fuzzification parameter values

---

$c_1 \leftarrow M_1 \vee L_3$
$c_1 \leftarrow M_1 \vee M_2$
$c_2 \leftarrow M_2 \vee M_3 \vee (H_1 \wedge M_2)$
$c_2 \leftarrow M_2 \vee H_3$
$c_3 \leftarrow (L_1 \wedge H_2) \vee (M_1 \wedge H_2)$
$c_3 \leftarrow (L_1 \wedge H_2) \vee (L_1 \wedge M_3)$
$c_4 \leftarrow (L_1 \wedge L_2) \vee (L_1 \wedge L_3) \vee (L_2 \wedge M_3) \vee (L_1 \wedge M_3)$
$c_5 \leftarrow (H_1 \wedge M_2) \vee (M_1 \wedge M_3) \vee (M_1 \wedge M_2) \vee (M_2 \wedge L_1)$
$c_5 \leftarrow (H_1 \wedge M_2) \vee (M_1 \wedge M_2) \vee (H_1 \wedge H_3) \vee (H_2 \wedge L_1)$
$c_5 \leftarrow (L_2 \wedge L_1) \vee (H_3 \wedge M_3) \vee M_1$
$c_6 \leftarrow L_1 \vee M_3 \vee L_2$
$c_6 \leftarrow M_1 \vee H_3$
$c_6 \leftarrow L_1 \vee H_3$
$c_6 \leftarrow M_1 \vee M_3 \vee L_2.$

Fuzzification Parameters:
Feature 1: $c_L = 0.348$, $c_M = 0.463$, $c_H = 0.613$,
    $\lambda_L = 0.115$, $\lambda_M = 0.150$, $\lambda_H = 0.134$
Feature 2: $c_L = 0.219$, $c_M = 0.437$, $c_H = 0.725$,
    $\lambda_L = 0.218$, $\lambda_M = 0.253$, $\lambda_H = 0.288$
Feature 3: $c_L = 0.396$, $c_M = 0.542$, $c_H = 0.678$,
    $\lambda_L = 0.146$, $\lambda_M = 0.140$, $\lambda_H = 0.135$

It is observed from Table 8.2 that Model S performs the best (except for Model R on Vowel data and Model F on Hepatobiliary data) with the least network size as well as the least number of sweeps. For Model R with Vowel data and Model F with Hepatobiliary data, the classification performance on test set is marginally better than that of Model S, but with a significantly higher number of links and training sweeps required. Comparing models F and R, we observe that the incorporation of domain knowledge in the latter through rough sets boosts its performance. Similarly, using the modular approach with GA (Model FM) improves the efficiency of Model F. Since Model S encompasses the principle of both models R and FM, it results in the least redundant yet most effective model. The variation of the classification accuracy of the models with iteration is also studied. As expected, Model S is found to have high recognition score at the very beginning of evolutionary training; the next values are attained by models R and FM and the lowest by models O and F using back-propagation. For example, in the case of Vowel data, these figures are 64% for S, 52% for R, 44% for FM, and 0% for F and O. Model S converges after about 90 iterations of the GA, providing the highest accuracy compared to all the other models. The back-propagation based models require about 2000–5000 iterations for convergence.

It may be noted that the modular training algorithm described is successful in imposing a structure among the connection weights. As seen from Figure 8.8, for Vowel data, the weight values for a fuzzy MLP trained with BP (Model F) is more or less uniformly distributed between the maximum and minimum values. On the other hand, the modular rough-fuzzy MLP (Model S) has most of its weight values zero, while the majority of its non-zero weights have a high value. Hence it can be inferred that the former model results in a dense network with weak links, while the incorporation of rough sets, modular concepts and GAs produces a sparse network with strong links. The latter is suitable for rule extraction. The connectivity (positive weights) of the trained network is shown in Figure 8.9.

8.8.2   Rule extraction

The algorithm explained in Section 8.7.1 is used to extract rules from the trained network (Model S). These rules are compared with those obtained by the *Subset* method [73], *M of N* method [273], a pedagogical method X2R [143] and a decision tree-based method C4.5 [232] in terms of the performance measures (Section 8.7.2). The set of rules extracted from the modular rough-fuzzy network (Model S) is presented in Tables 8.4–8.6 along with their certainty factors (*cf*) for Vowel, Hepatobiliary and Pat data. The values of the fuzzification parameters of the membership functions L, M and H are also mentioned. For the Hepatobiliary data the fuzzification parameters are presented only for those features that appear in the extracted rules.

A comparison of the performance indices of the extracted rules is presented in Table 8.3. Since the network obtained using Model S contains fewer links,

TABLE 8.2: Comparative performance of different models

Models	Model O		Model F		Model R		Model FM		Model S	
	Train	Test	Train	Test	Train	Test	Train	Test	Train	Test
Vowel data										
Accuracy(%) (Mean SD)	65.4 0.5	64.1 0.5	84.1 0.4	81.8 0.5	86.7 0.3	86.0 0.2	85.3 0.4	82.3 0.5	87.1 0.2	85.8 0.2
# links	131		210		152		124		84	
Sweeps	5600		5600		2000		200		90	
Pat data										
Accuracy(%) (Mean SD)	55.1 0.4	54.8 0.3	68.7 0.5	68.1 0.5	73.1 0.4	71.1 0.4	70.2 0.5	69.8 0.4	75.7 0.5	74.7 0.4
# links	62		105		82		84		72	
Sweeps	2000		2000		1500		150		90	
Hepatobiliary data										
Accuracy(%) (Mean SD)	70.1 0.4	60.0 0.3	66.1 0.4	69.8 0.5	76.9 0.4	68.0 0.5	76.8 0.4	67.4 0.5	78.4 0.4	68.9 0.5
# links	143		310		190		230		108	
Iterations	2500		2500		1500		200		110	

SD: Standard Deviation

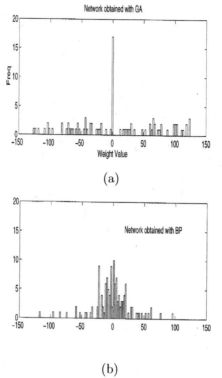

(a)

(b)

FIGURE 8.8:   Histogram plot of the distribution of weight values with (a) Model S and (b) Model F for Vowel data.

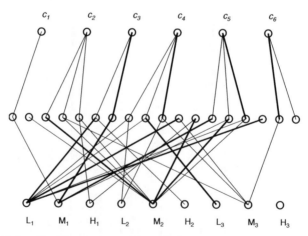

FIGURE 8.9:   Positive connectivity of the network obtained for the Vowel data, using Model S. (Bold lines indicate weights greater than $PThres_2$, while others indicate values between $PThres_1$ and $PThres_2$.)

TABLE 8.3: Comparison of the performance of the rules extracted by various methods for Vowel, Pat and Hepatobiliary data

	Algorithm	Accuracy (%)	Users' Accuracy (%)	Kappa (%)	Uncovered Region (%)	No. of Rules	CPU time (Sec)	*Conf*
V O W E L	Model S	81.02	83.31	78.17	3.10	10	1.1	1.4
	Subset	82.01	82.72	77.29	2.89	16	1.4	1.9
	M of N	79.00	80.01	74.55	2.10	14	1.2	1.9
	X2R	76.00	75.81	72.34	2.72	14	0.9	1.7
	C4.5	79.00	79.17	77.21	3.10	16	1.0	1.5
P A T	Model S	70.31	74.44	71.80	2.02	8	1.0	1.1
	Subset	71.02	73.01	70.09	1.91	16	1.1	1.5
	M of N	70.09	71.12	70.02	2.02	11	1.1	1.5
	X2R	67.82	68.23	67.91	1.91	10	0.9	1.4
	C4.5	71.02	73.44	72.00	2.02	11	1.1	1.2
H E P A TO	Model S	64.90	64.70	64.10	8.02	7	0.9	1.4
	Subset	65.00	65.41	64.44	7.52	11	1.0	1.8
	M of N	63.91	64.00	63.02	8.02	10	1.0	1.8
	X2R	61.02	60.90	60.90	7.91	9	0.9	1.7
	C4.5	64.01	64.23	64.90	7.91	10	0.9	1.4

TABLE 8.4: Rules extracted from trained networks (Model S) for Vowel data along with the input fuzzification parameter values

---

$c_1 \leftarrow M_1 \vee L_3 \vee M_2 \quad cf = 0.851$
$c_1 \leftarrow H_1 \vee M_2 \quad cf = 0.755$
$c_2 \leftarrow M_2 \vee M_3 \quad cf = 0.811$
$c_2 \leftarrow \neg M_1 \wedge \neg H_1 \wedge L_2 \wedge M_2 \quad cf = 0.846$
$c_3 \leftarrow L_1 \vee H_2 \quad cf = 0.778$
$c_4 \leftarrow L_1 \wedge L_2 \wedge \neg L_3 \quad cf = 0.719$
$c_5 \leftarrow M_1 \wedge H_2 \quad cf = 0.881$
$c_5 \leftarrow M_1 \wedge M_2 \quad cf = 0.782$
$c_5 \leftarrow H_1 \wedge M_2 \quad cf = 0.721$
$c_6 \leftarrow \neg H_2 \quad cf = 0.717.$

Fuzzification Parameters:
Feature 1: $c_L = 0.34, c_M = 0.502, c_H = 0.681$
Feature 1: $\lambda_L = 0.122, \lambda_M = 0.154, \lambda_H = 0.177$
Feature 2: $c_L = 0.217, c_M = 0.431, c_H = 0.725$
Feature 2: $\lambda_L = 0.211, \lambda_M = 0.250, \lambda_H = 0.288$
Feature 3: $c_L = 0.380, c_M = 0.540, c_H = 0.675$
Feature 3: $\lambda_L = 0.244, \lambda_M = 0.212, \lambda_H = 0.224$

TABLE 8.5: Rules extracted from trained networks (Model S) for Pat data along with the input fuzzification parameter values

---

$c_1 \leftarrow M_1 \wedge M_2 \quad cf = 0.674$
$c_1 \leftarrow M_1 \wedge H_1 \wedge \neg L_2 \quad cf = 0.875$
$c_2 \leftarrow L_2 \wedge H_1 \quad cf = 0.80$
$c_2 \leftarrow L_2 \wedge M_1 \quad cf = 0.778$
$c_3 \leftarrow L_1 \wedge L_2 \quad cf = 0.636$
$c_3 \leftarrow H_1 \wedge H_2 \quad cf = 0.674$
$c_3 \leftarrow M_1 \wedge M_2 \wedge \neg L_2 \quad cf = 0.636$
$c_3 \leftarrow M_1 \wedge M_2 \wedge \neg L_2 \quad cf = 0.636$

Fuzzification Parameters:
Feature 1: $c_L = 0.216, c_M = 0.499, c_H = 0.751$
Feature 1: $\lambda_L = 0.282, \lambda_M = 0.265, \lambda_H = 0.252$
Feature 2: $c_L = 1.266, c_M = 1.737, c_H = 2.511$
Feature 2: $\lambda_L = 0.244, \lambda_M = 0.235, \lambda_H = 0.226$

TABLE 8.6: Rules extracted from trained networks (Model S) for Hepatobiliary data along with the input fuzzification parameter values

---

$c_1 \leftarrow L_3 \wedge M_6 \wedge \neg L_1 \quad cf = 0.857$
$c_1 \leftarrow L_3 \wedge \neg L_6 \wedge L_1 \quad cf = 0.800$
$c_2 \leftarrow L_2 \wedge M_2 \wedge M_3 \quad cf = 0.846$
$c_2 \leftarrow M_6 \quad cf = 0.571$
$c_3 \leftarrow L_3 \wedge L_2 \wedge M_3 \quad cf = 0.800$
$c_4 \leftarrow L_3 \wedge L_6 \wedge \neg L_1 \quad cf = 0.833$
$c_4 \leftarrow M_2 \wedge L_2 \wedge \neg M_3 \quad cf = 0.833$

Fuzzification Parameters:
Feature 1: $c_L = 52.47, c_M = 112.88, c_H = 289.17$
Feature 1: $\lambda_L = 62.44, \lambda_M = 118.35, \lambda_H = 176.40$
Feature 2: $c_L = 24.04, c_M = 53.41, c_H = 125.35$
Feature 2: $\lambda_L = 29.15, \lambda_M = 55.14, \lambda_H = 72.08$
Feature 3: $c_L = 336.15, c_M = 477.95, c_H = 844.00$
Feature 3: $\lambda_L = 140.00, \lambda_M = 254.44, \lambda_H = 367.01$
Feature 6: $c_L = 12.15, c_M = 17.27, c_H = 25.52$
Feature 6: $\lambda_L = 5.11, \lambda_M = 7.18, \lambda_H = 9.25$

---

the generated rules are less in number and they have a high *certainty factor*. Accordingly, it possesses a relatively higher percentage of uncovered region, though the accuracy did not suffer much. Although the *Subset* algorithm achieves the highest *accuracy*, it requires the largest number of rules and computation time. In fact, the accuracy/computation time of Subset method is marginally better/worse than Model S, while the size of the rule base is significantly less for Model S.

The accuracy achieved by Model S is better than that of *M of N*, X2R, and C4.5, except for the *Pat* data with C4.5. Also considering *user's accuracy* and *kappa*, the best performance is obtained by Model S. The X2R algorithm requires least computation time but achieves least accuracy with more rules. The *Conf* index is the minimum for rules extracted by Model S; it also has high *fidelity* (e.g., 94.22%, 89.17% and 74.88% for Vowel, Pat, and Hepatobiliary, data, respectively).

It is observed that the rule extraction performance degrades substantially for Models O, R, and FM because these networks are less structured and hence less suitable, as compared to Model S, for rule extraction.

8.8.2.1 Rules for staging of cervical cancer with binary feature inputs

Investigation is also made to demonstrate the effectiveness of the aforesaid concept of modular rule evolution to the problem of staging of cervical cancer where the rules corresponding to four stages are validated by oncologists [163]. Here the symptoms (features) are binary valued. Therefore conventional MLP is used, instead of fuzzy MLP. Knowledge encoding is done using rough set theoretic rules which are generated directly from the feature values (without fuzzification). One thus obtains a modular rough MLP (denoted by Model RM, say), instead of the modular rough-fuzzy MLP (Model S) studied in earlier experiments. Before we present the experimental results, we describe, in brief, the problem of cancer staging, details of the features (clinical measurements) involved and the patient data used for building the modular rough MLP model.

Staging is a process that uses information learned about cancer through diagnostic processes, such as the size of the tumor, how deeply the tumor has invaded tissues at the site of the origin, the extent of any invasion into surrounding organs, and the extent of metastasis (spread) to lymph nodes or distant organs. This is a very important process because proper staging is the most important factor in selecting the right treatment plan. Cervical cancer is most frequently staged using the FIGO (International Federation of Gynecology and Obstetrics) System of Staging. This system classifies the disease in Stages I through IV.

The data used consists of a set of 221 cervical cancer patient cases obtained from the database of the Chittaranjan National Cancer Institute (CNCI), Calcutta. There are four classes corresponding to Stages I, II, III and IV of the cancer, containing 19, 41, 139, and 19 patient cases, respectively. The features of the model represent the presence or absence of the symptoms, and the signs observed upon physical examination. The 21 boolean input features refer to *Vulva: healthy (Vu(h)), Vulva: lesioned (Vu(l)), Vagina: healthy (Va(h)), Vagina: spread to upper part (Va(u)), Vagina: spread to middle part (Va(m)), Vagina: spread to lower part (Va(l)), Cervix: healthy (Cx(h)), Cervix: eroded (Cx(e)), Cervix: small ulcer (Cx(su)), Cervix: ulcerative growth (Cx(u)), Cervix: proliferative growth (Cx(p)), Cervix: ulceroproliferative growth (Cx(l)), Paracervix: free (PCx(f)), Paracervix: infiltrated (PCx(i)), Urinary bladder base: soft (BB(s)), Urinary bladder base: hard (BB(h)), Rectrovaginal septum: free (RVS(f)), Rectrovaginal septum: infiltrated (RVS(i)), Parametrium: free (Para(f)), Parametrium: spread, but not up to (Para(nu))* and *Parametrium: spread up to (Para(u))*, respectively.

The dependency rules generated via rough set theory and used in the encoding scheme are provided in Table 8.7. The evolved network is found to have (for recognition score around 80%) 118 links in 50 iterations, vis-a-vis 175 links in 90 iteration for the conventional MLP (Model O). A sample set of refined rules extracted from the network is presented in Table 8.8.

The expertise obtained from oncologists regarding different stages is provided below. In Stage I the cancer has spread from the lining of the cervix into the deeper connective tissue of the cervix. But it is still confined within the cervix. Stage II signifies the spread of cancer beyond the cervix to nearby areas like parametrial tissue, that are still inside the pelvic area. In Stage III the cancer has spread to the lower part of the vagina or the pelvic wall. It may be blocking the ureters (tubes that carry urine from the kidneys to the

TABLE 8.7: Crude rules obtained via rough set theory for staging of cervical cancer

I	Cx(su) ∨ Para(f), Cx(p) ∨ Para(f), Cx(su) ∨ Para(nu)
II	Va(h) ∨ Cx(u), Va(h) ∨ Cx(l), Va(u) ∨ Cx(u), Para(nu), Pcx(f)
III	Para(nu), Para(u), Va(u) (Va(u) ∧ Cx(u)) ∨ Cx(l) ∨ Va(m) (Va(h) ∧ Cx(u)) ∨ (Va(u) ∧ Cx(u)) ∨ Cx(l) (Va(u) ∧ Cx(p)) ∨ Va(m) ∨ Cx(l)
IV	(Va(l) ∧ Cx(u)) ∨ (Cx(u) ∧ Va(u)) ∨ (Va(l) ∧ Para(u)) (Va(l) ∧ Cx(p)) ∨ Va(m).

TABLE 8.8: Rules extracted from the modular rough MLP for staging of cervical cancer

I	←	$(Va(h) \wedge Para(f)) \vee (Cx(h) \wedge Cx(u) \wedge BB(s))$
II	←	$(PCx(f) \wedge PCx(i)) \vee Para(f) \vee Para(nu)$
III	←	$Va(h) \wedge Cx(u) \wedge Cx(l) \wedge Para(u)$
IV	←	$Va(m) \vee (Cx(u) \wedge Cx(p)) \vee (Para(nu) \wedge Para(u))$

bladder). Stage IV is the most advanced stage of cervical cancer. Now the cancer has spread to other parts of the body, like rectum, bladder or lungs. It may be mentioned here that the rules generated by the algorithm (Table 8.8) conform to the experts' opinion.

The performance of the popular C4.5 machine learning system [232] on the data set was also studied as a benchmark. Sample rules generated by C4.5 are:

I ← Va(h) ∧ PCx(f) ∧ Para(f)
II ← Para(f)
II ← BB(s)
III ← BB(s) ∧ Para(u)

Note that the rules obtained using C4.5 are significantly poorer than those obtained by the modular rough-fuzzy methodology. This is due to the fact that only statistically significant instances of the stages are represented in the rules by C4.5. On the other hand, in the modular rough-fuzzy model the rare patient cases are also preserved and incorporated into the network in the process of knowledge encoding and structured training. This leads to a more complete rule base.

8.9 Summary

The problem of classification, rule generation and rule evaluation in a soft-computing framework is addressed. At first, different algorithms for discovering association and classification rules are provided. Then a methodology for modular evolution of a rough-fuzzy MLP using genetic algorithms for designing a knowledge-based network for pattern classification and rule generation is described. The algorithm involves synthesis of several MLP modules, each encoding the rough set rules for a particular class. These knowledge-based modules are refined using a GA. The genetic operators are implemented in such a way that they help preserve the modular structure already evolved. It is seen that this methodology along with modular network decomposition results in accelerated training and more sparse (compact) network with comparable classification accuracy, as compared to earlier hybridizations.

The aforesaid model is used to extract classification rules. The performance of the rules is evaluated with some quantitative indices. These indices reflect the knowledge discovery aspect. It is observed that the modular rough-fuzzy methodology extracts rules that are fewer in number, yet accurate, and have high certainty factor and low confusion with less computation time. The model, besides having significance in soft-computing research, has potential for application to large scale problems involving knowledge discovery tasks, particularly related to mining of linguistic classification rules.

The modular rough-fuzzy MLP generates a structured network providing high classification accuracy. This is achieved by constrained evolution of the network, implemented by a modified genetic algorithm. In other words, the search is performed over a restricted hypothesis space. It is observed that the weight values of the solution network obtained using the above approach are not uniformly distributed; there is presence of a few strong links, others being mostly nonexistent. Such networks are known to have better generalization capability. Its VC-dimension is likely to be lower than that of the ordinary MLP. Establishing this theoretically may constitute an interesting future research problem. Again, one may investigate the sensitivity of the rule evaluation indices with respect to network weights.

Some of the indices (e.g., fidelity, coverage, confusion, certainty) used for extracting linguistic rules may be used in a suitable combination to act as the objective function of the network, instead of classification accuracy, for generating a knowledge-based connectionist system. This formulation is geared towards maximizing the utility of the network with respect to knowledge discovery tasks.

Appendix A

Role of Soft-Computing Tools in KDD

The main constituents of soft computing, at this juncture, include fuzzy logic, neural networks, genetic algorithms, and rough sets. Each of them contributes a distinct methodology for addressing problems in its domain. This is done in a cooperative, rather than a competitive, manner. The result is a more intelligent and robust system providing a human-interpretable, low-cost, approximate solution, as compared to traditional techniques. A review of the role of various soft-computing tools for different data mining tasks has recently been reported in [175]. Here we provide it in brief.

A.1 Fuzzy Sets

The modeling of imprecise and qualitative knowledge, as well as the transmission and handling of uncertainty at various stages, is possible through the use of fuzzy sets. Fuzzy logic is capable of supporting, to a reasonable extent, human-type reasoning in *natural* form. It is the earliest and most widely reported constituent of soft computing. The development of fuzzy logic has led to the emergence of soft computing. In this section we provide a glimpse of the available literature pertaining to the use of fuzzy sets in data mining [175].

Knowledge discovery in databases is mainly concerned with identifying interesting patterns and describing them in a concise and meaningful manner [65]. Fuzzy models can be said to represent a prudent and user-oriented sifting of data, qualitative observations and calibration of common-sense rules in an attempt to establish meaningful and useful relationships between system variables [217]. Despite a growing versatility of knowledge discovery systems, there is an important component of human interaction that is inherent to any process of knowledge representation, manipulation, and processing. Fuzzy sets are inherently inclined towards coping with linguistic domain knowledge and producing more interpretable solutions.

The notion of *interestingness*, which encompasses several features such as validity, novelty, usefulness, and simplicity, can be quantified through fuzzy sets. Fuzzy dissimilarity of a discovered pattern with a user-defined vocabulary has been used as a measure of this interestingness [139]. As an extension to the above methodology *unexpectedness* can also be defined in terms of a *belief system*, where if a belief b is based on previous evidence ξ then $d(b|\xi)$ denotes the degree of belief b. In soft belief systems, a weight w_i is attached to each belief b_i. The degree of a belief may be measured with conditional probability, Dempster-Shafer belief function or frequency of the raw data. Here, the interestingness of a pattern E relative to a belief system B and evidence ξ may be formally defined as

$$I(E, B, \xi) = \sum_{b_i \in B} w_i \left| d(b_i | E, \xi) - d(b_i | \xi) \right|. \tag{A.1}$$

This definition of interestingness measures the amount by which the degrees of belief change as a result of a new pattern E.

There is a growing indisputable role of fuzzy set technology in the realm of data mining [283]. Various data browsers have been implemented using fuzzy set theory [16]. Analysis of real-world data in data mining often necessitates simultaneously dealing with different types of variables, viz., categorical/symbolic data and numerical data. Nauck [183] has developed a learning algorithm that creates *mixed* fuzzy rules involving both categorical and numeric attributes. Pedrycz [217] discusses some constructive and fuzzy set-driven computational vehicles of knowledge discovery and establishes the relationship between data mining and fuzzy modeling. The role of fuzzy sets is categorized below based on the different functions of data mining that are modeled.

A.1.1   Clustering

Data mining aims at sifting through large volumes of data in order to reveal useful information in the form of new relationships, patterns, or clusters, for decision making by a user [224]. Fuzzy sets support a focused search, specified in linguistic terms, through data. They also help discover dependencies between the data in qualitative/semiqualitative format. In data mining, one is typically interested in a focused discovery of structure and an eventual quantification of functional dependencies existing therein. This helps prevent searching for meaningless or trivial patterns in a database. Researchers have developed fuzzy clustering algorithms for this purpose [274]. Russell and Lodwick [244] have explored fuzzy clustering methods for mining telecommunications customer and prospect databases to gain residential and business customer market share. Pedrycz has designed fuzzy clustering algorithms [216] using (a) contextual information and (b) induced linguistic space for better focusing of the search procedure in KDD.

Achieving focus is important in data mining because there are too many attributes and values to be considered and can result in combinatoric explosion. Most unsupervised data mining approaches try to achieve attribute focus by first recognizing the most interesting features. Mazlack [156] suggests a converse approach of progressively reducing the data set by partitioning and eliminating the least important attributes to reduce intra-item dissonance within the partitions. A *soft* focus is used to handle both crisp and imprecise data. It works by progressive reduction of cognitive dissonance, leading to an increase in useful information. The objective is to generate cohesive and comprehensible information *nuggets* by sifting out uninteresting attributes. A combined distance metric takes care of different types of attributes simultaneously, thus avoiding any taxonomic structure. Non-crisp values are handled by granularization followed by partitioning.

Increased granularity reduces attribute distinctiveness, resulting in loss of useful information, while finer grains lead to partitioning difficulty. Soft granules can be defined in terms of membership functions. *Granular computing* [288] is useful in finding meaningful patterns in data by expressing and processing chunks of information (granules). These are regarded as essential entities in all cognitive pursuits geared toward establishing meaningful patterns in data. The concept of granular computing allows one to concentrate all computational effort on some specific and problem-oriented subsets of a complete database. It also helps split an overall computing effort into several subtasks, leading to a *modularization* effect.

A.1.2 Association rules

An important area of data mining research deals with the discovery of *association rules* [2]. An association rule describes an interesting association relationship among different attributes. A boolean association involves binary attributes, a generalized association involves attributes that are hierarchically related, and a quantitative association involves attributes that can take on quantitative or categorical values. The use of fuzzy techniques has been considered to be one of the key components of data mining systems because of the affinity with human knowledge representation [149]. Wei and Chen [278] have mined generalized association rules with fuzzy taxonomic structures. A crisp taxonomy assumes that a child belongs to its ancestor with degree one. A fuzzy taxonomy is represented as a directed acyclic graph, each of whose edges represents a fuzzy *IS-A* relationship with degree μ ($0 \leq \mu \leq 1$). The partial belonging of an item in a taxonomy is taken into account while computing the degrees of support and confidence.

Au and Chan [14] utilize an *adjusted difference* between observed and expected frequency counts of attributes for discovering fuzzy association rules in relational databases. Instead of dividing quantitative attributes into fixed intervals, they employ linguistic terms to represent the revealed regularities and exceptions. Here no user-supplied thresholds are required, and quantitative values can be directly inferred from the rules. The linguistic representation leads to the discovery of *natural* and more understandable rules. The algorithm allows one to discover both *positive* and *negative* rules and can deal with fuzzy class boundaries as well as missing values in databases. The use of fuzzy techniques buries the boundaries of adjacent intervals of numeric quantities, resulting in resilience to noises such as inaccuracies in physical measurements of real life entities. The effectiveness of the algorithm was demonstrated on a transactional database of a PBX system and a database concerning industrial enterprises in mainland China.

A.1.3 Functional dependencies

Fuzzy logic has been used for analyzing inference based on functional dependencies (FDs), between variables, in database relations. Fuzzy inference generalizes both imprecise (set-valued) and precise inference. Similarly, fuzzy relational databases generalize their classical and imprecise counterparts by supporting fuzzy information storage and retrieval [86]. Inference analysis is performed using a special abstract model which maintains vital links to classical, imprecise and fuzzy relational database models. These links increase the utility of the inference formalism in practical applications involving "catalytic inference analysis," including knowledge discovery and database security. FDs are an interesting notion from a knowledge discovery standpoint since they allow one to express, in a condensed form, some properties of the real world which are valid on a given database. These properties can then be used in various applications such as reverse engineering or query optimization. Bosc et al. [28] use a data mining algorithm to extract/discover extended FDs, represented by gradual rules composed of linguistic variables.

A.1.4 Data summarization

Summary discovery is one of the major components of knowledge discovery in databases. This provides the user with comprehensive information for grasping the essence from a large amount of information in a database. Fuzzy set theory is also used for data summarization [133]. Typically, fuzzy sets are used for an interactive top-down summary discovery process which utilizes fuzzy *IS-A* hierarchies as domain knowledge. Here generalized tuples are used as a representational form of a database summary including fuzzy concepts. By virtue of fuzzy *IS-A* hierarchies, where fuzzy *IS-A* relationships common in actual domains are naturally expressed, the discovery process comes up with more accurate database summaries.

Linguistic summaries of large sets of data are derived as linguistically quantified propositions with a degree of validity [282]. This corresponds to the preference criterion involved in the mining task. The system consists of a summarizer (like, *young*), a quantity in agreement (like, *most*), and the truth/validity (say, 0.7). Single-attribute simple summarizers often need to be extended for some confluence of attribute values, implying combinatorial problems due to the huge number (all possible combinations) of summaries involved and the determination of the most appropriate/valid one.

It is found that often the most interesting linguistic summaries are non-trivial and human-consistent concepts, involving complicated combinations of attributes. In practice, this cannot be generated automatically and *human assistance/interaction* is required. Kacprzyk and Zadrozny [103] have developed *FQUERY*, a fuzzy querying add-on for *Access*, for an interactive linguistic summarization using *natural* terms and *comprehensible* quantifiers. It supports various fuzzy elements in queries, including interval attributes with membership for matching in a fuzzy relation and importance coefficients. First the user has to formulate a set of linguistic summaries of interest. The system then retrieves records from the database and calculates the validity of each summary. Finally, a most appropriate linguistic summary is selected. The scheme has also been used for fuzzy querying over the Internet, using a web browser such as Microsoft Explorer or Netscape Navigator. The definition of fuzzy values, fuzzy relations, and linguistic quantifiers is via Java applets.

Chiang et al. [41] have used fuzzy linguistic summary for mining time series data. The system provides a human interface, in the form of a graphic display tool, to help users premine a database and determine what knowledge could be discovered. The model is used to predict the on-line utilization ranks of different resources, including CPU and real storage.

A.1.5 Web application

Mining typical user profiles and URL associations from the vast amount of access logs is an important component of Web personalization, that deals with tailoring a user's interaction with the Web information space based on information about him/her. Nasraoui et al. [182] have defined a *user session* as a temporally compact sequence of Web accesses by a user and used a dissimilarity measure between two Web sessions to capture the organization of a Web site. Their goal is to categorize these sessions using Web mining.

A.1.6 Image retrieval

Recent increase in the size of *multimedia* information repositories, consisting of mixed media data, has made content-based image retrieval (CBIR) an active research area [195]. Unlike traditional database techniques which retrieve images based on exact matching of keywords, CBIR systems represent the information content of an image by visual features such as color, texture, and shape, and retrieve images based on similarity of features. Frigui [71] has developed an *interactive* and *iterative* image retrieval system that takes into account the *subjectivity* of human perception of visual content. The feature relevance weights are learned from the user's positive and negative feedback, and the Choquet integral is used as a dissimilarity measure. The smooth transition in the user's feedback is modeled by continuous fuzzy membership functions. Medasani and Krishnapuram [157] have designed a fuzzy approach to handle complex linguistic queries consisting of multiple attributes. Such queries are usually more *natural, user-friendly*, and *interpretable* for image retrieval. The degree to which an image satisfies an attribute is given by the membership value of the feature vector corresponding to the image in the membership function for the attribute. Fuzzy connectives are used to combine the degrees of satisfaction of multiple attributes in a complex query to arrive at an overall degree of satisfaction while ranking images for retrieval.

A.2   Neural Networks

Neural networks were earlier thought to be unsuitable for data mining because of their inherent *black-box* nature. No information was available from them in symbolic form, suitable for verification or interpretation by humans. Recently there has been widespread activity aimed at redressing this situation, by extracting the embedded knowledge in trained networks in the form of symbolic rules [270]. This serves to identify the attributes that, either individually or in a combination, are the most significant determinants of the decision or classification. Unlike fuzzy sets, the main contribution of neural nets towards data mining stems from rule extraction and clustering [175].

A.2.1   Rule extraction

In general, the primary input to a connectionist rule extraction algorithm is a representation of the trained neural network, in terms of its nodes, links and sometimes the data set. One or more hidden and output units are used to automatically derive the rules, which may later be combined and simplified to arrive at a more comprehensible rule set. These rules can also provide new insights into the application domain. The use of neural nets helps in (i) incorporating parallelism and (ii) tackling optimization problems in the data domain. The models are usually suitable in *data-rich* environments.

Typically a network is first trained to achieve the required accuracy rate. Redundant connections of the network are then removed using a pruning algorithm. The link weights and activation values of the hidden units in the network are analyzed, and classification rules are generated [148, 270].

A.2.2   Clustering and self organization

One of the big challenges of data mining is the organization and retrieval of documents from archives. Kohonen et al. [120] have demonstrated the utility of a huge self-organizing map (SOM) with more than one million nodes to partition a little less than seven million patent abstracts where the documents are represented by 500-dimensional feature vectors. Vesanto and Alhoniemi

[276] employ a stepwise strategy by partitioning the data with a SOM, followed by its clustering. Alahakoon et al. [8] perform hierarchical clustering of SOMs, based on a spread factor which is independent of the dimensionality of the data.

Shalvi and De Claris [255] have designed a data mining technique, combining Kohonen's self-organizing neural network with data visualization, for clustering a set of pathological data containing information regarding the patients' drugs, topographies (body locations) and morphologies (physiological abnormalities). Koenig [116] has combined SOM and Sammon's nonlinear mapping for reducing the dimension of data representation for visualization purposes.

A.2.3 Regression

Neural networks have also been used for a variety of classification and regression tasks [42]. Time series prediction has been attempted by Lee and Liu [134]. They have employed a neural oscillatory elastic graph matching model with hybrid radial basis functions for tropical cyclone identification and tracking.

A.3 Neuro-fuzzy Computing

Neuro-fuzzy computation [204] is one of the most popular hybridizations widely reported in literature. It comprises a judicious integration of the merits of neural and fuzzy approaches, enabling one to build more intelligent decision-making systems. This incorporates the generic advantages of artificial neural networks such as massive parallelism, robustness, and learning in *data-rich* environments into the system. The modeling of imprecise and qualitative knowledge in natural/linguistic terms as well as the transmission of uncertainty are possible through the use of fuzzy logic. Besides these generic advantages, the neuro-fuzzy approach also provides the corresponding application specific merits as highlighted earlier.

The rule generation aspect of neural networks is utilized to extract more *natural* rules from fuzzy neural networks [170]. The fuzzy MLP [173] and fuzzy Kohonen network [174] have been used for linguistic rule generation and inferencing. Here the input, besides being in quantitative, linguistic, or set forms, or a combination of these, can also be incomplete. The components of the input vector consist of membership values to the overlapping partitions of linguistic properties *low, medium,* and *high* corresponding to each input feature. Output decision is provided in terms of class membership values.

The models are capable of

- Inferencing based on complete and/or partial information

- Querying the user for unknown input variables that are key to reaching a decision

- Producing justification for inferences in the form of IF–THEN rules.

The connection weights and node activation values of the trained network are used in the process. A *certainty factor* determines the confidence in an output decision. Note that this certainty refers to the preference criterion for the extracted rules and is different from the notion of certain patterns of Equation (1.1).

Zhang et al. [292] have designed a granular neural network to deal with numerical-linguistic data fusion and granular knowledge discovery in numerical-linguistic databases. The network is capable of learning internal granular relations between input and output and predicting new relations. Low-level granular data can be compressed to generate high-level granular knowledge in the form of rules.

A neuro-fuzzy knowledge-based network by Mitra et al. [169] is capable of generating both *positive* and *negative* rules in linguistic form to justify any decision reached. In the absence of positive information regarding the belonging of a pattern to class C_k, the complementary information about the pattern not belonging to class $C_{k'}$ is used for generating the negative rules. The a priori class information and the distribution of pattern points in the feature space are taken into account while encoding the crude *domain knowledge* from the data set among the connection weights. Fuzzy intervals and linguistic sets are used in the process. The network topology is automatically determined, followed by refinement using growing and/or pruning of links and nodes. The knowledge-based network converges earlier, resulting in more meaningful rules.

A.4 Genetic Algorithms

GAs are adaptive, robust, efficient and global search methods, suitable in situations where the search space is large. They optimize a *fitness function*, corresponding to the preference criterion of data mining, to arrive at an optimal solution using certain genetic operators. Knowledge discovery systems have been developed using genetic programming concepts [68, 237]. The *MAS-SON* system [245], where intentional information is extracted for a given set of objects, is popular. The problem addressed is to find the common characteristics of a set of objects in an object-oriented database. Genetic programming is used to automatically generate, evaluate, and select object-oriented queries. GAs are also used for several other purposes like fusion of multiple data types in *multimedia* databases and automated program generation for mining multimedia data [269].

However, the literature in the domain of GA-based data mining is not as rich as that of fuzzy sets. We provide below a categorization of a few such interesting systems based on the functions modeled [175].

Besides discovering human-interpretable patterns data mining also encompasses prediction [65], where some variables or attributes in the database are used to determine unknown or future values of other variables of interest. The traditional weighted average or linear multi-regression models for prediction require a basic assumption that there is no interaction among the attributes. GAs, on the other hand, are able to handle attribute interaction in a better manner. Xu et al. [281] have designed a multi-input single-output system using a nonlinear integral. An adaptive GA is used for learning the nonlinear multi-regression from a set of training data.

Noda et al. [185] used GAs to discover *interesting* rules in a dependence modeling task, where different rules can predict different goal attributes. Generally attributes with high information gain are good predictors of a class when considered individually. However, attributes with low information gain could become more relevant when attribute interactions are taken into account. This phenomenon is associated with rule interestingness. The degree of interestingness of the consequent is computed based on the relative frequency of the value predicted by it. In other words, the rarer the value of a goal attribute, the more interesting a rule it predicts. The algorithm can discover a few interesting rules (knowledge nuggets) instead of a large set of accurate (but not necessarily interesting) rules.

Lopes et al. [146] evolved association rules of IF C THEN P type, which provide a high degree of accuracy and coverage. While the *accuracy* of a rule measures its degree of confidence, its *coverage* is interpreted as the comprehensive inclusion of all the records that satisfy the rule. Hence $Accuracy = \frac{|C \bigcap P|}{|C \bigcap P| + |C \bigcap \overline{P}|}$ and $Coverage = \frac{|C \bigcap P|}{|C \bigcap P| + |\overline{C} \bigcap P|}$ are defined. Note that various quantitative measures for rule evaluation have been discussed in Section 8.7.2, with reference to neural networks.

A.5 Rough Sets

The theory of rough sets [214] has emerged as a major mathematical tool for managing uncertainty that arises from granularity in the domain of discourse, i.e., from the indiscernibility between objects in a set, and has proved to be useful in a variety of KDD processes [175]. It offers mathematical tools to discover hidden patterns in data, and therefore its importance, as far as data mining is concerned, can in no way be overlooked. A fundamental principle of a rough set-based learning system is to discover redundancies and dependencies between the given features of a problem to be classified. It approximates a given concept from below and from above, using *lower* and *upper approximations*.

A rough set learning algorithm can be used to obtain a set of rules in IF–THEN form, from a *decision table*. The rough set method provides an effective tool for extracting knowledge from databases. Here one first creates a knowledge base, classifying objects and attributes within the created decision tables. Then a knowledge discovery process is initiated to remove some undesirable attributes. Finally the data dependency is analyzed, in the reduced database, to find the minimal subset of attributes called *reduct*.

Rough set applications to data mining generally proceed along the following directions.

1. *Decision rule induction from attribute value table* [98, 176, 256, 259]. Most of these methods are based on generation of discernibility matrices and reducts.

2. *Data filtration by template generation* [227]. This mainly involves extracting elementary blocks from data based on equivalence relation. Genetic algorithms are also sometimes used in this stage for searching, so that the methodologies can be used for large data sets.

Besides these, reduction of memory and computational requirements for rule generation, and working on dynamic databases [256] are also considered.

A.6   Other Hybridizations

Banerjee et al. [17] have used a *rough–neuro-fuzzy* integration to design a knowledge-based system, where the theory of rough sets is utilized for extracting domain knowledge. In the said rough–fuzzy MLP, the extracted crude domain knowledge is encoded among the connection weights. Rules are generated from a decision table by computing relative reducts. The network topology is automatically determined and the dependency factors of these rules are encoded as the initial connection weights. The hidden nodes model the conjuncts in the antecedent part of a rule, while the output nodes model the disjuncts. Various other *rough–fuzzy* hybridizations for intelligent system design are reported in [209].

George and Srikanth [76] have used a *fuzzy–genetic* integration, where GAs are applied to determine the most appropriate data summary. Kiem and Phuc [111] have developed a *rough–neuro–genetic* hybridization for discovering conceptual clusters from a large database.

Appendix B

Data Sets Used in Experiments

We present below the details of the data sets used in empirical evaluation and comparison of the algorithms described. They are listed in the order of their size (number of samples and dimensions), along with their sources.

1. *Forest cover type*: The data represents forest cover types of 30m × 30m cells obtained from US Forest Service (USFS) Region 2 Resource Information System (RIS). There are 581012 instances, with 54 attributes representing cartographic variables (hillshade, distance to hydrology, elevation, soil type, etc.), of which 10 are quantitative and 44 binary. The task is to classify the observations into seven categories representing the forest cover types, namely, Spruce/Fir, Lodgepole Pine, Ponderosa Pine, Cottonwood/Willow, Aspen, DouglasFir, Krummholz. Source: UCI KDD Archive [95].

2. *PUMS census*: Population census data for the Los Angeles and Long Beach area. The data contains 320,000 samples and 133 attributes (mostly categorical or integer valued). The task is to identify two groups of population, namely those who have undergone/not undergone 'higher education,' measured in terms of number of years in college. Source: UCI KDD Archive [95].

3. *Satellite image*: Gray level images of four different spectral bands obtained by the Indian Remote Sensing satellite of the city of Calcutta in India [201]. Each image is 512 × 512 pixels in size. Source: NRSA data center, India, http://www.isical.ac.in/~miu.

4. *Isolet*: The data consists of several spectral coefficients of utterances of English alphabets by 150 subjects. There are 617 features all real in the range [0, 1], 7797 instances and 26 classes. Source: UCI Machine Learning Repository [25].

5. *Multiple features*: This data set consists of features of handwritten numerals (0−9) extracted from a collection of Dutch utility maps. There are a total 2000 patterns, 649 features and 10 classes. Source: UCI Machine Learning Repository [25].

6. *Twonorm*: Artificial data [32] having 20000 samples, 20 features and 2 classes. Each class follows multivariate normal distribution with covari-

211

ance matrix as the identity matrix. Class 1 has mean $(a, a, \ldots, a)$ and class 2 has mean $(-a, -a, \ldots, -a)$. $a = \frac{2}{20^{\frac{1}{2}}}$. Source: UCI Machine Learning Repository [25].

7. *Ringnorm*: Artificial data [32] having 20000 samples, 20 features and 2 classes. Each class is multivariate normal. Class 1 has mean $(0, 0, \ldots, 0)$ and covariance matrix as 4 time the identity matrix, class 2 has mean $(a, a, \ldots, a)$ and covariance matrix as the identity matrix. $a = \frac{2}{20^{\frac{1}{2}}}$. Source: UCI Machine Learning Repository [25].

8. *Waveform*: Noisy artificial data [32]. It consists of 5000 instances having 40 attributes each. The attributes are continuous valued, and some of them are noise. The task is to classify an instance into one of the 3 categories of waves. Source: UCI Machine Learning Repository [25].

9. *Spambase*: Word frequencies of email, used to classify an email into spam or non-spam category. There are 4601 instances, 57 continuous valued attributes denoting word frequencies, and 2 classes. Source: UCI Machine Learning Repository [25].

10. *Arrhythmia*: Parameters of ECG measurements used to classify a patient into classes of cardiac arrhythmia. It contains 452 samples, each having 279 attributes. Among the attributes 195 are real valued and are used for our experiments. Source: UCI Machine Learning Repository [25].

11. *Heart*: Diagnostic measurements of Cleveland heart disease patients. It contains 1535 data points belonging to 2 classes. Number of features is 16. Source: UCI Machine Learning Repository [25].

12. *Vowel*: Formant frequencies of Indian Telugu vowels [199] uttered in consonant-vowel-consonant context by 3 male speakers in the age group of 30–35 years. It contains 871 samples, 3 features and 6 classes. Source: Machine Intelligence Unit, Indian Statistical Institute, Calcutta, http://www.isical.ac.in/~miu.

13. *Pat*: Artificial linearly nonseparable data as shown in Figure 6.3 [204]. There are 880 samples, 2 features and 2 classes. Source: Machine Intelligence Unit, Indian Statistical Institute, Calcutta, http://www.isical.ac.in/~miu.

14. *Pima*: Clinical measurements to detect diabetes disease of Pima Indian tribe. There are 768 samples, 8 features and 2 classes. Source: UCI Machine Learning Repository [25].

15. *Wisconsin cancer*: Clinical measurements to detect breast cancer. It contains 9 features, 684 instances and 2 classes. Source: UCI Machine Learning Repository [25].

16. *Hepatobiliary:* Results of biochemical tests (e.g., glutamic oxalacetic transaminate, glutamic pyruvic transaminase, lactate dehydrase, gamma glutamyl transpeptidase, blood urea nitrogen) used to detect Hepatobiliary disorders such as alcoholic liver damage, primary hepatoma, liver cirrhosis and cholelithiasis [93]. There are 536 samples, 9 features and 4 classes.

17. *Monks-2:* AI game-playing moves data having 432 samples, 6 features and 2 classes. Source: UCI Machine Learning Repository [25].

18. *Ionosphere:* The data represents autocorrelation functions of radar measurements. The task is to classify them into 2 classes denoting passage or obstruction in ionosphere. There are 351 instances and 34 attributes, all continuous. Source: UCI Machine Learning Repository [25].

19. Cervical cancer: Clinical measurements for staging of cervical cancer [163]. There are 221 samples, 21 features and 4 classes. Source: Machine Intelligence Unit, Indian Statistical Institute, Calcutta.

20. *Iris:* Measurements of iris flowers. There are 150 samples, 4 features and 3 classes. Source: UCI Machine Learning Repository [25].

21. *Norm:* Artificial bivariate normal data with zero mean and covariance matrix as the identity matrix [165]. It contains 500 samples and 2 features.

References

[1] R. Agrawal, J. Gehrke, D. Gunopulos, and P. Raghavan. Automatic subspace clustering of high dimensional data for data mining applications. In *Proc. ACM SIGMOD Conf.*, pages 94–105, Washington, 1998.

[2] R. Agrawal, T. Imielinski, and A. Swami. Mining association rules between sets of items in large databases. In *Proc. 1993 ACM SIGMOD Intl. Conf. Management of Data*, pages 207–216, Washington D.C., May 1993.

[3] R. Agrawal, H. Mannila, R. Srikant, H. Toivonen, and I. Verkamo. Fast discovery of association rules. In U. M. Fayyad, G. Piatetsky-Shapiro, P. Smyth, and R. Uthuruswamy, editors, *Advances in Knowledge Discovery and Data Mining*, pages 307–328. MIT Press, Cambridge, MA, 1996.

[4] D. W. Aha. Tolerating noisy, irrelevant and novel attributes in instance based learning algorithms. *International Journal of Man Machine Studies*, 36:266–287, 1992.

[5] D. W. Aha. Editorial on lazy learning. *AI Review, Spl. issue on lazy learning*, 11(1-5):7–10, 1997.

[6] D. W. Aha and R. L. Bankert. A comparative evaluation of sequential feature selection algorithms. In D. Fisher and J.-H. Lenz, editors, *Artificial Intelligence and Statistics V*. Springer Verlag, New York, 1996.

[7] D. W. Aha, D. Kibler, and M. K. Albert. Instance-based learning algorithms. *Machine Learning*, 6:37–66, 1991.

[8] D. Alahakoon, S. K. Halgamuge, and B. Srinivasan. Dynamic self organizing maps with controlled growth for knowledge discovery. *IEEE Transactions on Neural Networks*, 11:601–614, 2000.

[9] R. Andrews, J. Diederich, and A. B. Tickle. A survey and critique of techniques for extracting rules from trained artificial neural networks. *Knowledge-Based Systems*, 8:373–389, 1995.

[10] D. Angluin. Queries and concept learning. *Machine Learning*, 2:319–342, 1988.

[11] S. Arya, D. M. Mount, N. S. Netanyahu, R. Silverman, and A. Y. Wu. An optimal algorithm for approximate nearest neighbor searching. *Journal of the ACM*, 45:891–923, 1998.

[12] A. Aspin. Tables for use in comparisons whose accuracy involves two variances. *Biometrika*, 36:245–271, 1949.

[13] M. M. Astrahan. Speech analysis by clustering, or the hyperphoneme method. In *Stanford A.I. Project Memo*. Stanford University, CA, 1970.

[14] W. H. Au and K. C. C. Chan. An effective algorithm for discovering fuzzy rules in relational databases. In *Proc. IEEE Intl. Conf. Fuzzy Systems FUZZ IEEE 98*, pages 1314–1319, Alaska, 1998.

[15] P. Baldi and S. Brunak. *Bioinformatics: The Machine Learning Approach*. MIT Press, Boston, MA, 1998.

[16] J. F. Baldwin. Knowledge from data using fuzzy methods. *Pattern Recognition Letters*, 17:593–600, 1996.

[17] M. Banerjee, S. Mitra, and S. K. Pal. Rough fuzzy MLP: Knowledge encoding and classification. *IEEE Trans. Neural Networks*, 9(6):1203–1216, 1998.

[18] D. Barbará, W. DuMouchel, C. Faloutsos, P. J. Haas, J. M. Hellerstein, Y. E. Ioannidis, H. V. Jagadish, T. Johnson, R. T. Ng, V. Poosala, K. A. Ross, and K. C. Sevcik. The New Jersey data reduction report. *IEEE Data Engineering Bulletin*, 20(4):3–45, 1997.

[19] E. B. Baum and D. Haussler. What size nets give valid generalization? *Neural Computation*, 1:151–160, 1989.

[20] L. M. Belue and K. W. Bauer. Determining input features for multilayer perceptrons. *Neurocomputing*, 7:111–121, 1995.

[21] Y. Bengio, J. M. Buhmann, M. Embrechts, and J. M. Zurada. Introduction to the special issue on neural networks for data mining and knowledge discovery. *IEEE Transactions on Neural Networks*, 11:545–549, 2000.

[22] J. L. Bentley. Multidimensional divide and conquer. *Comm. ACM*, 23(4):214–219, 1980.

[23] M. Berthold and D. J. Hand, editors. *Intelligent Data Analysis: An Introduction*. Spinger-Verlag, Berlin, 1999.

[24] J. C. Bezdek and S. K. Pal, editors. *Fuzzy Models for Pattern Recognition: Methods that Search for Structures in Data*. IEEE Press, New York, 1992.

[25] C. L. Blake and C. J. Merz. *UCI Repository of machine learning databases*. University of California, Irvine, Dept. of Information and Computer Sciences, http://www.ics.uci.edu/~mlearn/MLRepository.html, 1998.

[26] H. Blockeel and L. De Raedt. Top-down induction of first-order logical decision trees. *Artificial Intelligence*, 101(1-2):285–297, 1997.

[27] R. L. Blum. *Discovery and Representation of Causal Relationships from a Large Time-Oriented Clinical Database: The RX Project*, volume 19 of *Lecture Notes in Medical Informatics*. Spinger-Verlag, 1982.

[28] P. Bosc, O. Pivert, and L. Ughetto. Database mining for the discovery of extended functional dependencies. In *Proc. NAFIPS 99*, pages 580–584, New York, USA, 1999. IEEE Press, Piscataway, NJ.

[29] P. Bradley, U. M. Fayyad, and C. Reina. Scaling clustering algorithms to large databases. In *Proc. 4th Intl. Conf. Knowledge Discovery and Data Mining*, pages 9–15, NY, 1998. AAAI Press, Menlo Park, CA.

[30] P. S. Bradley and O. L. Mangasarian. Massive data discrimination via linear support vector machines. *Optimization Methods and Software*, 13(1):1–10, 2000.

[31] L. Breiman. Arcing classifiers. *Annals of Statistics*, 26(3):801–849, 1998.

[32] L. Breiman, J. H. Friedman, R. A. Olshen, and C. J. Stone. *Classification and Regression Trees*. Wadsworth and Brooks/Cole, Monterey, CA, 1984.

[33] S. Brin, R. Motwani, J. D. Ullman, and S. Tsur. Dynamic itemset counting and implication rules for market basket data. In *SIGMOD 1997, Proc. ACM SIGMOD Int. Conf. Management of Data*, pages 255–264, Tucson, AR, 1997. ACM Press, NY.

[34] H. Bunke and A. Kandel, editors. *Neuro-Fuzzy Pattern Recognition*. World Scientific, Singapore, 2001.

[35] C. J. C. Burges. A tutorial on support vector machines for pattern recognition. *Data Mining and Knowledge Discovery*, 2(2):1–47, 1998.

[36] C. Campbell, N. Cristianini, and A. Smola. Query learning with large margin classifiers. In *Proc. 17th Intl. Conf. Machine Learning*, pages 111–118, Stanford, CA, 2000. Morgan Kaufmann, San Mateo, CA.

[37] J. Catlett. *Megainduction: Machine learning on very large databases*. PhD thesis, Department of Computer Science, University of Sydney, Australia, 1991.

[38] C. Chatterjee and V. P. Roychowdhury. On self-organizing algorithms and networks for class-separability features. *IEEE Trans. Neural Networks*, 8:663–678, 1997.

[39] D. Chaudhuri, C. A. Murthy, and B. B. Chaudhuri. Finding a subset of representative points in a dataset. *IEEE Trans. Syst. Man. Cybern.*, 24:1416–1424, 1994.

[40] P. Cheeseman, J. Kelly nad M. Self, and J. Stutz. Autoclass: A bayesian classification system. In *Proc. 5th Intl. Conf. Machine Learning*, Ann Arbor, MI, 1988. Morgan Kaufmann, San Mateo, CA.

[41] D.-A. Chiang, L. R. Chow, and Y.-F. Wang. Mining time series data by a fuzzy linguistic summary system. *Fuzzy Sets and Systems*, 112:419–432, 2000.

[42] V. Ciesielski and G. Palstra. Using a hybrid neural/expert system for database mining in market survey data. In *Proc. Second Intl. Conf. Knowledge Discovery and Data Mining (KDD-96)*, page 38, Portland, OR, 1996. AAAI Press, Menlo Park, CA.

[43] K. Cios, W. Pedrycz, and R. Swiniarski. *Data Mining Methods for Knowledge Discovery*. Kluwer Academic Publishers, Boston, MA, 1998.

[44] K. J. Cios, W. Pedrycz, and R. M. Swiniarski. Data mining methods for knowledge discovery. *IEEE Trans. Neural Networks*, 9(6):1533–1534, 1998.

[45] D. Cohn, L. Atlas, and R. Ladner. Improving generalization with active learning. *Machine Learning*, 15:201–221, 1994.

[46] M. Craven and J. Shavlik. Using neural networks for data mining. *Future Generation Computer Systems*, 13:211–219, 1997.

[47] S. K. Das. Feature selection with a linear dependence measure. *IEEE Trans. Computers*, 20:1106–1109, 1971.

[48] B. V. Dasarathy. *Nearest Neighbor (NN) Norms: NN Patterns Classification Techniques*. IEEE Computer Society Press, Los Alamitos, 1991.

[49] R. K. De, J. Basak, and S. K. Pal. Neuro-fuzzy feature evaluation with theoretical analysis. *Neural Networks*, 12(10):1429–1455, 1999.

[50] R. K. De, J. Basak, and S. K. Pal. Unsupervised feature extraction using neuro-fuzzy approaches. *Fuzzy Sets and Systems*, 176:277–291, 2002.

[51] R. K. De and S. K. Pal. A connectionist model for selection of cases. *Information Sciences*, 132:179–194, 2001.

[52] P. Demartines and J. Herault. Curvilinear component analysis: A self-organizing neural network for nonlinear mapping of data sets. *IEEE Trans. Neural Network*, 8:148–160, 1997.

[53] A. P. Dempster, N. M. Laird, and D. B. Rubin. Maximum likelihood from incomplete data via the EM algorithm. *Journal of the Royal Statistical Society, Series B*, 39:1–38, 1977.

[54] K. Deng and A. W. Moore. Multiresolution instance-based learning. In *Proc. Intl. Joint Conf. Artificial Intelligence (IJCAI-95)*, pages 1233–1242, Montreal, Canada, 1995. Morgan Kaufmann, San Mateo, CA.

[55] P. A. Devijver and J. Kittler. *Pattern Recognition: A Statistical Approach.* Prentice Hall, Englewood Cliffs, 1982.

[56] S. Dick. Granular computing in neural networks. In W. Pedrycz, editor, *Granular Computing*, pages 275–305. Physica Verlag, Heidelberg, 2001.

[57] C. Domeniconi and D. Gunopulos. Adaptive nearest neighbor classification using support vector machines. In *Advances in Neural Information Processing System 14 (NIPS'2001)*, Vancouver, Canada, 2001. MIT Press, Boston, MA.

[58] G. Dong and J. Li. Interestingness of discovered association rules in terms of neighborhood-based unexpectedness. In *Proc. 2nd Pacific-Asia Conf. Knowledge Discovery and Data Mining*, pages 72–86. Springer Verlag, Singapore, 1998.

[59] R. O. Duda, P. E. Hart, and D. G. Stork. *Pattern Classification (2nd Edition).* Wiley-Interscience, New York, 2000.

[60] W. DuMouchel, C. Volinsky, T. Johnson, C. Cortes, and D. Pregibon. Squashing flat files flatter. In *Proc. 5th ACM Conf. Knowledge Discovery and Data Mining*, pages 6–15, San Diego, CA, 1999. ACM Press, NY.

[61] J. Ester, H.-P. Kriegel, J. Sander, and X. Xu. A density-based algorithm for discovering clusters in large spatial databases with noise. In *Proc. 2nd Intl. Conf. Knowledge Discovery and Data Mining (KDD'96)*, pages 226–231, Portland, OR, 1996. AAAI Press, Menlo Park, CA.

[62] O. Etzioni. The world-wide web: Quagmire or goldmine? *Comm. ACM*, 39:65–68, 1996.

[63] A. Faragó, T. Linder, and G. Lugosi. Nearest neighbor search and classification in $\mathcal{O}(1)$ time. *Problems of Control and Information Theory*, 20(6):383–395, 1991.

[64] U. M. Fayyad, D. Haussler, and P. Stolorz. Mining scientific data. *Comm. ACM*, 39:51–57, 1996.

[65] U. M. Fayyad, G. Piatetsky-Shapiro, P. Smyth, and R. Uthurusamy, editors. *Advances in Knowledge Discovery and Data Mining.* MIT Press, Menlo Park, CA, 1996.

[66] U. M. Fayyad and R. Uthurusamy. Data mining and knowledge discovery in databases. *Comm. ACM*, 39(11):24–27, 1996.

[67] D. Fisher. Knowledge aquistion via conceptual clustering. *Machine Learning*, 2:139–172, 1987.

[68] I. W. Flockhart and N. J. Radcliffe. A genetic algorithm-based approach to data mining. In *The 2nd Intl. Conf. Knowledge Discovery and Data*

Mining (KDD-96), page 299, Portland, OR, 1996. AAAI Press, Menlo Park, CA.

[69] Y. Freund and R. E. Schapire. Large margin classification using the perceptron algorithm. *Machine Learning*, 37(3):277–296, 1999.

[70] T. Friess, N. Cristianini, and C. Campbell. The kernel adatron algorithm: A fast and simple learning procedure for support vector machine. In *Proc. 15th Intl. Conf. Machine Learning*, pages 188–196, Madison, WI, 1998. Morgan Kaufmann, San Mateo, CA.

[71] H. Frigui. Adaptive image retrieval using the fuzzy integral. In *Proc. NAFIPS 99*, pages 575–579, New York, 1999. IEEE Press, Piscataway, NJ.

[72] K. S. Fu. *Syntactic Pattern Recognition and Applications*. Academic Press, London, 1982.

[73] L. M. Fu. Knowledge-based connectionism for revising domain theories. *IEEE Trans. Systems, Man, and Cybernetics*, 23:173–182, 1993.

[74] K. Fukunaga and J. M. Mantock. Nonparametric data reduction. *IEEE Trans. Pattern Analysis and Machine Intelligence*, 6:115–118, 1984.

[75] J. Gehrke, R. Ramakrishnan, and V. Ganti. RainForest – a framework for large decision tree construction for large datasets. In *Proc. 24th Intl. Conf. Very Large Databases*, pages 416–427, San Francisco, 1998. Morgan Kaufmann, San Mateo, CA.

[76] R. George and R. Srikanth. Data summarization using genetic algorithms and fuzzy logic. In F. Herrera and J. L. Verdegay, editors, *Genetic Algorithms and Soft Computing*, pages 599–611. Physica-Verlag, Heidelberg, 1996.

[77] J. Ghosh. Multiclassifier systems: Back to the future. In J. Kittler and F. Roli, editors, *Multiple Classifier Systems*, volume 2364 of *Lecture Notes in Computer Science*, pages 1–15. Springer Verlag, London, 2002.

[78] A. Giani, F. Baiardi, and A. Starita. PANIC: A parallel evolutionary rule based system. In D. Fogel, J. McDonell, and R. Reynolds, editors, *Evolutionary Programming IV. Proc. Fourth Annual Conf. Evolutionary Programming*, pages 753–771, San Diego, CA, 1995. MIT Press, Cambridge, MA.

[79] C. Glymour, D. Madigan, D. Pregibon, and P. Smyth. Statistical inference and data mining. *Comm. ACM*, 39:35–41, 1996.

[80] D. E. Goldberg. *Genetic Algorithms in Search, Optimization and Machine Learning*. Addison-Wesley, Reading, MA, 1989.

[81] B. Gray and M.E. Orlowska. CCAIIA: Clustering categorical attributes into interesting association rules. In *Proc. 2nd Pacific-Asia Conf.*

Knowledge Discovery and Data Mining, pages 132–143. Springer Verlag, Singapore, 1998.

[82] J. Gray, S. Chaudhuri, A. Bosworth, A. Layman, D. Reichart, M. Venkatrao, F. Pellow, and H. Pirahesh. Data cube: A relational aggregation operator generalizing group-by, cross-tab, and sub-totals. *Data Mining and Knowledge Discovery*, 1(1):29–53, 1997.

[83] R. M. Gray. Vector quantization. *IEEE ASSP Mag.*, 1:4–29, 1984.

[84] S. Guha, R. Rastogi, and K. Shim. CURE: An efficient clustering algorithm for large databases. In *Proc. ACM SIGMOD Intl. Conf. Management of Data*, pages 73–84, New York, 1998. ACM Press, NY.

[85] D. Gusfield. *Algorithms on Strings, Trees, and Sequences: Computer Science and Computational Biology*. Cambridge University Press, Cambridge, UK, 1997.

[86] J. Hale and S. Shenoi. Analyzing FD inference in relational databases. *Data and Knowledge Engineering*, 18:167–183, 1996.

[87] M. A. Hall. Correlation based feature selection for discrete and numeric class machine learning. In *Proc. 17th Intl. Conf. Machine Learning*, Stanford, CA, 2000. Morgan Kaufmann, CA.

[88] J. Han and M. Kamber. *Data Mining: Concepts and Techniques*. Morgan Kaufmann, San Mateo, CA, 2000.

[89] D. Hand, H. Mannila, and P. Smyth. *Principles of Data Mining*. MIT Press, Menlo Park, CA, 2001.

[90] B. M. Happel and J. J. Murre. Design and Evolution of Modular Neural Network Architectures. *Neural Networks*, 7:985–1004, 1994.

[91] P. E. Hart. The condensed nearest neigbor rule. *IEEE Trans. Information Theory*, 14:515–516, 1968.

[92] T. Hastie, R. Tibshirani, and J. Friedman. *The Elements of Statistical Learning: Data Mining, Inference, and Prediction*. Springer Verlag, NY, 2001.

[93] Y. Hayashi. A neural expert system with automated extraction of fuzzy if-then rules and its application to medical diagnosis. In R. P. Lippmann, J. E. Moody, and D. S. Touretzky, editors, *Advances in Neural Information Processing Systems*, pages 578–584. Morgan Kaufmann, Los Altos, CA, 1991.

[94] R. Heider. Troubleshooting CFM 56-3 engines for the Boeing 737 – using CBR and data-mining. *Lecture Notes in Computer Science*, 1168:512–523, 1996.

[95] S. Hettich and S. D. Bay. *The UCI KDD Archive.* University of California, Irvine, Dept. of Information and Computer Sciences, http://kdd.ics.uci.edu, 1999.

[96] R. P. Heydorn. Redundancy in feature extraction. *IEEE Trans. Computers*, 21:1051–1054, 1971.

[97] K. Hornik and C.-M. Kuan. Convergence analysis of local feature extraction algorithms. *Neural Networks*, 5:229–240, 1992.

[98] X. Hu and N. Cercone. Mining knowledge rules from databases: A rough set approach. In *Proceedings of the 12th International Conference on Data Engineering*, pages 96–105, Washington, February 1996. IEEE Computer Society Press, NY.

[99] T. Imeliensky and H. Mannila. A database perspective on knowledge discovery. *Comm. ACM*, 39:58–64, 1996.

[100] C. Z. Jaikow. A knowledge intensive genetic algorithm for supervised learning. *Machine Learning*, 13:198–228, 1993.

[101] A. K. Jain, R. P. W. Duin, and J. Mao. Statistical pattern recognition: A review. *IEEE Trans. Pattern Analysis and Machine Intelligence*, 22:4–37, 2000.

[102] F. V. Jensen. *Bayesian Networks and Decision Diagrams.* Springer Verlag, New York, 2001.

[103] J. Kacprzyk and S. Zadrozny. Data mining via linguistic summaries of data: An interactive approach. In *Proc. IIZUKA 98*, pages 668–671, Fukuoka, Japan, 1998.

[104] L. Kanal. Patterns in pattern recognition. *IEEE Trans. Information Theory*, 20:697–722, 1974.

[105] A. Kandel. *Fuzzy Techniques in Pattern Recognition.* Wiley Interscience, New York, 1982.

[106] H. Kargupta and P. Chan, editors. *Advances in Distributed and Parallel Knowledge Discovery.* MIT/AAAI Press, Menlo Park, CA, 2001.

[107] L. Kaufmann. Solving the quadratic programming problem arising in support vector classification. In B. Scholkopf, C. J. C. Burges, and A. J. Smola, editors, *Advances in Kernel Methods – Support Vector Learning*, pages 147–168. MIT Press, Boston, MA, 1998.

[108] M. J. Kearns. Efficient noise-tolerant learning from statistical queries. In *Proc. 25th ACM Symposium on Theory of Computing*, pages 392–401, San Diego, CA, 1993. ACM Press, NY.

[109] R. L. Kennedy, Y. Lee, B. van Roy, C. D. Reed, and R. P. Lippman. *Solving Data Mining Problems Through Pattern Recognition.* Prentice Hall, NJ, 1998.

[110] R. Khosla and T. S. Dillon. Welding symbolic AI systems with neural networks and their applications. In *Proc. IEEE Int. Joint Conf. Neural Networks (IJCNN'98)*, pages 29–34, Anchorage, AL, 1998. IEEE Press, NJ.

[111] H. Kiem and D. Phuc. Using rough genetic and Kohonen's neural network for conceptual cluster discovery in data mining. In *Proc. RSFD-GrC'99*, pages 448–452, Yamaguchi, Japan, 1999.

[112] B. King. Step-wise clustering procedures. *Journal of American Statistical Association*, 62:86–101, 1967.

[113] K. Kira and L. Rendell. A practical approach to feature selection. In *Proc. 9th Intl. Workshop on Machine Learning*, pages 249–256, San Mateo, CA, 1992. Morgan Kaufmann, San Mateo, CA.

[114] J. Kivinen and H. Mannila. The power of sampling in knowledge discovery. In *Proc. 1994 ACM SIGACT-SIGMOD Symposium on Principles of Database Theory (PODS'94)*, pages 77–85, Minneapolis, MN, 1994. ACM Press, NY.

[115] M. Klemettinen, H. Mannila, P. Ronkainen, H. Toivonen, and A. Inkeri Verkamo. Finding interesting rules from large sets of discovered association rules. In *Proc. 3rd Intl. Conf. Information and Knowledge Management (CIKM'94)*, pages 401–407. ACM Press, NY, 1994.

[116] A. Koenig. Interactive visualization and analysis of hierarchical neural projections for data mining. *IEEE Trans. Neural Networks*, 11:615–624, 2000.

[117] R. Kohavi and G. John. Wrappers for feature selection. *Artificial Intelligence*, 97(1-2):273–324, 1997.

[118] T. Kohonen. The Self-Organizing Map. *Proc. IEEE*, 78:1464–1480, 1990.

[119] T. Kohonen. *Self-Organizing Maps*. Springer, Heidelberg, 2001.

[120] T. Kohonen, S. Kaski, K. K. Lagusand J. Salojarvi, V. Paatero, and A. Saarela. Organization of a massive document collection. *IEEE Trans. Neural Networks*, 11(3):574–585, 2000.

[121] D. Koller and M. Sahami. Towards optimal feature selection. In *Proc. 13th Intl. Conf. Machine Learning*, pages 284–292, San Fransico, CA, 1996. Morgan Kaufmann, San Mateo, CA.

[122] J. L. Kolodner. *Case-Based Reasoning*. Morgan Kaufmann, San Mateo, 1993.

[123] J. Komorowski, Z. Pawlak, L. Polkowski, and A. Skowron. A rough set perspective on data and knowledge. In W. Klosgen and J. Zytkow, ed-

itors, *The Handbook of Data Mining and Knowledge Discovery*. Oxford University Press, Oxford, UK, 1999.

[124] I. Kononenko. Estimating attributes: Analysis and extension of Relief. In *Proc. 7th European Machine Learning Conference*, pages 171–182, Berlin, 1994. Springer Verlag, Berlin.

[125] M. A. Kraaijveld, J. Mao, and A. K. Jain. A non-linear projection method based on Kohonen's topology preserving maps. *IEEE Trans. Neural Networks*, 6:548–559, 1995.

[126] M. Kudo and J. Sklansky. Comparison of algorithms that selects features for pattern classifiers. *Pattern Recognition*, 33:25–41, 2000.

[127] L. I. Kuncheva. Combining classifiers: Soft computing solutions. In S. K. Pal and A. Pal, editors, *Pattern Recognition: From Classical to Modern Approaches*, pages 429–448. World Scientific, Singapore, 2001.

[128] J. Lampinen and E. Oja. Distortion tolerant pattern recognition based on self-organizing feature extraction. *IEEE Trans. Neural Networks*, 6:539–547, 1995.

[129] M. Last, A. Kandel, and O. Maimon. Information-theoretic algorithm for feature selection. *Pattern Recognition Letters*, 22(6/7):799–811, 2001.

[130] M. Last, Y. Klein, and A. Kandel. Knowledge discovery in time series databases. *IEEE Trans. Systems, Man, and Cybernetics*, 31(1):160–169, 2001.

[131] C. Lee and D. A. Landgrebe. Feature extraction based on decision boundaries. *IEEE Trans. Patt. Anal. and Mach. Intell.*, 15:388–400, 1993.

[132] C. Lee and D. A. Landgrebe. Decision boundary feature extraction for neural networks. *IEEE Trans. Neural Network*, 8:75–83, 1997.

[133] D. H. Lee and M. H. Kim. Database summarization using fuzzy ISA hierarchies. *IEEE Trans. Systems Man and Cybernetics B*, 27:68–78, 1997.

[134] R. S. T. Lee and J. N. K. Liu. Tropical cyclone identification and tracking system using integrated neural oscillatory leastic graph matching and hybrid RBF network track mining techniques. *IEEE Trans. Neural Networks*, 11:680–689, 2000.

[135] Y. Leung, J.-S. Zhang, and Z.-B. Xu. Clustering by scale-space filtering. *IEEE Trans. Pattern Analysis and Machine Intelligence*, 22:1396–1410, 2000.

[136] D. D. Lewis and J. Catlett. Heterogeneous uncertainty sampling for supervised learning. In *Proc. 11th Intl. Conf. Machine Learning (ICML-1994)*, pages 148–156, San Francisco, CA, 1994. Morgan Kaufmann, CA.

[137] T. Y. Lin and N. Cercone, editors. *Rough Sets and Data Mining: Analysis of Imprecise Data*. Kluwer Academic Publications, Boston, MA, 1997.

[138] T. Y. Lin, Y. Y. Yao, and L. Zadeh, editors. *Data Mining, Rough Sets and Granular Computing*. Physica Verlag, Berlin, 2002.

[139] B. Liu, W. Hsu, L.-F. Mun, and H. Y. Lee. Finding interesting patterns using user expectation. *IEEE Trans. Knowledge and Data Engineering*, 11:817–832, 1999.

[140] H. Liu, H. Lu, L. Feng, and F. Hussain. Efficient search of reliable exceptions. In *Pacific-Asia Conf. Knowledge Discovery and Data Mining*, pages 194–203. Springer Verlag, 1999.

[141] H. Liu and H. Motoda. *Feature Selection for Knowledge Discovery and Data Mining*. Kluwer Academic Publication, Boston, MA, 1998.

[142] H. Liu and H. Motoda. On issues of instance selection. *Data Mining and Knowledge Discovery, Spl. issue on instance selection*, 6(2):115–130, 2002.

[143] H. Liu and S. T. Tan. X2R: A fast rule generator. In *Proc. IEEE Intl. Conf. System Man Cybernetics*, pages 215–220, Vancouver, Canada, 1995.

[144] J. N. K. Liu, B. N. L. Li, and T. S. Dillon. An improved naive Bayesian classifier technique coupled with a novel input solution method. *IEEE Trans. Systems, Man and Cybernetics*, 31(2):249–256, 2001.

[145] D. O. Loftsgaarden and C. P. Quesenberry. A nonparametric estimate of a multivariate density function. *Annals of Math. Statistics*, 36:1049–1051, 1965.

[146] C. Lopes, M. Pacheco, M. Vellasco, and E. Passos. Rule-evolver: An evolutionary approach for data mining. In *Proc. RSFDGrC'99*, pages 458–462, Yamaguchi, Japan, 1999.

[147] D. Lowe and A. R. Webb. Optimized feature extraction and Bayes decision in feed-forward classifier networks. *IEEE Trans. Pattern Analysis and Machine Intelligence*, 13:355–364, 1991.

[148] H. Lu, R. Setiono, and H. Liu. Effective data mining using neural networks. *IEEE Trans. Knowledge and Data Engineering*, 8(6):957–961, 1996.

[149] A. Maeda, H. Ashida, Y. Taniguchi, and Y. Takahashi. Data mining system using fuzzy rule induction. In *Proc. IEEE Intl. Conf. Fuzzy Systems FUZZ IEEE 95*, pages 45–46, Yokohama, Japan, 1995.

[150] J. Main, T. S. Dillon, and R. Khosla. Use of fuzzy feature vectors and neural networks for case retrieval in case based systems. In *Proc. Biennial Conf. North American Fuzzy Information Processing Society (NAFIPS'96)*, pages 438–443, Berkeley, CA, 1996. IEEE Press, NJ.

[151] J. A. Major and D. R. Riedinger. EFD – A hybrid knowledge statistical-based system for the detection of fraud. *International Journal of Intelligent Systems*, 7:687–703, 1992.

[152] D. P. Mandal, C. A. Murthy, and S. K. Pal. Determining the shape of a pattern class from sampled points in R^2. *International Journal of General Systems*, 20(4):307–339, 1992.

[153] H. Mannila. Theoretical frameworks for data mining. *SIGKDD Explorations*, 1(2):30–32, 2000.

[154] J. Mao and A. K. Jain. Artificial neural networks for feature extraction and multivariate data projection. *IEEE Trans. Neural Networks*, 6:296–317, 1995.

[155] P. Masson and W. Pieczynski. SEM algorithm and unsupervised statistical segmentation of satellite images. *IEEE Trans. Geoscience and Remote Sensing*, 31:618–633, 1993.

[156] L. J. Mazlack. Softly focusing on data. In *Proc. NAFIPS 99*, pages 700–704, New York, 1999. IEEE Press, Piscataway, NJ.

[157] S. Medasani and R. Krishnapuram. A fuzzy approach to complex linguistic query based image retrieval. In *Proc. NAFIPS 99*, pages 590–594, New York, 1999. IEEE Press, Piscataway, NJ.

[158] M. Mehta, R. Agrawal, and J. Rissanen. SLIQ: A fast scalable classifier for data mining. In *Intl. Conf. Extending Database Technology*, pages 18–32, Avignon, France, 1996.

[159] M. Meila and D. Heckerman. An experimental comparison of several clustering and initialization methods. *Microsoft Research Technical Report*, MSR-TR-98-06, ftp://ftp.research.microsoft.com/pub/tr/TR-98-06.PS, 1998.

[160] S. Mika, B. Schölkopf, A. J. Smola, K.-R. Müller, M. Scholz, and G. Rätsch. Kernel PCA and de–noising in feature spaces. In M. S. Kearns, S. A. Solla, and D. A. Cohn, editors, *Advances in Neural Information Processing Systems 11*, pages 536–542, Denver, CO, 1999. MIT Press, Cambridge, MA.

[161] T. Mitchell. Machine learning and data mining. *Comm. ACM*, 42(11):30–36, 1999.

[162] P. Mitra, S. Mitra, and S. K. Pal. Rough fuzzy MLP: Evolutionary design. In N. Zhong, A. Skowron, and S. Ohsuga, editors, *Recent Advances in Rough Sets, Fuzzy Sets, Data Mining and Granular Computing*, volume 1711 of *Lecture Notes in Artificial Intelligence*, pages 128–136. Springer Verlag, Singapore, 1999.

[163] P. Mitra, S. Mitra, and S. K. Pal. Staging of cervical cancer with soft computing. *IEEE Trans. Biomedical Engineering*, 47(7):934–940, 2000.

[164] P. Mitra, C. A. Murthy, and S. K. Pal. Data condensation in large databases by incremental learning with support vector machines. In *Proc. Intl. Conf. Pattern Recognition (ICPR2000)*, pages 712–715, Barcelona, Spain, 2000.

[165] P. Mitra, C. A. Murthy, and S. K. Pal. Density based multiscale data condensation. *IEEE Trans. Pattern Analysis and Machine Intelligence*, 24(6):734–747, 2002.

[166] P. Mitra, C. A. Murthy, and S. K. Pal. Unsupervised feature selection using feature similarity. *IEEE Trans. Pattern Analysis and Machine Intelligence*, 24(3):301–312, 2002.

[167] P. Mitra, C. A. Murthy, and S. K. Pal. A probabilistic active support vector learning algorithm. *IEEE Trans. Pattern Analysis and Machine Intelligence*, 26(2), 2004.

[168] P. Mitra, S. K. Pal, and M. A. Siddiqi. Nonconvex clustering using expectation maximization algorithm with rough set initialization. *Pattern Recognition Letters*, 24(6):863–873, 2003.

[169] S. Mitra, R. K. De, and S. K. Pal. Knowledge-based fuzzy MLP for classification and rule generation. *IEEE Trans. Neural Networks*, 8:1338–1350, 1997.

[170] S. Mitra and Y. Hayashi. Neuro-fuzzy rule generation: Survey in soft computing framework. *IEEE Trans. Neural Network*, 11:748–768, 2000.

[171] S. Mitra, P. Mitra, and S. K. Pal. Evolutionary modular design of rough knowledge-based network using fuzzy attributes. *Neurocomputing*, 36:45–66, 2001.

[172] S. Mitra and S. K. Pal. Self-organizing neural network as a fuzzy classifier. *IEEE Trans. Systems, Man and Cybernetics*, 24(3):385–399, 1994.

[173] S. Mitra and S. K. Pal. Fuzzy multi-layer perceptron, inferencing and rule generation. *IEEE Trans. Neural Networks*, 6:51–63, 1995.

[174] S. Mitra and S. K. Pal. Fuzzy self organization, inferencing and rule generation. *IEEE Trans. Systems, Man and Cybernetics, Part A: Systems and Humans*, 26:608–620, 1996.

[175] S. Mitra, S. K. Pal, and P. Mitra. Data mining in soft computing framework: A survey. *IEEE Trans. Neural Networks*, 13(1):3–14, 2002.

[176] T. Mollestad and A. Skowron. A rough set framework for data mining of propositional default rules. In Z. W. Ras and M. Michalewicz, editors, *Foundations of Intelligent Systems*, volume 1079 of *Lecture Notes in Computer Science*, pages 448–457. Springer Verlag, Berlin, 1996.

[177] A. W. Moore and M. S. Lee. Cached sufficient statistics for efficient machine learning with large datasets. *Journal of Artificial Intelligence Research*, 8:67–91, 1998.

[178] A. W. Moore, J. Schneider, and K. Deng. Efficient locally weighted polynomial regression predictions. In *Proc. 14th Int. Conf. Machine Learning*, pages 236–244, Nashville, TN, 1997. Morgan Kaufmann, San Mateo, CA.

[179] S. Muggleton, editor. *Inductive Logic Programming*. Academic Press, London, 1992.

[180] S. Muggleton. Inverse entailment and PROGOL. *New Generation Computing*, 13:245–286, 1995.

[181] S. Muggleton and C. Feng. Efficient induction of logic programs. In *Proc. 1st Conf. Algorithmic Learning Theory*, pages 368–381. Ohmsma, Tokyo, Japan, 1990.

[182] O. Nasraoui, R. Krishnapuram, and A. Joshi. Relational clustering based on a new robust estimator with application to web mining. In *Proc. NAFIPS 99*, pages 705–709, New York, 1999.

[183] D. Nauck. Using symbolic data in neuro-fuzzy classification. In *Proc. NAFIPS 99*, pages 536–540, New York, 1999.

[184] R. T. Ng and J. Han. Efficient and effective clustering methods for spatial data mining. In *Proc. 20th Intl. Conf. Very Large Databases*, pages 144–155, San Francisco, 1994. Morgan Kaufmann, San Mateo, CA.

[185] E. Noda, A. A. Freitas, and H. S. Lopes. Discovering interesting prediction rules with a genetic algorithm. In *Proc. IEEE Congress on Evolutionary Computation CEC 99*, pages 1322–1329, Washington DC, 1999.

[186] D. W. Opitz and J. W. Shavlik. Generating accurate and diverse members of a neural-network ensemble. In *Advances in Neural Information*

Processing Systems, volume 8, pages 535–541. MIT Press, Cambridge, MA, 1996.

[187] D. W. Opitz and J. W. Shavlik. Connectionist theory refinement: Genetically searching the space of network topologies. *Journal of Artificial Intelligence Research*, 6:177–209, 1997.

[188] E. Osuna, R. Freund, and F. Girosi. An improved training algorithm for support vector machines. In *Proc. IEEE Workshop on Neural Networks for Signal Processing*, pages 276–285, Brisbane, Australia, 1997. IEEE Press, NJ.

[189] A. Pal and S. K. Pal. Pattern recognition: Evolution of methodologies and data mining. In S. K. Pal and A. Pal, editors, *Pattern Recognition: From Classical to Modern Approaches*, pages 1–23. World Scientific, Singapore, 2001.

[190] S. K. Pal. Soft computing pattern recognition: Principles, integrations and data mining. In T. Terano, T. Nishida, A. Namatame, S. Tsumoto, Y. Ohswa, and T. Washio, editors, *Advances in Artificial Intelligence*, volume 2253 of *Lecture Notes in Artificial Intelligence*, pages 261–268. Springer Verlag, Berlin, 2002.

[191] S. K. Pal. Soft data mining, computational theory of perceptions, and rough-fuzzy approach. *Information Sciences*, 2004 (to appear).

[192] S. K. Pal and D. Bhandari. Selection of optimum set of weights in a layered network using genetic algorithms. *Information Sciences*, 80:213–234, 1994.

[193] S. K. Pal, B. Dasgupta, and P. Mitra. Rough self organizing map. *Applied Intelligence*, 2004 (to appear).

[194] S. K. Pal, R. K. De, and J. Basak. Unsupervised feature evaluation: A neuro-fuzzy approach. *IEEE Trans. Neural Networks*, 11(2):366–376, 2000.

[195] S. K. Pal, T. S. Dillon, and D. S. Yeung, editors. *Soft Computing in Case Based Reasoning*. Springer Verlag, London, 2000.

[196] S. K. Pal and A. Ghosh. Image segmentation using fuzzy correlation. *Information Sciences*, 62:223–250, 1992.

[197] S. K. Pal and A. Ghosh. Neuro-fuzzy computing for image processing and pattern recognition. *International Journal of System Science*, 27(12):1179–1193, 1996.

[198] S. K. Pal, A. Ghosh, and B. Uma Shankar. Segmentation of remotely sensed images with fuzzy thresholding, and quantitative evaluation. *International Journal of Remote Sensing*, 21(11):2269–2300, 2000.

[199] S. K. Pal and D. Dutta Majumder. Fuzzy sets and decision making approaches in vowel and speaker recognition. *IEEE Trans. Systems, Man, and Cybernetics*, 7:625–629, 1977.

[200] S. K. Pal and D. Dutta Majumder. *Fuzzy Mathematical Approach to Pattern Recognition*. John Wiley (Halsted Press), New York, 1986.

[201] S. K. Pal and P. Mitra. Multispectral image segmentation using rough set initialized EM algorithm. *IEEE Trans. Geoscience and Remote Sensing*, 40(11):2495–2501, 2002.

[202] S. K. Pal and P. Mitra. Case generation using rough sets with fuzzy representation. *IEEE Trans. Knowledge and Data Engineering*, 16(3), 2004.

[203] S. K. Pal and S. Mitra. Multi-layer perceptron, fuzzy sets and classification. *IEEE Trans. Neural Networks*, 3:683–697, 1992.

[204] S. K. Pal and S. Mitra. *Neuro-fuzzy Pattern Recognition: Methods in Soft Computing*. John Wiley, New York, 1999.

[205] S. K. Pal, S. Mitra, and P. Mitra. Rough fuzzy MLP: Modular evolution, rule generation and evaluation. *IEEE Trans. Knowledge and Data Engineering*, 15(1):14–25, 2003.

[206] S. K. Pal and A. Pal, editors. *Pattern Recognition: From Classical to Modern Approaches*. World Scientific, Singapore, 2001.

[207] S. K. Pal, L. Polkowski, and A. Skowron, editors. *Rough-Neuro Computing: Techniques for Computing with Words*. Springer, Heidelberg, 2003.

[208] S. K. Pal and S. C. K. Shiu. *Foundations of Soft Case Based Reasoning*. John Wiley, New York, 2004.

[209] S. K. Pal and A. Skowron, editors. *Rough-Fuzzy Hybridization: New Trends in Decision Making*. Springer Verlag, Singapore, 1999.

[210] S. K. Pal, V. Talwar, and P. Mitra. Web mining in soft computing framework: Relevance, state of the art and future directions. *IEEE Trans. Neural Networks*, 13(5):1163–1177, 2002.

[211] S. K. Pal and P. P. Wang, editors. *Genetic Algorithms for Pattern Recognition*. CRC Press, Boca Raton, 1996.

[212] D. Pavlov, J. Mao, and B. Dom. Scaling-up support vector machines using boosting algorithm. In *Proc. 15th Intl. Conf. Pattern Recognition*, pages 219–222, Barcelona, Spain, 2000.

[213] Z. Pawlak. Rough sets. *International Journal on Computer and Information Sciences*, 11:341–356, 1982.

[214] Z. Pawlak. *Rough Sets, Theoretical Aspects of Reasoning About Data.* Kluwer Academic, Dordrecht, 1991.

[215] Z. Pawlak. Rough sets and decision algorithms. In *Proc. Intl. Conf. Rough Sets and Current Trends in Computing (RSTC'2000)*, pages 1–16, Banff. Canada, 2000.

[216] W. Pedrycz. Conditional fuzzy c-means. *Pattern Recognition Letters,* 17:625–632, 1996.

[217] W. Pedrycz. Fuzzy set technology in knowledge discovery. *Fuzzy Sets and Systems,* 98:279–290, 1998.

[218] W. Pedrycz. Shadowed sets: Representing and processing fuzzy sets. *IEEE Trans. Systems, Man and Cybernetics B,* 28:103–109, 1998.

[219] W. Pedrycz. Granular computing in data mining. In M. Last and A. Kandel, editors, *Data Mining and Computational Intelligence.* Springer Verlag, Singapore, 2001.

[220] W. Pedrycz and A. Bargiela. Granular clustering: A granular signature of data. *IEEE Trans. Systems, Man and Cybernetics,* 32(2):212–224, 2002.

[221] W. Pedrycz and Z. A. Sosnowski. Designing decision trees with the use of fuzzy granulation. *IEEE Trans. Systems, Man, and Cybernetics,* 30(2):151–159, 2000.

[222] W. Pedrycz and G. Vukovich. Abstraction and specialization of information granules. *IEEE Trans. Systems, Man and Cybernetics,* 31(1):106–111, 2001.

[223] J. F. Peters, A. Skowron, L. Han, and S. Ramanna. Towards rough neural computing based on rough neural networks. In *Proc. Intl. Conf. Rough Sets and Current Trends in Computing (RSTC'2000)*, pages 572–579, Banff, Canada, 2000. Springer Verlag, Berlin.

[224] P. Piatetsky-Shapiro and W. J. Frawley, editors. *Knowledge Discovery in Databases.* AAAI/MIT Press, Menlo Park, CA, 1991.

[225] J. C. Platt. Fast training of support vector machines using sequential minimal optimisation. In B. Scholkopf, C. J. C. Burges, and A. J. Smola, editors, *Advances in Kernel Methods – Support Vector Learning*, pages 185–208. MIT Press, Cambridge, MA, 1998.

[226] M. Plutowski and H. White. Selecting concise training sets from clean data. *IEEE Trans. Neural Networks,* 4(2)(2):305–318, 1993.

[227] L. Polkowski and A. Skowron, editors. *Rough Sets in Knowledge Discovery 1 and 2.* Physica-Verlag, Heidelberg, 1998.

[228] L. Polkowski, A. Skowron, and J. Komorowski. Approximate case-based reasoning: A rough mereological approach. In H.D. Burkhard and M. Lenz, editors, *Proc. 4th German Workshop on Case-Based Reasoning, System Deveolpment and Evaluation*, pages 144–151, Humboldt University, Berlin, 1996.

[229] K. L. Priddy, S. K. Rogers, D. W. Ruck, G. L. Tarr, and M. Kabrisky. Bayesian selection of important features for feedforward neural networks. *Neurocomputing*, 5:91–103, 1993.

[230] F. Provost and V. Kolluri. A survey of methods for scaling up inductive algorithms. *Data Mining and Knowledge Discovery*, 2:131–169, 1999.

[231] P. Pudil, J. Novovicova, and J. Kittler. Floating search methods in feature selection. *Pattern Recognition Letters*, 15:1119–1125, 1994.

[232] J. R. Quinlan. *C4.5, Programs for Machine Learning*. Morgan Kaufmann, San Mateo, CA, 1993.

[233] J. R. Quinlan and R. M. Cameron-Jones. Induction of logic programs: FOIL and related systems. *New Generation Computing*, 13:287–312, 1995.

[234] N. Ramakrishnan and A. Y. Grama. Data mining: From serendipity to science. *IEEE Computer*, 34(8):34–37, 1999.

[235] V. Ramamurti and J. Ghosh. Structurally adaptive modular networks for non-stationary environments. *IEEE Trans. Neural Networks*, 10(1):152–160, 1999.

[236] C. R. Rao. *Linear Statistical Inference and its Applications*. John Wiley, New York, 1973.

[237] M. L. Raymer, W. F. Punch, E. D. Goodman, and L. A. Kuhn. Genetic programming for improved data mining: An application to the biochemistry of protein interactions. In *Genetic Programming 1996: Proc. First Annual Conf.*, pages 375–380, Stanford University, CA, 1996. MIT Press, Cambridge, MA.

[238] M. L. Raymer, W. F. Punch, E. D. Goodman, L. A. Kuhn, and A. K. Jain. Dimensionality reduction using genetic algorithm. *IEEE Trans. Evolutinary Computation*, 4:164–172, 2000.

[239] F. Ricci and P. Avesani. Data compression and local metrics for nearest neighbor classification. *IEEE Trans. Pattern Analysis and Machine Intelligence*, 21:380–384, 1999.

[240] G. H. Rosenfeld and K. Fitzpatrick-Lins. Coefficient of agreement as a measure of thematic classification accuracy. *Photogrammetric Engineering and Remote Sensing*, 52:223–227, 1986.

[241] N. Roy and A. McCallum. Towards optimal active learning through sampling estimation of error reduction. In *Proc. 18th Intl. Conf. Machine Learning (ICML-2001)*, pages 441–448, Williams College, MA, 2001. Morgan Kaufmann, San Mateo, CA.

[242] J. Rubner and P. Tavan. A self-organizing network for principal component analysis. *Europhysics Letters*, 10:693–698, 1989.

[243] D. W. Ruck, S. K. Rogers, and M. Kabrisky. Feature selection using a multilayer perceptron. *Neural Network Computing*, 20:40–48, 1990.

[244] S. Russell and W. Lodwick. Fuzzy clustering in data mining for telco database marketing campaigns. In *Proc. NAFIPS 99*, pages 720–726, New York, 1999. IEEE Press, Piscataway, NJ.

[245] T. Ryu and C. F. Eick. MASSON: Discovering commonalities in collection of objects using genetic programming. In *Genetic Programming 1996: Proc. First Annual Conf.*, pages 200–208, Stanford University, CA, 1996. MIT Press, Cambridge, MA.

[246] R. Sasisekharan, V. Seshadri, and Sholom M. Weiss. Data mining and forecasting in large-scale telecommunication networks. *IEEE Intelligent Systems*, 11(1):37–43, 1996.

[247] E. Saund. Dimensionality-reduction using connectionist networks. *IEEE Trans. Pattern Analysis and Machine Intelligence*, 11:304–314, 1989.

[248] A. Savasere, E. Omiecinski, and S. B. Navathe. An efficient algorithm for mining association rules in large databases. In *Proc. 21st Intl. Conf. Very Large Database*, pages 432–444, Zurich, Switzerland, 1995. Morgan Kaufmann, San Mateo, CA.

[249] N. A. Sayeed, H. Liu, and K. K. Sung. A sudy of support vectors on model independent example selection. In *Proc. 1st Intl. Conf. Knowledge Discovery and Data Mining*, pages 272–276, San Diego, CA, 1999. AAAI Press, CA.

[250] R. Schapire, Y. Freund, P. Bartlett, and W. S. Lee. Boosting the margin: A new explanation for the effectiveness of voting methods. *Annals of Statistics*, 26(5):1651–1686, 1998.

[251] W. A. C. Schmidt and J. P. Davis. Pattern recognition properties of various feature spaces for higher order neural networks. *IEEE Trans. Pattern Analysis and Machine Intelligence*, 15:795–801, 1993.

[252] G. Schohn and D. Cohn. Less is more: Active learning with support vector machines. In *Proc. 17th Intl. Conf. Machine Learning*, pages 839–846, Stanford, CA, 2000. Morgan Kaufmann, CA.

[253] B. Scholkopf, S. Mika, C.J.C. Burges, P. Knirsch, K.-R. Müller, G. Ratsch, and A.J. Smola. Input space versus feature space in kernel-based methods. *IEEE Trans. Neural Networks*, 10(5):1000–1017, 1999.

[254] J. Shafer, R. Agrawal, and M. Mehta. SPRINT: A scalable parallel classifier for data mining. In *Proc. 22nd Intl. Conf. Very Large Databases*, pages 544–555, San Francisco, 1996. Morgan Kaufmann, San Mateo, CA.

[255] D. Shalvi and N. De Claris. Unsupervised neural network approach to medical data mining techniques. In *Proc. IEEE Intl. Joint Conf. Neural Networks*, pages 171–176, Alaska, 1998.

[256] N. Shan and W. Ziarko. Data-based acquisition and incremental modification of classification rules. *Computational Intelligence*, 11:357–370, 1995.

[257] A. Silberschatz and A. Tuzhilin. What makes patterns interesting in knowledge discovery systems. *IEEE Trans. Knowledge and Data Engineering*, 8:970–974, 1996.

[258] D. Skalak. Prototype and feature selection by sampling and random mutation hill climbing algorithms. In *Proc. 11th Intl. Conf. Machine Learning*, pages 293–301, New Brunswick, NJ, 1994. Morgan Kaufmann, San Mateo, CA.

[259] A. Skowron. Extracting laws from decision tables – A rough set approach. *Computational Intelligence*, 11:371–388, 1995.

[260] A. Skowron and C. Rauszer. The discernibility matrices and functions in information systems. In R. Slowiński, editor, *Intelligent Decision Support, Handbook of Applications and Advances of the Rough Sets Theory*, pages 331–362. Kluwer Academic, Dordrecht, 1992.

[261] A. Skowron and R. Swiniarski. Rough sets in pattern recognition. In S. K. Pal and A. Pal, editors, *Pattern Recognition: From Classical to Modern Approaches*, pages 385–428. World Scientific, Singapore, 2001.

[262] Spl. issue on soft case based reasoning. T. Dillon, S. K. Pal, and S.C.K Shiu, editors, *Applied Intelligence*, volume 24(3). 2004.

[263] Spl. issue on soft data mining. S. K. Pal and A. Ghosh, editors, *Information Sciences*. 2004 (to appear).

[264] Spl. issue on rough-neuro computing. S. K. Pal, W. Pedrycz, A. Skowron, and R. Swiniarski, editors, *Neurocomputing*, volume 36(1-4). 2001.

[265] Spl. issue on rough sets, pattern recognition and data mining. S. K. Pal and A. Skowron, editors, *Pattern Recognition Letters*, volume 24(6). 2003.

[266] Spl. issue on neural networks for data mining and knowledge discovery. Y. Bengio, J. M. Buhmann, M. Embrechts, and J. M. Zurada, editors, *IEEE Trans. Neural Networks*, volume 11(3). 2000.

[267] R. Srikant, Q. Vu, and R. Agrawal. Mining association rules with item constraints. In *Proc. 3rd Intl. Conf. Knowledge Discovery and Data Mining, KDD*, pages 67–73. AAAI Press, Menlo Park, CA, 14–17 1997.

[268] I. A. Taha and J. Ghosh. Symbolic interpretation of artificial neural networks. *IEEE Trans. Knowledge and Data Engineering*, 11(3):448–463, 1999.

[269] A. Teller and M. Veloso. Program evolution for data mining. *The International Journal of Expert Systems*, 8:216–236, 1995.

[270] A. B. Tickle, R. Andrews, M. Golea, and J. Diederich. The truth will come to light: Directions and challenges in extracting the knowledge embedded within trained artificial neural networks. *IEEE Trans. Neural Networks*, 9:1057–1068, 1998.

[271] H. Toivonen. Sampling large databases for association rules. In *Proc. 1996 Int. Conf. Very Large Data Bases*, pages 134–145. Morgan Kaufman, San Mateo, CA, 1996.

[272] S. Tong and D. Koller. Support vector machine active learning with application to text classification. *Journal of Machine Learning Research*, 2:45–66, 2001.

[273] G. G. Towell and J. W. Shavlik. Extracting refined rules from knowledge-based neural networks. *Machine Learning*, 13:71–101, 1993.

[274] I. B. Turksen. Fuzzy data mining and expert system development. In *Proc. IEEE Intl. Conf. Systems, Man, and Cybernetics*, pages 2057–2061, San Diego, CA, 1998.

[275] V. Vapnik. *Statistical Learning Theory*. Wiley, New York, 1998.

[276] J. Vesanto and E. Alhoniemi. Clustering of the self-organizing map. *IEEE Transactions on Neural Networks*, 11:586–600, 2000.

[277] W. Wang, J. Yang, and R. R. Muntz. STING: A statistical information grid approach to spatial data mining. In *Intl. Conf. Very Large Data Bases*, pages 186–195, Athens, Greece, 1997. Morgan Kaufmann, San Mateo, CA.

[278] Q. Wei and G. Chen. Mining generalized association rules with fuzzy taxonomic structures. In *Proc. NAFIPS 99*, pages 477–481, New York, 1999.

[279] D. R. Wilson and T. R. Martinez. Reduction techniques for instance-based learning algorithms. *Machine Learning*, 38(3):257–286, 2000.

[280] J. Wroblewski. Genetic algorithms in decomposition and classification. In *Rough Sets in Knowledge Discovery 1 and 2*. Physica-Verlag, Heidelberg, 1998.

[281] K. Xu, Z. Wang, and K. S. Leung. Using a new type of nonlinear integral for multi-regression: An application of evolutionary algorithms in data mining. In *Proc. IEEE Intl. Conf. Systems, Man, and Cybernetics*, pages 2326–2331, San Diego, CA, 1998.

[282] R. R. Yager. On linguistic summaries of data. In W. Frawley and G. Piatetsky-Shapiro, editors, *Knowledge Discovery in Databases*, pages 347–363. AAAI/MIT Press, Menlo Park, CA, 1991.

[283] R. R. Yager. Database discovery using fuzzy sets. *International Journal of Intelligent Systems*, 11:691–712, 1996.

[284] Y. Y. Yao. Granular computing: Basic issues and possible solutions. In *Proc. 5th Joint Conf. Information Sciences*, pages 186–189, Atlantic City, NJ, 2000. Association for Intelligent Machinery.

[285] L. A. Zadeh. Fuzzy sets. *Information and Control*, 8:338–353, 1965.

[286] L. A. Zadeh. Outline of a new approach to the analysis of complex systems and decision processes. *IEEE Trans. Systems, Man, and Cybernetics*, 3:28–44, 1973.

[287] L. A. Zadeh. Fuzzy logic, neural networks, and soft computing. *Comm. ACM*, 37:77–84, 1994.

[288] L. A. Zadeh. Toward a theory of fuzzy information granulation and its centrality in human reasoning and fuzzy logic. *Fuzzy Sets and Systems*, 90:111–127, 1997.

[289] L. A. Zadeh. A new direction in AI: Toward a computational theory of perceptions. *AI Magazine*, 22:73–84, 2001.

[290] C. T. Zahn. Graph-theoretical methods for detecting and describing Gestalt clusters. *IEEE Trans. on Computer*, 20:68–86, 1971.

[291] T. Zhang, R. Ramakrishnan, and M. Livny. BIRCH: An efficient data clustering method for large databases. In *Proc. ACM SIGMOD Intl. Conf. Management of Data*, pages 103–114, New York, 1996. ACM Press, NY.

[292] Y. Q. Zhang, M. D. Fraser, R. A. Gagliano, and A. Kandel. Granular neural networks for numerical-linguistic data fusion and knowldege discovery. *IEEE Trans. Neural Networks*, 11:658–667, 2000.

[293] Q. Zhao. A Co-Evolutionary Algorithm for Neural Network Learning. In *Proc. IEEE Intl. Conf. Neural Networks*, pages 432–437, Houston, TX, 1997. IEEE Press, NJ.

[294] N. Zhong, Y. Y. Yao, and S. Oshuga. Peculiarity oriented multi-database mining. In *Proc. PKDD'99*, pages 136–146, Prague, Czech Republic, 1999. Springer Verlag, Berlin.

Index

About the Authors

Sankar K. Pal is a Professor and Distinguished Scientist at the Indian Statistical Institute, Calcutta. He is also the Founding Head of the Machine Intelligence Unit. He received a Ph.D. in Radio Physics and Electronics from the University of Calcutta in 1974, and another Ph.D. in Electrical Engineering along with DIC from Imperial College, University of London in 1982.

He worked at the University of California, Berkeley and the University of Maryland, College Park 1986–87 and at the NASA Johnson Space Center, Houston, Texas 1990–92 and 1994. Since 1997 he has been serving as a Distinguished Visitor of IEEE Computer Society (USA) for the Asia-Pacific Region and has held several visiting positions in Hong Kong and Australian universities.

Prof. Pal is a Fellow of the IEEE, USA, Third World Academy of Sciences, Italy, International Association for Pattern Recognition, USA, and all the four National Academies for Science/Engineering in India. He is a co-author of ten books and about three hundred research publications in the areas of pattern recognition and machine learning, image processing, data mining, soft computing, neural nets, genetic algorithms, fuzzy sets, and rough sets.

He received the 1990 S.S. Bhatnagar Prize (which is the most coveted award for a scientist in India) and many prestigious awards in India and abroad, including the 1999 G.D. Birla Award, 1998 Om Bhasin Award, 1993 Jawaharlal Nehru Fellowship, 2000 Khwarizmi International Award from the Islamic Republic of Iran, 2000-2001 FICCI Award, 1993 Vikram Sarabhai Research Award, 1993 NASA Tech Brief Award (USA), 1994 *IEEE Trans. Neural Networks* Outstanding Paper Award (USA), 1995 NASA Patent Application Award (USA), 1997 IETE-R.L. Wadhwa Gold Medal, and the 2001 INSA-S.H. Zaheer Medal.

Prof. Pal is an Associate Editor of *IEEE Trans. Pattern Analysis and Machine Intelligence, IEEE Trans. Neural Networks, Pattern Recognition Letters, Neurocomputing, Applied Intelligence, Information Sciences, Fuzzy Sets and Systems, Fundamenta Informaticae* and *Int. J. Computational Intelligence and Applications*; a Member, Executive Advisory Editorial Board, *IEEE Trans. Fuzzy Systems, Int. Journal on Image and Graphics*, and *Int. Journal of Approximate Reasoning*; and a Guest Editor of *IEEE Computer*.

Pabitra Mitra obtained his B. Tech in Electrical Engineering from Indian Insitute of Technology, Kharagpur in 1996 and Ph.D in Computer Science form Indian Statistical Institute, Calcutta in 2003. Currently he is an Assistant Professor at the Department of Computer Science and Engineering, Indian Institute of technology, Kanpur. His research interests are in the areas of data mining and knowledge discovery, pattern recognition, learning theory, and soft computing.